I0793178

IMAGES
of America

ZELIENOPLE

On the Cover: This 1898 photograph shows the Cyrus Harper Mill in operation along the Connoquenessing Creek in a similar location to other earlier mills. A wooden dam at that location provided the waterpower to run the milling equipment that processed various grains into flour and corn meal. The mill burned in 1911 and was rebuilt, but when it burned again in 1912, it was not. This location is now along Halstead Boulevard. (William Harper.)

IMAGES
of America

ZELIENOPLE

Tom Nesbitt for the
Zelienople Historical Society

ARCADIA
PUBLISHING

ISBN 978-1-4671-3445-3

Published by Arcadia Publishing
Charleston, South Carolina

Printed in the United States of America

Library of Congress Control Number: 2015950078

For all general information, please contact Arcadia Publishing:
Telephone 843-853-2070
Fax 843-853-0044
E-mail sales@arcadiapublishing.com
For customer service and orders:
Toll-Free 1-888-313-2665

Visit us on the Internet at www.arcadiapublishing.com

This work is dedicated to the founders and early settlers of Zelienople and to the local historians who have recorded our history for future generations.

Contents

Acknowledgments

No project of this size can be completed alone. I received valuable information and many photographs from the Zelienople Historical Society, and several residents contributed their photographs. May Lutz and Bruce Zeigler made available the photograph collection of the late Blair Zeigler, who for many years photographed houses and buildings in town. Shelby Ruch of Historic Harmony was very helpful in getting started on this historical quest. Thanks go to all who helped in any way.

Photograph credits are as follows: ZHS (Zelienople Historical Society), BZC (Blair Zeigler Collection), and other individuals by name. Space and pages were limited by the publisher, so not all photographs submitted could be used in the book.

INTRODUCTION

In 1753, a 21-year-old George Washington traveled from Logstown (near Ambridge) to Murdering Town (near Harmony) and became the first white man to map the Connoquenessing Creek area that would eventually become Zelienople. This was done while Washington and his guide, Christopher Gist, traveled north to meet the French commander Jacques Legardeur at Fort LeBoeuf near Lake Erie.

In 1802, a wealthy German diplomat named Dettmar William Frederic Basse landed in America and purchased 10,000 acres from the Philadelphia Land Company. He traveled with wagons full of goods to the frontier village of Pittsburgh, where he mingled with the aristocracy. A short time later, he traveled north on Indian trails to his new lands. His goal was to establish a barony unequalled in this new world, similar to the ones he had known in Germany.

He started building his barony with a large wooden mansion he called Bassenheim (Basse's home in German). He built his mansion on a hill overlooking the Connoquenessing Creek where he could command a view of the surrounding land. Then he built a perfectly straight road, 50 feet wide, from the base of his mansion into the village—now New Castle Street. He established a grain mill, sawmill, and brickyard, and laid out streets for a small town. While Bassenheim was still under construction, Dettmar returned to Germany to bring back his daughter Fredericka "Zelie" Wilhelmina Basse, who had married Philipp Passavant of French Huguenot ancestry. As he was born in Germany, the "Philipp" spelling is used in this text.

In 1807, the party arrived in Philadelphia and set out in large Conestoga wagons for the five-week journey west. The travelers' baggage consisted of 70 cases of household goods, including rare china, paintings, and two highly valued Merino sheep. Arriving at Bassenheim in the depth of winter in its still unfinished state, the young bride was heartbroken at the primitive conditions around her. On her first morning, she awoke with snow on her bed. Baron Dettmar Basse soon built the young couple a two-story log house on Main Street. The first floor was fitted for a store with dry goods, hardware, and groceries, with the second floor serving as their residence. Philipp Passavant became the town's first merchant, and in 1808, he built a brick house beside his store, which now serves as the headquarters of the Zelienople Historical Society.

By 1810, several more German, Scottish, and English settlers had built log cabins and the town was starting to grow. Dettmar Basse discovered iron ore on his property and built his Bassenheim Furnace in 1813. His business ventures did not prosper well, so in 1818 he turned over his interests to his son-in-law Philipp Passavant. After a long, tedious voyage on the Ohio and Mississippi Rivers to New Orleans, the baron set sail for Germany. He died in Mannheim, Germany, in 1836, ending the eventful career of this adventurous pioneer and founder of Zelienople. He named it "City of Zelie" after his daughter, using a derivative of the Greek *polis* (city). Zelienople is the only "-nople" in America.

Christian Buhl arrived in America from Germany in 1802 and traveled across Pennsylvania on horseback. He built the Buhl House in 1805, which is now Zelienople's oldest existing structure.

Buhl was the town's hatter and furrier and was later appointed an associate judge of Butler County. Buhl and his wife, Fredericka Goehring, raised their 11 children in this house, which is now owned by the historical society. Their descendants pursued business enterprises in many parts of the country and abroad—eventually assuming leadership roles in politics, commerce, and philanthropy.

In 1810, Andrew McClure built the first tavern where the Kaufman House now stands. His tavern also served as the first post office, but his sympathy for the British during the War of 1812 led to him being tarred and feathered and the post office being moved to nearby Harmony. Several more homes and shops of tradesmen and merchants were constructed along the Main Street during this time. Most were one- or two-story wooden shops and stores, and almost all those early buildings are gone today.

The town remained a trading center for the many farms in the area during the 1800s and the population continued to grow. Residents built early schools, churches, orphanages, and stately homes, and expanded their businesses. During the late 1800s, improved roads and the railroad came to town, making Zelienople a village of importance in the county. William Passavant, a descendant of Zelie Passavant, founded the Passavant Orphans Home in Zelienople in 1852. He eventually founded 40 other institutions in the United States, including the Passavant Hospital in Pittsburgh.

Christian Buhl's grandson Henry Buhl Jr. formed a close friendship with Zelienople youth Russell Boggs, who was to become his brother-in-law, his business partner, and his lifelong associate. In 1869, Buhl Jr. and Boggs moved to Old Allegheny City, and with $3,500 they opened a dry goods store on Federal Street. When Buhl Jr. died in 1927, he left an $11 million endowment to the city of Pittsburgh as the Buhl Foundation. Boggs and Buhl also constructed the first modern commuter rail service in this area. The Harmony Short Line railroad operated successfully from 1908 to 1931, providing commuter access into Pittsburgh and delivering fresh produce into the city.

In the beginning of the 20th century, many manufacturing facilities were built in Zelienople, bringing young men in from the farms, anxious to earn a steady wage. Main Street businesses offered goods and services of every sort. Hotels, taverns, banks, liveries, wagon and automobile dealers, shops of all kinds, and a movie theater were built during the early 1900s. A new high school was built in 1909 and there were churches of almost every denomination. New infrastructure was added to create a town from a frontier village—including natural gas, electricity, telephone, water service, and bricked streets.

When men returned home after World War II, the factories were booming with business and families were growing just as fast. New borough facilities and services were needed, like the community park, swimming pool, sports fields, library, fire and police departments, paved streets, and new elementary and secondary schools. Even though the steel industry is past its prime and some of the local factories have closed, Zelienople continues to hold its own due to its location along a four-lane interstate highway with proximity to ever-expanding Pittsburgh.

The Zelienople Revitalization Initiative is hard at work trying to improve the business district while keeping the historic structures preserved. It hopes to bring the town up to standards set by other communities in the area and to bring more life and energy into the Main Street businesses.

The early settlers of Zelienople worked very hard to establish and build their little community in the wilderness, and their descendants continued to build upon their efforts. In viewing these photographs and the information provided, the reader should gain a healthy respect for those who came before us. Today's residents should strive to maintain our history and historical structures, for the future generations that will appreciate our current preservation efforts.

One

Early Adventurers and Settlers

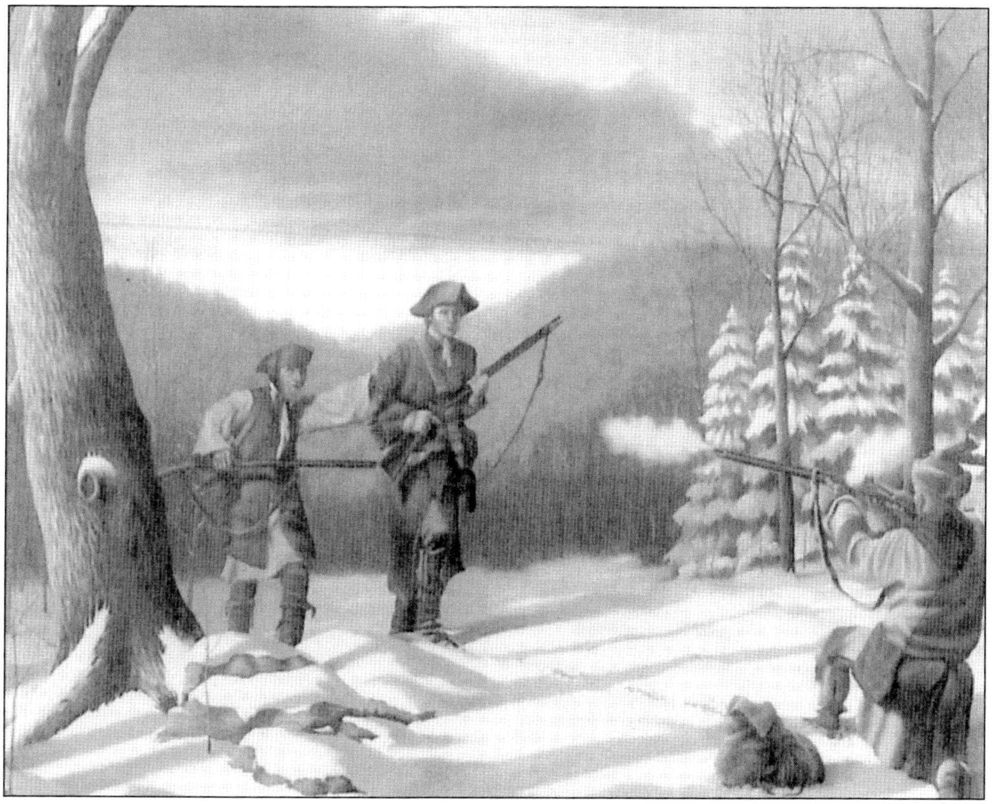

When George Washington was a 21-year-old major in the Virginia Militia, he became the first white man to enter what would become Zelienople. The painting pictured, *The First Shot*, was commissioned by retired Butler County judge Martin O'Brien. It depicts an incident in which Washington and his guide, Christopher Gist, were fired upon during their return trip through this area. (Painting by Martin O'Brien, photograph courtesy Historic Harmony.)

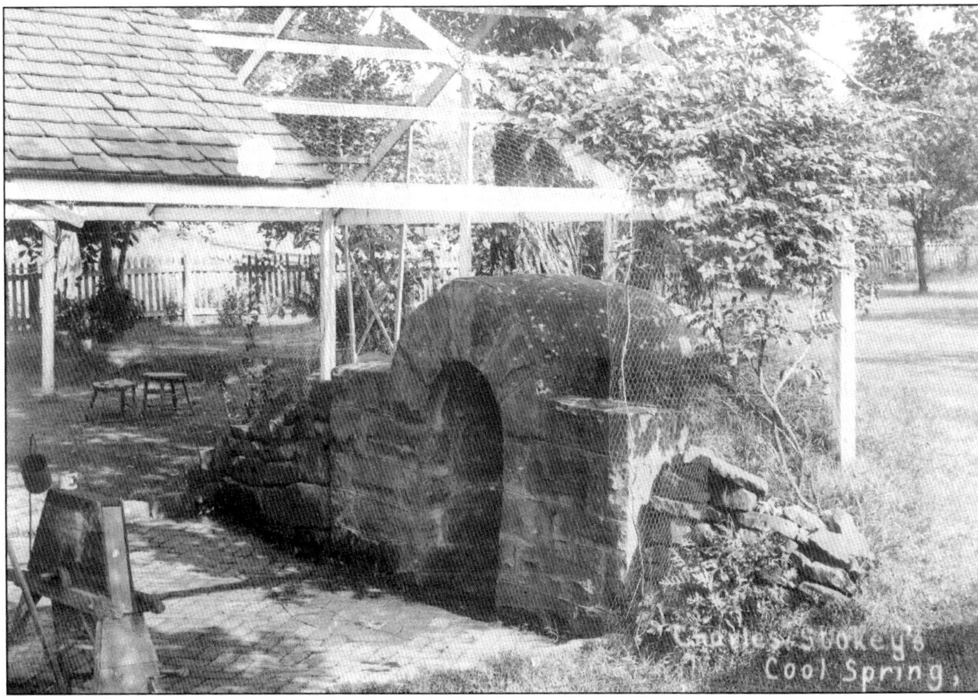

After leaving the Indian village of Logstown (now Ambridge) with guides, bearers, and several Indian chiefs, Washington's party traveled 14 miles to Zelienople, where legend says the men drank from this spring. They continued along the Connoquenessing another two miles to the Indian village called Murdering Town, where they were given meat and corn and camped for the night on November 30, 1753. (ZHS.)

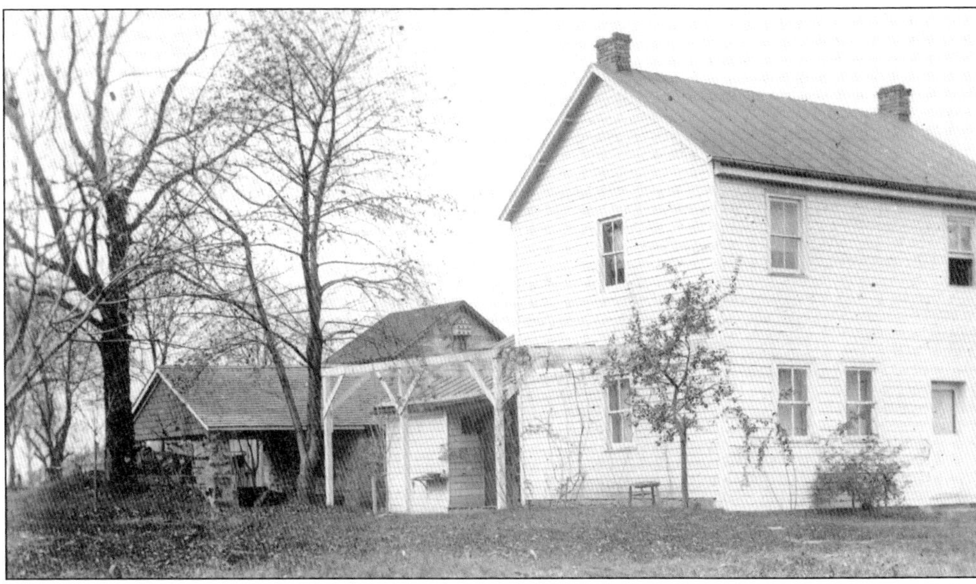

The small outdoor shelter shown on the left in this photograph is the location of the spring. This modest house was located on Jefferson Street. It was a log farmhouse that was moved to Mercer Street in Harmony, across the street from the Weaver's Cabin. The shelter and spring have been restored, but visitors must ask permission from the owner to view. (ZHS.)

Baron Dettmar Basse (right) arrived in 1802 and started building his dream: a baronial estate like the ones he knew in Germany. The Bassenheim (Basse's Home) took seven years to build and cost $7,000. No photographs of the structure exist, but the sketch shown below was done using known descriptions. The main portion of the house was three stories and the roof was flat with railings. It had two porches in front, one above the other, and the front door was reached by a long flight of steps. Attached to the house were two wings, each of two stories. The mansion faced east towards the village and stood on the hill across the Connoquenessing Creek. From the mansion to the village, Basse cut a road through the woods that was perfectly straight and three rods in width (50 feet); it is now called New Castle Street. (Both, ZHS.)

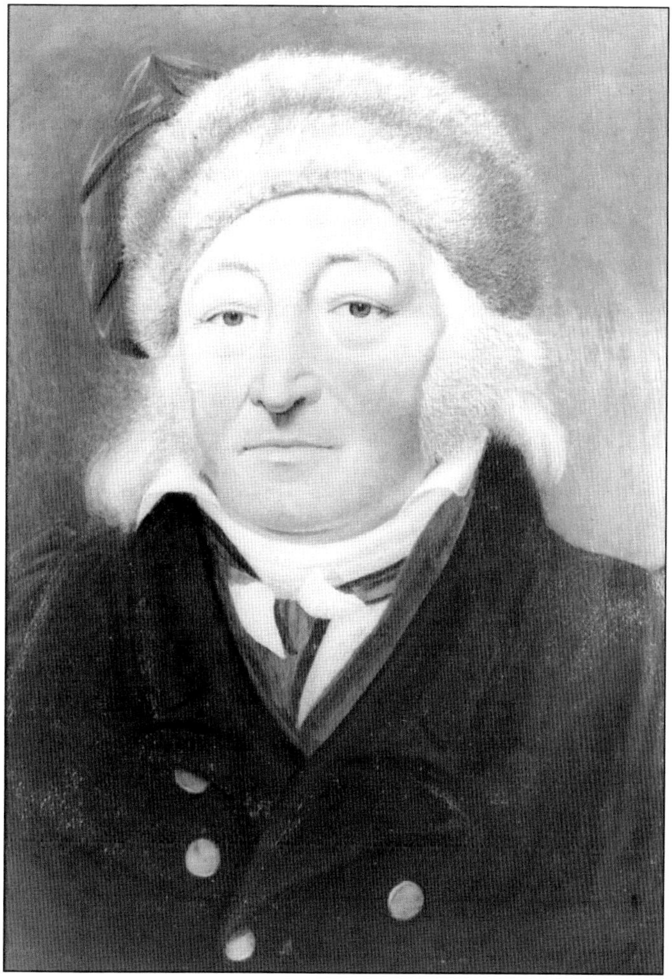

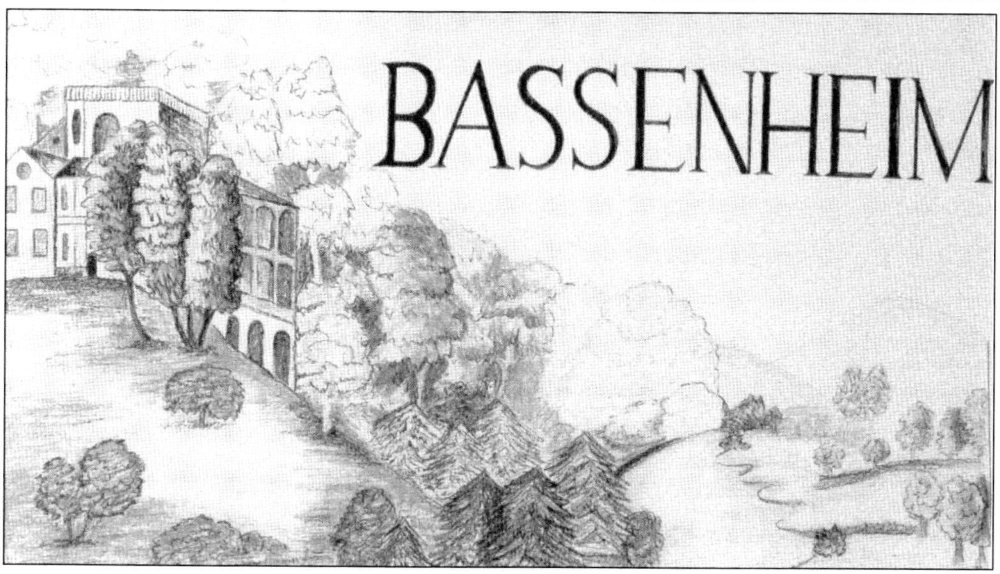

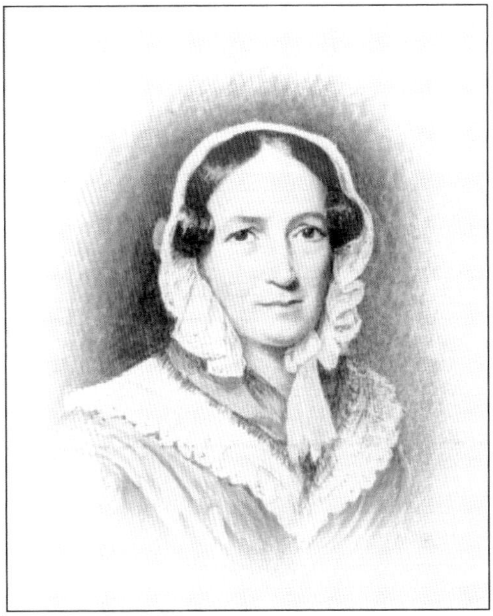

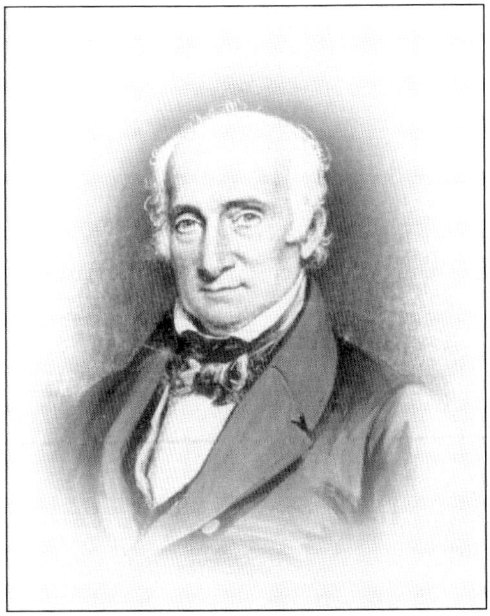

In 1806, Dettmar Basse returned to Germany for his daughter Zelie (left) and her new husband, Philipp Passavant (right), who was of French ancestry. They arrived in Philadelphia and set out in large Conestoga wagons for the long journey west. Their baggage consisted of 70 cases of household goods, rare china, paintings, and two highly valued Merino sheep. During the early years, Zelie wrote letters complaining of the harsh and primitive conditions she had to endure. Philipp became the town's first merchant when he built the log store on Main Street, and in 1808 he built a better brick home next door. Philipp's grandson Charles S. Passavant Jr. built the exquisite home shown below at 230 South Main Street. Charles and his wife, Lillian, can be seen in the 1900 photograph. (All, ZHS.)

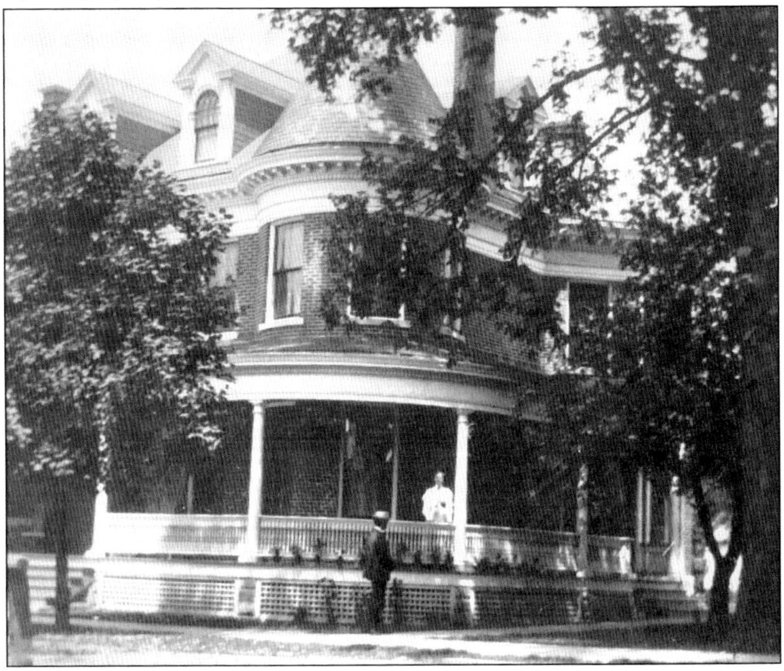

Since 1807, there have been 18 members of the Passavant family who have lived in Zelienople. The photograph on the right shows the Charles S. Passavant Sr. family around 1892. In front are Jane and Charles Sr., with children Emma Virginia and Charles Jr. in the rear. They lived in the old homestead at 243 South Main Street. The last Passavant to live in the house was Emma, who died in 1956 having never married. The photograph below shows the familiar Passavant house after it was expanded with additions to the rear and to the side porch. The lot was very large with flower and vegetable gardens all the way to Clay Street. It was saved from the wrecking ball by Lester Mohr and the Zelienople Historical Society in 1975 and is now used as its museum, library, and office. (Both, ZHS.)

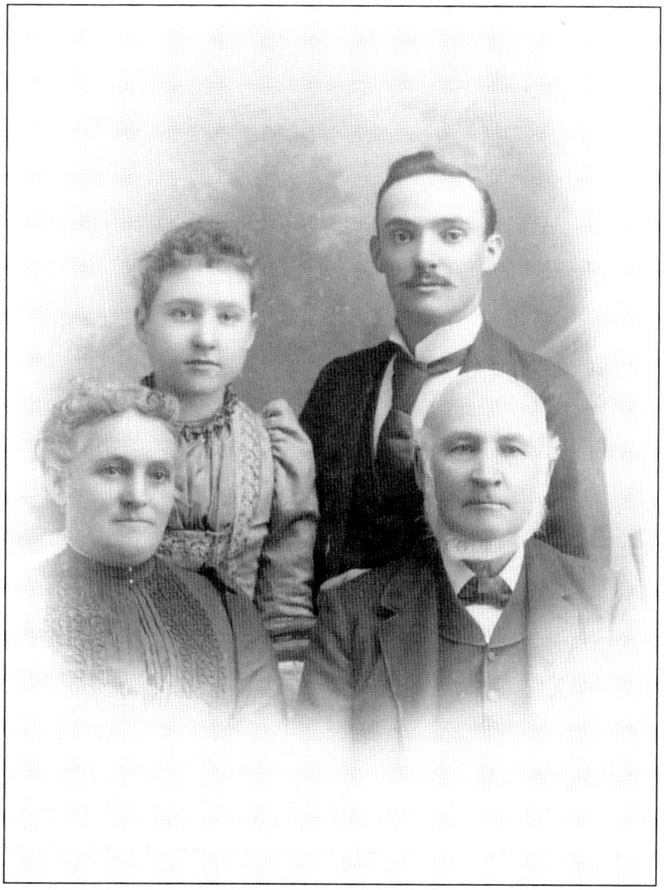

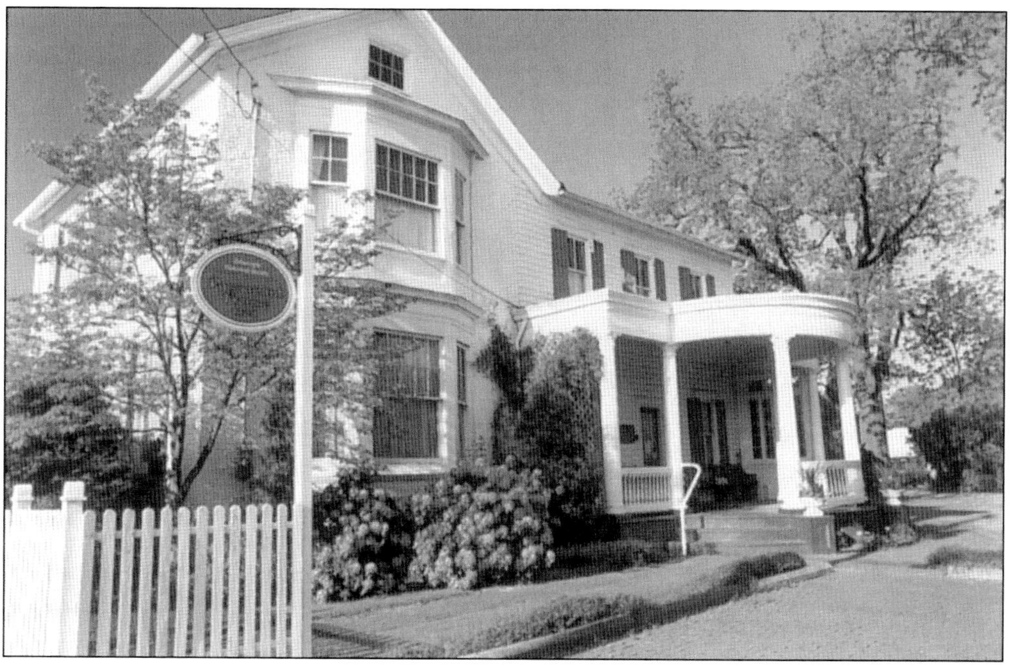

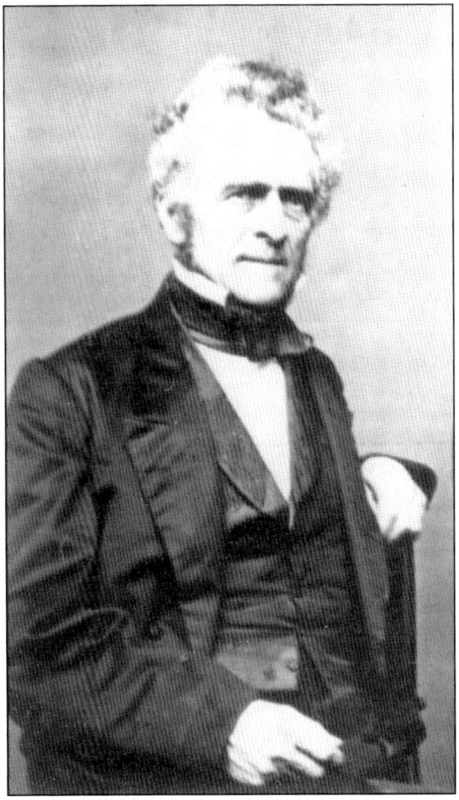

For nine generations, the Buhl family had been merchants in Bavaria, Germany. Christian Buhl (1776–1864), a hatter and fur trader, came to the frontier settlement of Zelienople around 1802. When he arrived, there were only two log cabins there. He was married the following year to Dorothy Goehring, also a native of Germany. They were the parents of 11 children, many of whom pursued business enterprises in many parts of the country and abroad, eventually assuming leadership roles in politics, commerce, and philanthropy. Their home at 221 South Main Street is the oldest building in Zelienople and is owned by the historical society. It has recently been restored by the Zelienople Historical Society, which offers tours and other functions as a second museum site. The c. 1890s photograph below shows Henry Buhl Sr. and his family outside on the sidewalk on a warm day. The wooden addition on the left is no longer present. (Both, ZHS.)

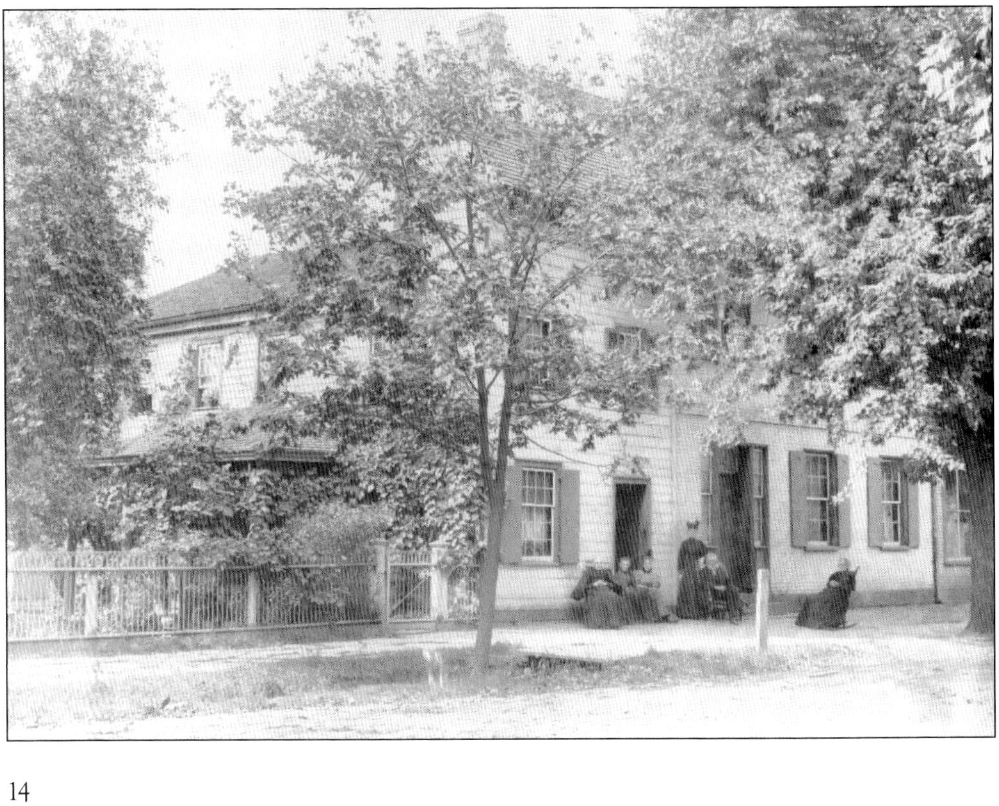

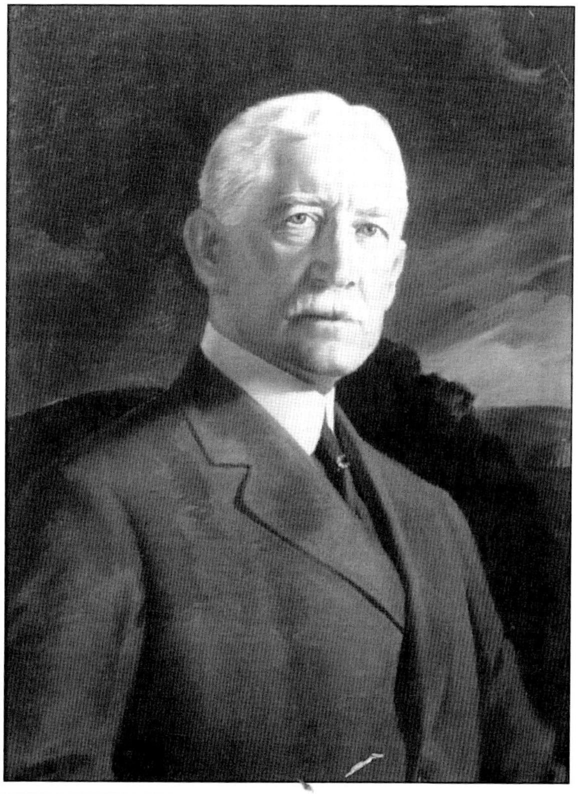

Christian Buhl's grandson Henry Buhl Jr., right, was born in 1848 on his family's farm near Evans City. His father, Henry Buhl Sr., was a builder of steam engines and an engineer on the river for many years. Henry Jr. was educated in a local school, and trained in business methods by his father and grandfather. In 1869, Henry Jr. and Russell Boggs, a childhood friend, started a small dry goods business in Pittsburgh and turned it into the multimillion dollar business called Boggs and Buhl. When Henry Jr. died, he left an $11 million endowment to the city of Pittsburgh as the Buhl Foundation. The photograph below shows his grandfather Christian's carriage house that dates to the early 1800s; it still stands today behind the Buhl House at 221 South Main Street. (Both, ZHS.)

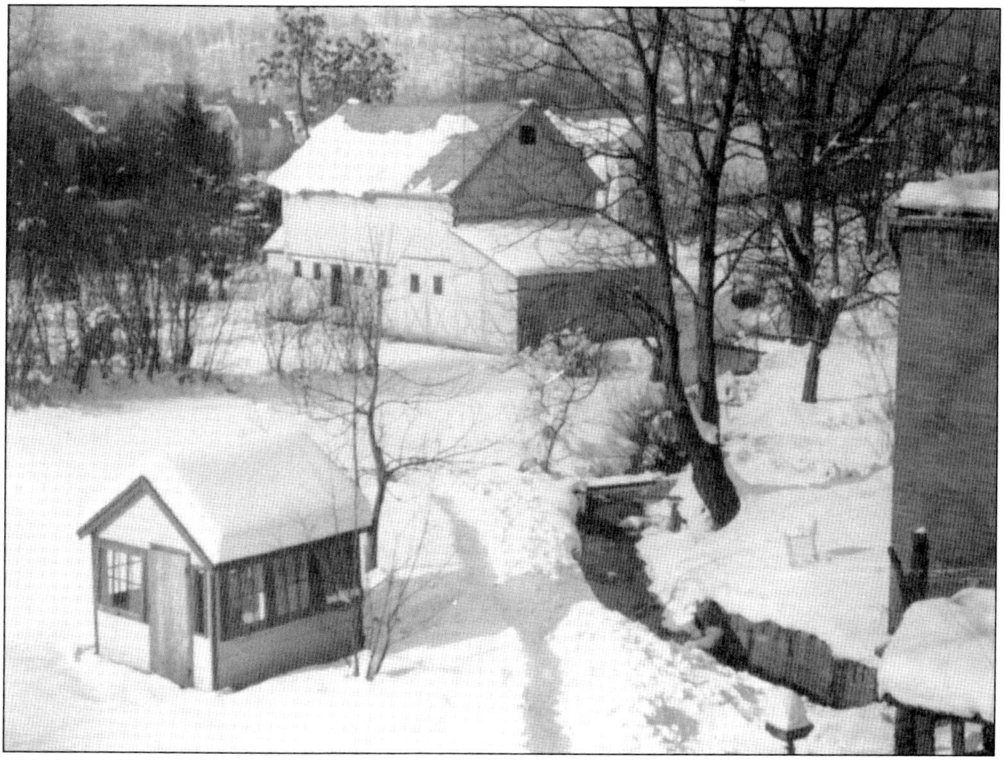

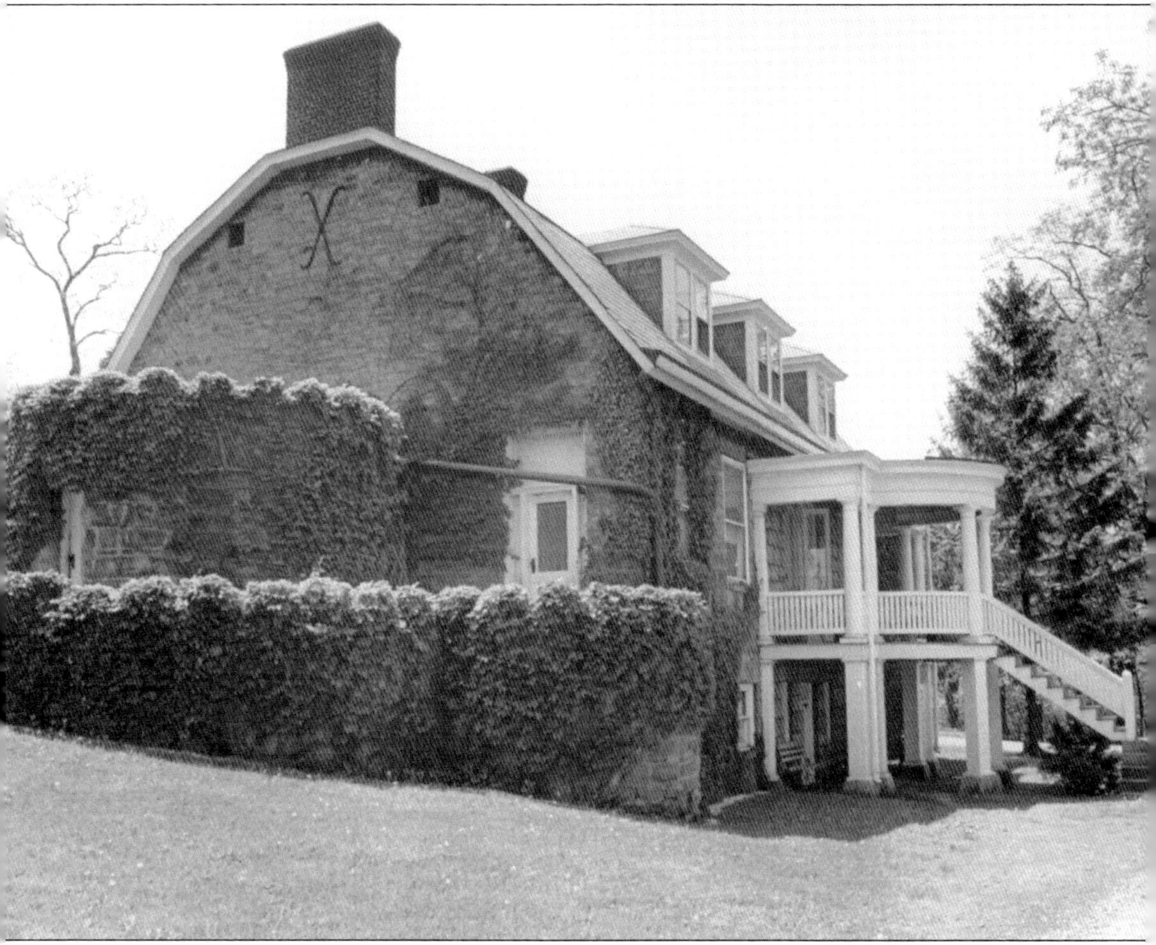

In 1815, George Henry Muller (1778–1873), a native of Hamburg, Germany, purchased 200 acres of land from Dettmar Basse, just west of Zelienople. The old Indian trail used by George Washington and his party in 1753 went through the property. Muller built a beautiful home on a hill overlooking the valley and the stone was quarried directly from the property. Muller and Basse would communicate across the valley using flashing lights or signals, as both their homes were on hills. In 1821, St. Paul Church was organized in this home, meeting in the foyer with its 13-foot ceiling. In 1902, the house was purchased by the Bethany Bible Society, which printed free Bibles in many languages here for 60 years. In 1963, it was purchased by the Hogan family and old gaslights and a coal furnace were still in use at that time. After updating, the Hogans raised beef cattle and later operated a bed-and-breakfast here. The home is now a private residence, and there have only been three owners in 200 years. Other early settlers in Zelienople included Henry and George Muntz in 1804; Daniel Fiedler, who ran a ferry service heading north across the Connoquenessing Creek; Andrew Diemer and Jacob Heberling, who were stonemasons; and Andrew McClure, who was a tavern keeper. By 1826, Zelienople contained 50 houses, 3 churches, 2 tanneries, 2 gristmills, 2 general stores, a brickyard, a sawmill, a public school, a distillery, a village inn, and various trade shops. (ZHS.)

Two

The Borough and Transportation

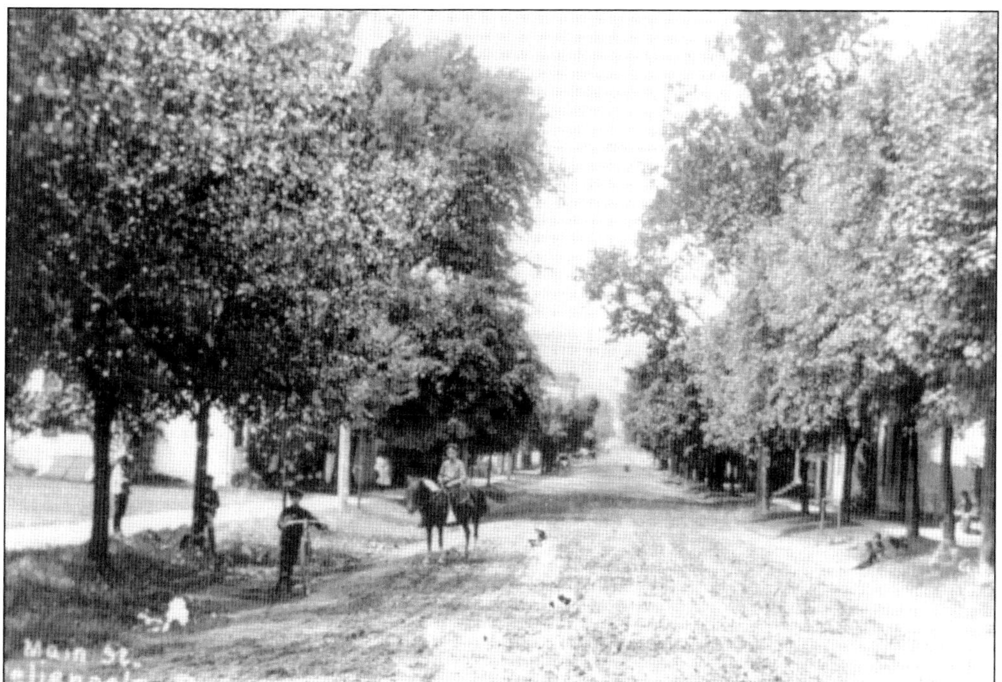

Main Street was just a dirt road when this 1905 photograph was taken. There is not a motorized vehicle in sight, only horses, carriages, and a relatively new invention called the safety bicycle. It was developed for children in the 1890s to replace the more dangerous adult high-wheeler. This photograph shows Charles S. Passavant III (1895–1985) on his pony in front of the Passavant house. (Delsa White.)

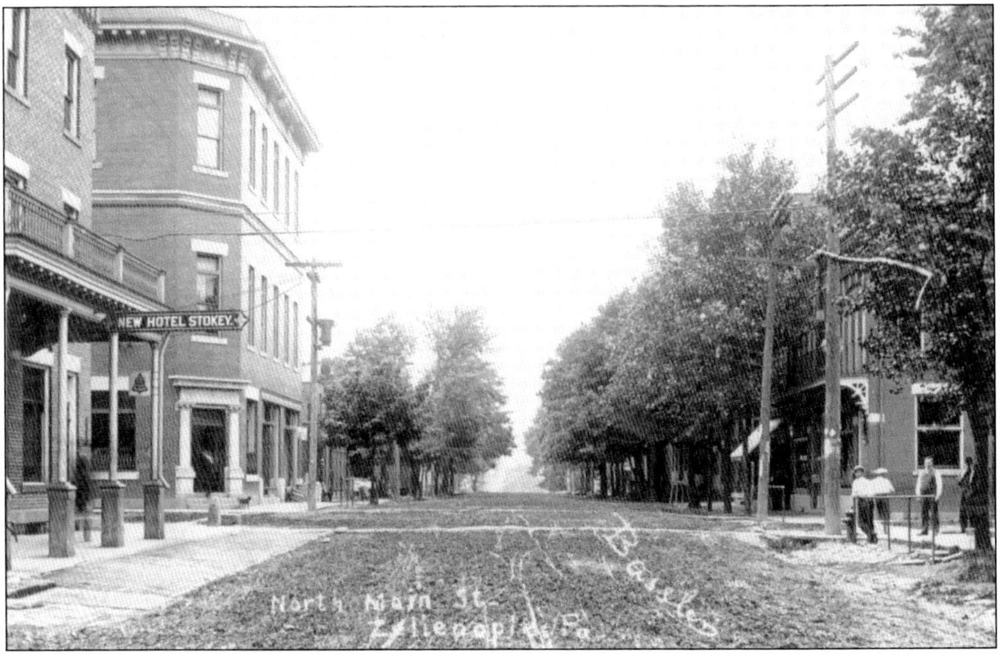

When this 1905 image was taken, Main Street was still a dirt road and not very passable in wet weather. This William Bassler photograph shows the recently built New Hotel Stokey and the primary intersection in town. The older Grand Central Hotel, made of wood, burned down in 1902. The First National Bank building on the left has a beveled corner, and the famous town clock has not yet been installed. (ZHS.)

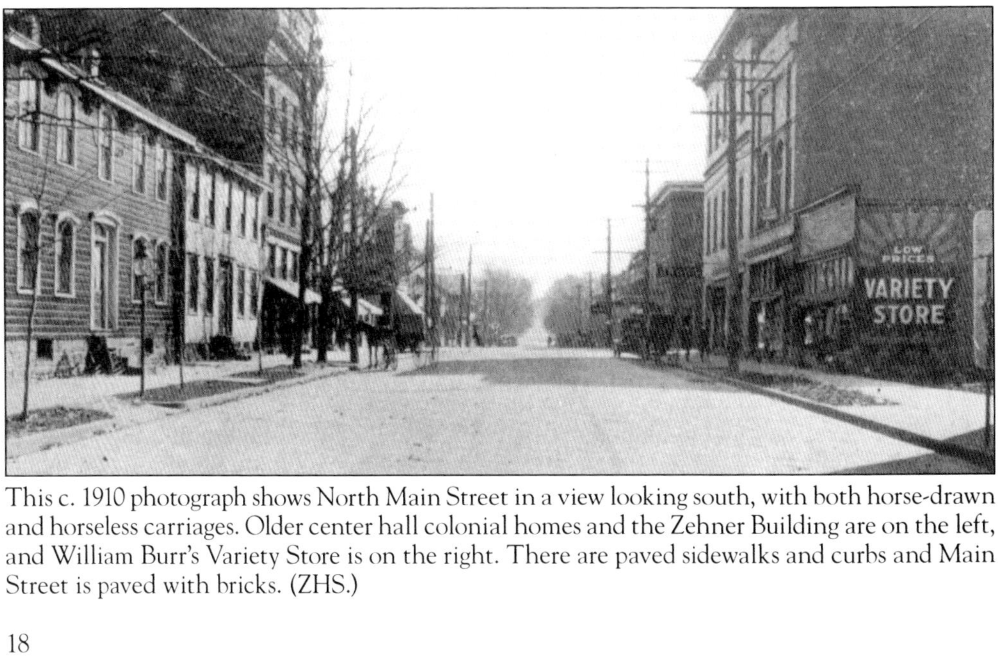

This c. 1910 photograph shows North Main Street in a view looking south, with both horse-drawn and horseless carriages. Older center hall colonial homes and the Zehner Building are on the left, and William Burr's Variety Store is on the right. There are paved sidewalks and curbs and Main Street is paved with bricks. (ZHS.)

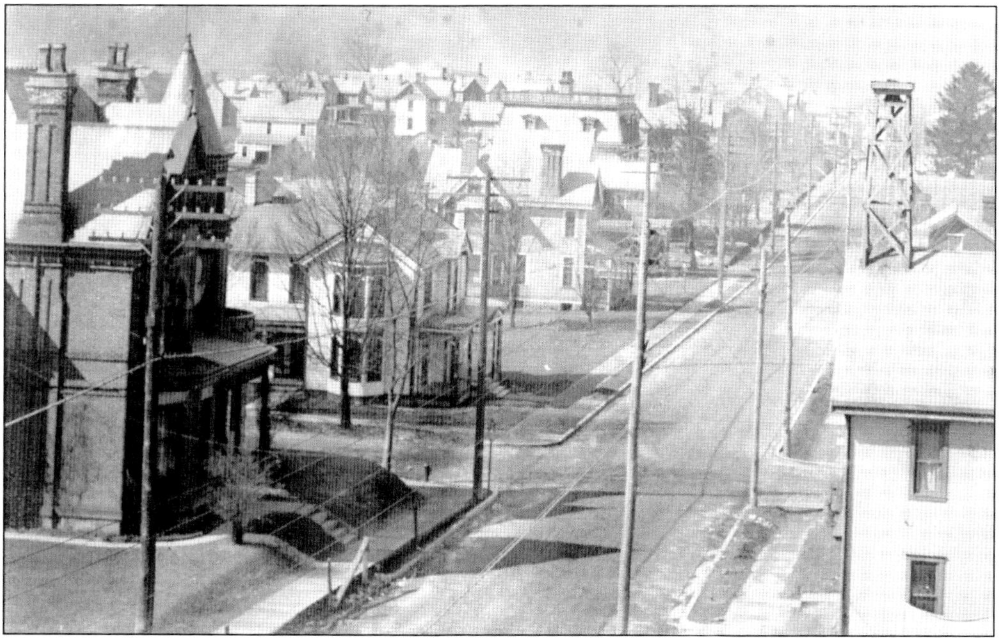

This view looking west on New Castle Street shows the stately Albert Goehring home on the left and other Victorian homes in this neighborhood. On the right is the original fire department and borough building of the early 1900s, including a fire siren mounted on the roof. (Gregory Cowell.)

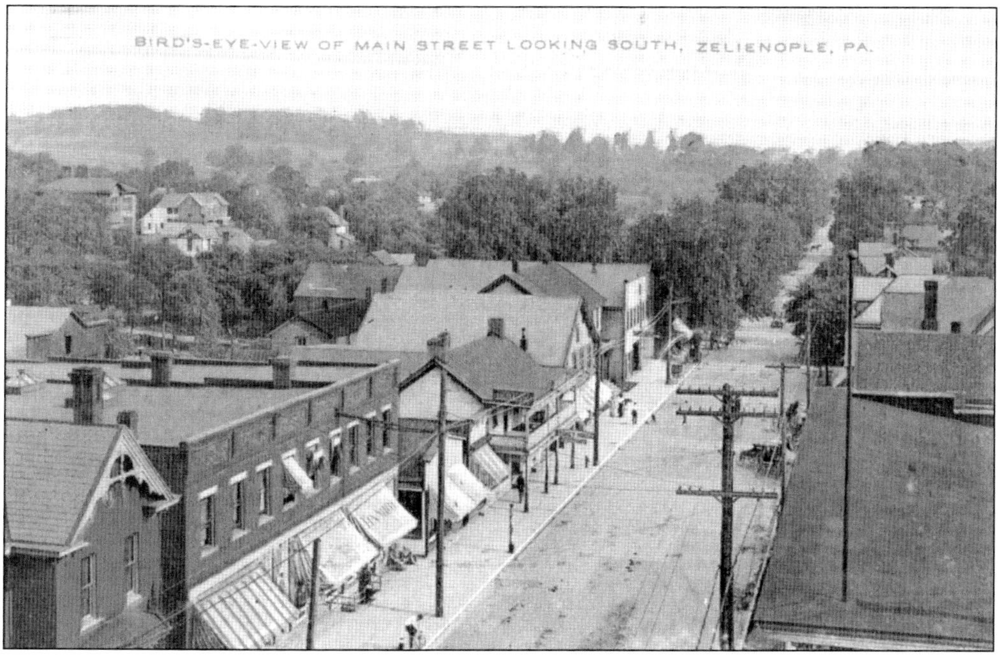

A rare rooftop view looking south into the center block of Main Street is seen in this c. 1920 image. Of interest in center left is the Stokey House before it was demolished; further south, there are were livery stables. In the upper left background is the original high school building constructed in 1909. (BZC.)

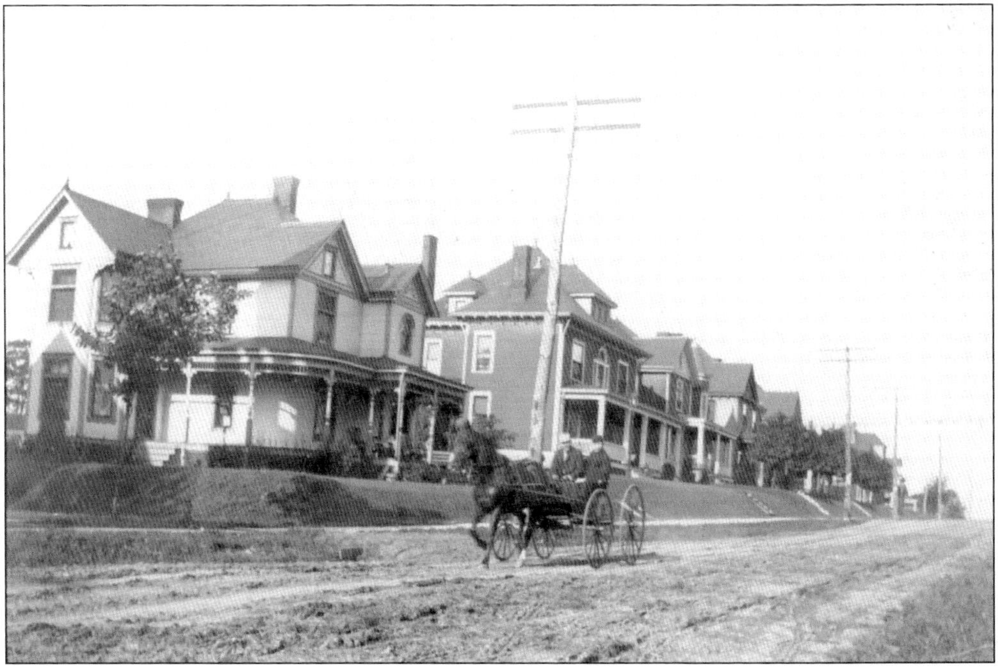

In 1900, the Mill Street sidewalks were paved, though the street was not. As more prestigious homes were built along it, a request to change the name was made, and it became Grandview Avenue. The homes seen in this view looking east from Main Street remain today. The first home on the left is now the Park Presbyterian Church parsonage. (ZHS.)

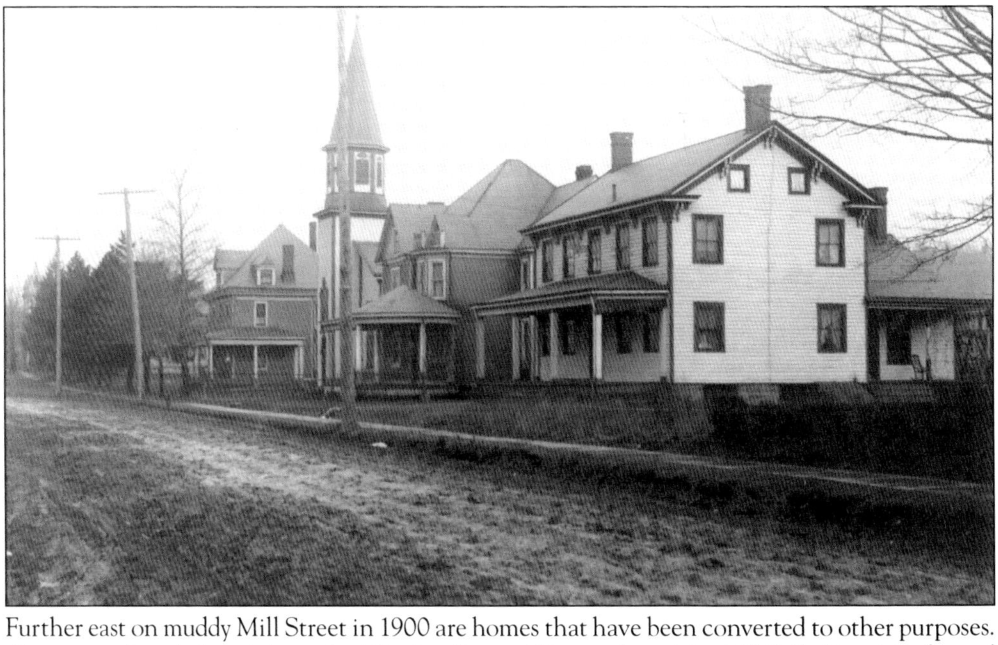

Further east on muddy Mill Street in 1900 are homes that have been converted to other purposes. Shown are, from left to right, today's Boylan Funeral Home, the original 1860 St. Peter's Reformed Church, today's St. Peter's Church offices, and today's Butler County Tourism Bureau building, which was a stagecoach stop and tavern in the 1800s. It was moved to its current location from the corner at Oliver Avenue in the late 1800s. (Gregory Cowell.)

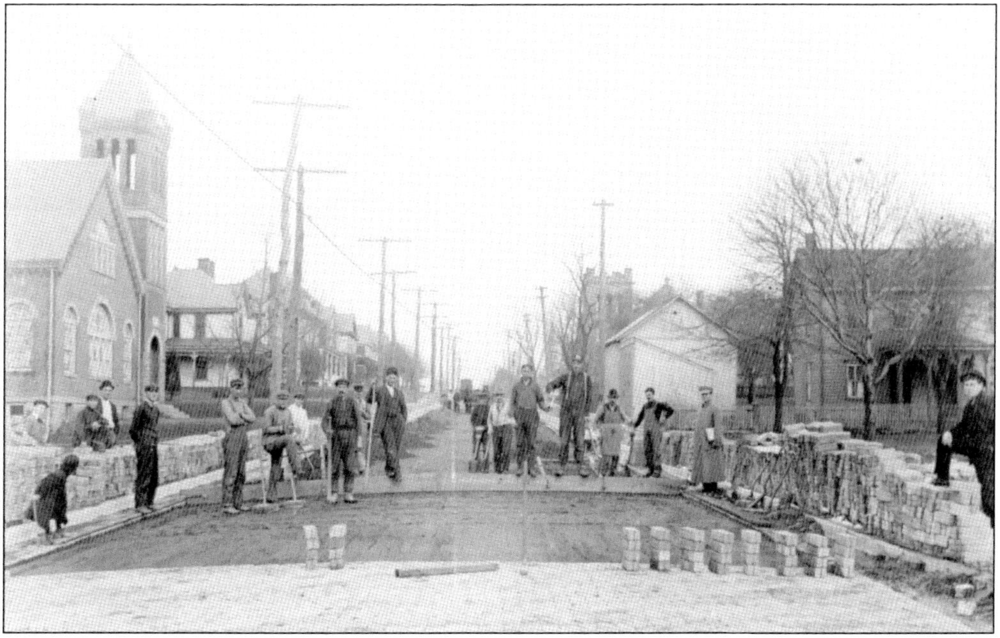

Sun-dried bricks date back to at least 7500 BC, but they were not used to pave Zelienople's muddy streets until 1900. This classic photograph shows the paving of Grandview Avenue, all being done by laborers using brooms and shovels. Layers of stone, sand, and bricks, contoured by the men standing on that wooden plank, made for better streets. Today, all streets in Zelienople are paved with asphalt. (ZHS.)

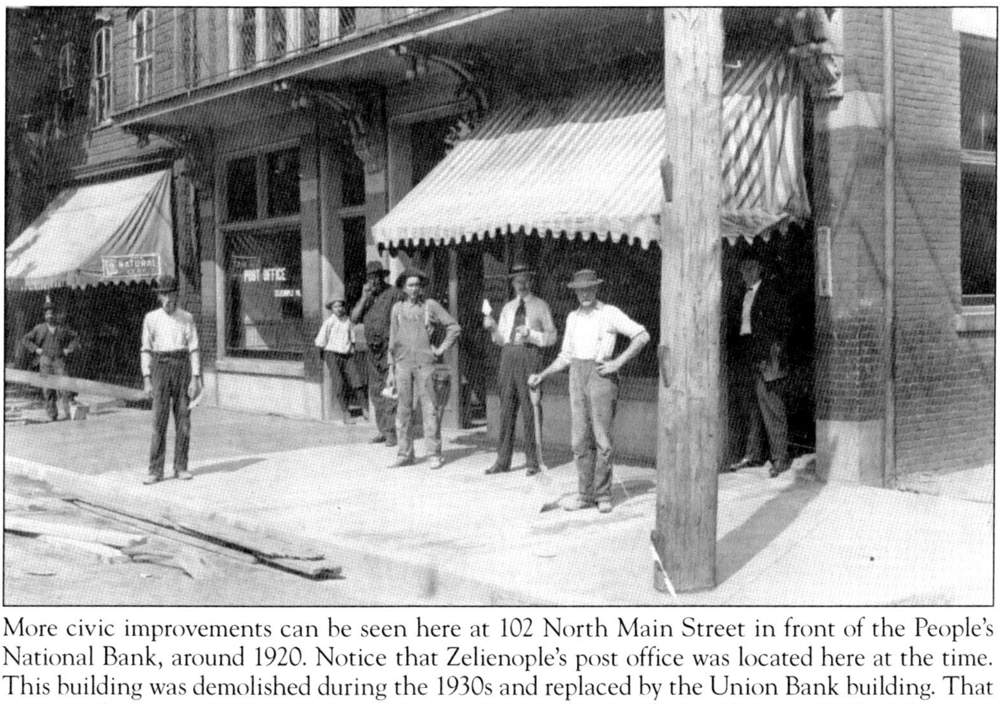

More civic improvements can be seen here at 102 North Main Street in front of the People's National Bank, around 1920. Notice that Zelienople's post office was located here at the time. This building was demolished during the 1930s and replaced by the Union Bank building. That structure became a Mellon Bank and is now Citizens Bank. The building on the far left is now home to Mussig Florist. (ZHS.)

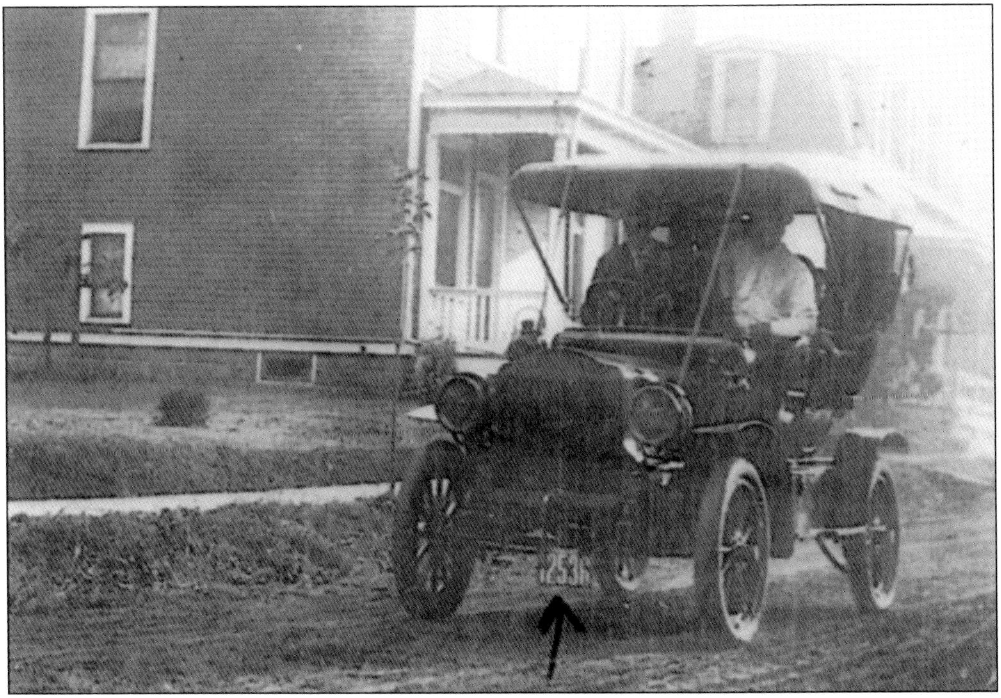

Zelienople's first horseless carriage was the 1906 version seen here at 207 East New Castle Street. Dirt streets and roads must have been a challenge on narrow, hard rubber tires. The carriage was owned by William Henry Gelbach (1852–1927), who was a justice of the peace. In 1892, William and Jacob Gelbach organized the banking firm of Gelbach Brothers, which later sold out to First National Bank. (ZHS.)

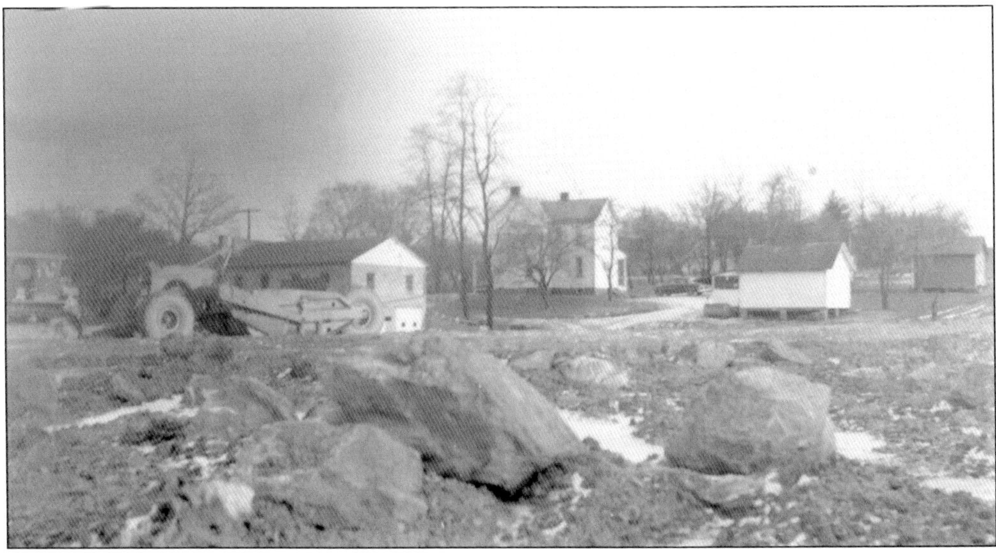

By the 1940s, the two-lane Perry Highway heading south became obsolete, so the state constructed a new four-lane highway on a slightly different path. This 1947 photograph shows the construction going through the William Sohn farm. Sohn raised turkeys and sold Case farm machinery. Later, he opened an Atlantic service station along the new highway in his former field. That location is now the new showroom for Baierl Motors. (Barbara Brizendine.)

The Pittsburgh, New Castle & Lake Erie Railroad finally came to town in 1879 on New Year's Day. In 1879, Zelienople was the end of the line. The railroad did not continue westward from Zelienople. The two-story station was located along Front Street near Herman Pneumatic and was demolished by the railroad company after passenger service was discontinued in the 1950s. Railroad company storage containers now occupy this location. (ZHS.)

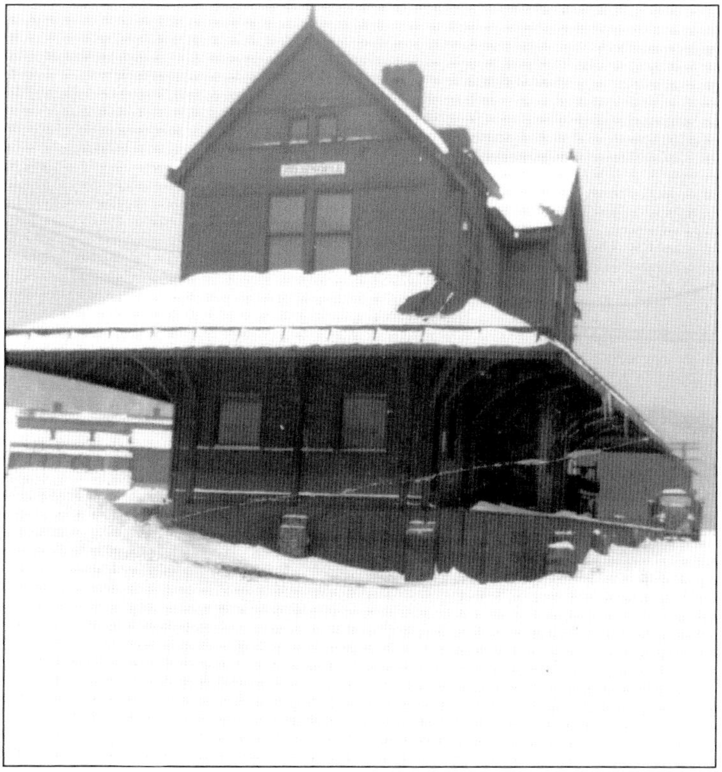

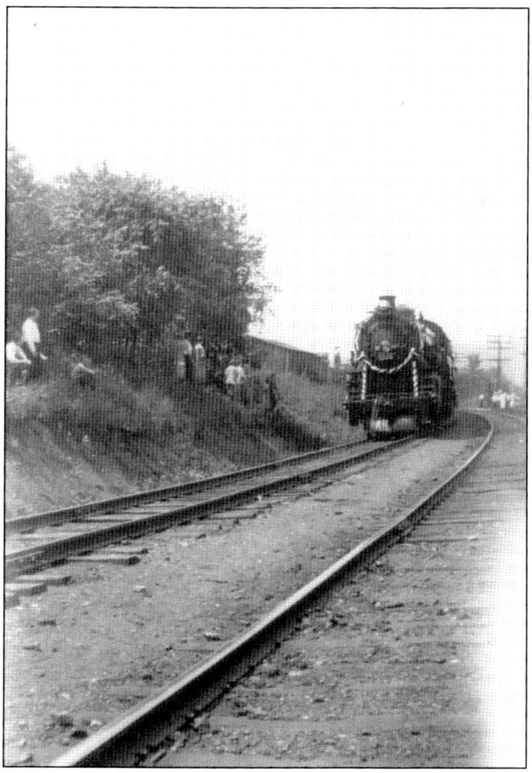

Warren G. Harding was born in rural Ohio in 1865 and served as the 29th president of the United States. He died prematurely, having served only two years—from 1921 to 1923. The news of President Harding's death came to the White House by telephone on August 2, 1923. The president had fallen ill and died suddenly of a heart attack in San Francisco. Due to massive crowds across the country, it took a week to return his body to Washington, DC. On August 7, 1923, President Harding's funeral train passed through Zelienople, as seen in this image. (Jack McMichael.)

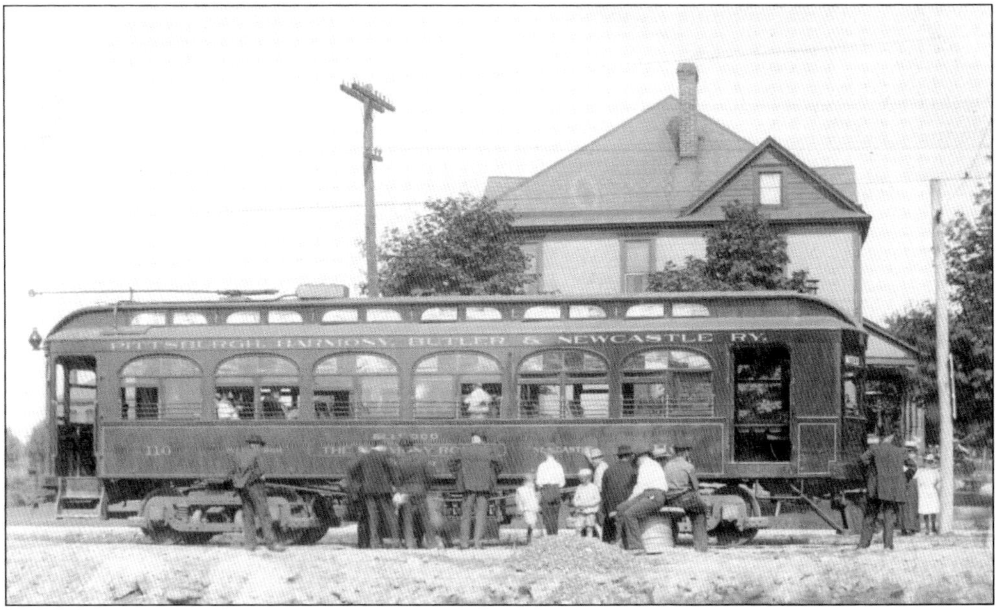

The Harmony Short Line was formed by Pittsburgh business partners Henry Buhl and Russell Boggs, both of whom grew up in Zelienople. The electric railcar service started in 1908 and transported farm products into Pittsburgh's produce market. From Pittsburgh, there was one route to Butler and another to Harmony, Zelienople, and New Castle. Farmers granted a right-of-way through their lands and were guaranteed a stop at their farms. It was used daily for passengers and small freight—until 1931, when automobiles made it obsolete. The photograph above shows passengers at one of the 100 stops on the line. The rare postcard below shows Zelienople's freight station on the left (now the site of Hearth and Home) and the small passenger station on the right (now the site of the St. Paul Church parking lot). Grandview Avenue houses are visible on the right. (Above, Gregory Cowell; below, BZC.)

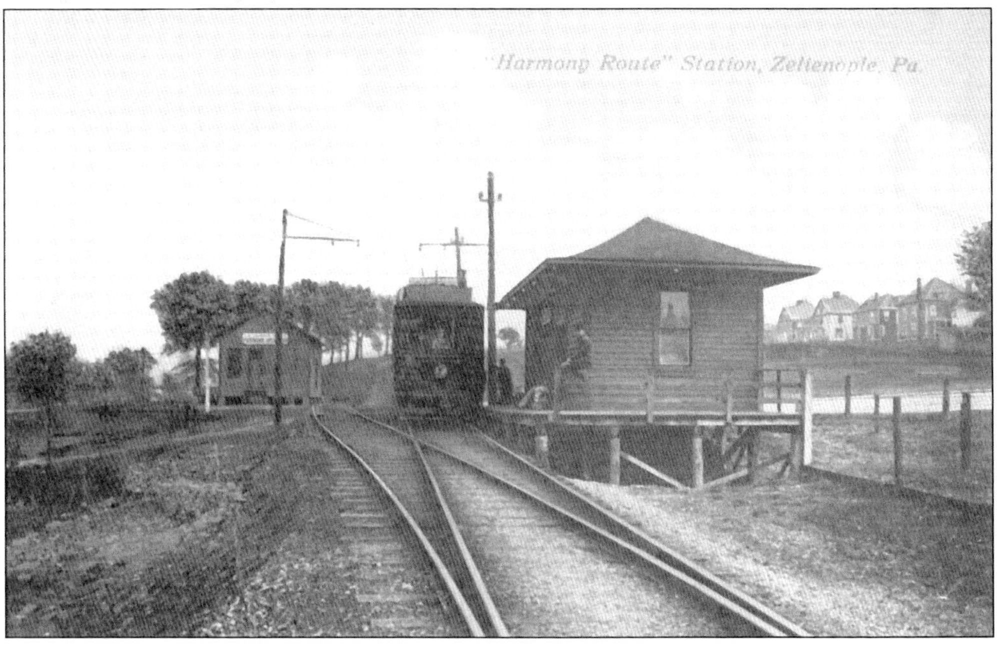

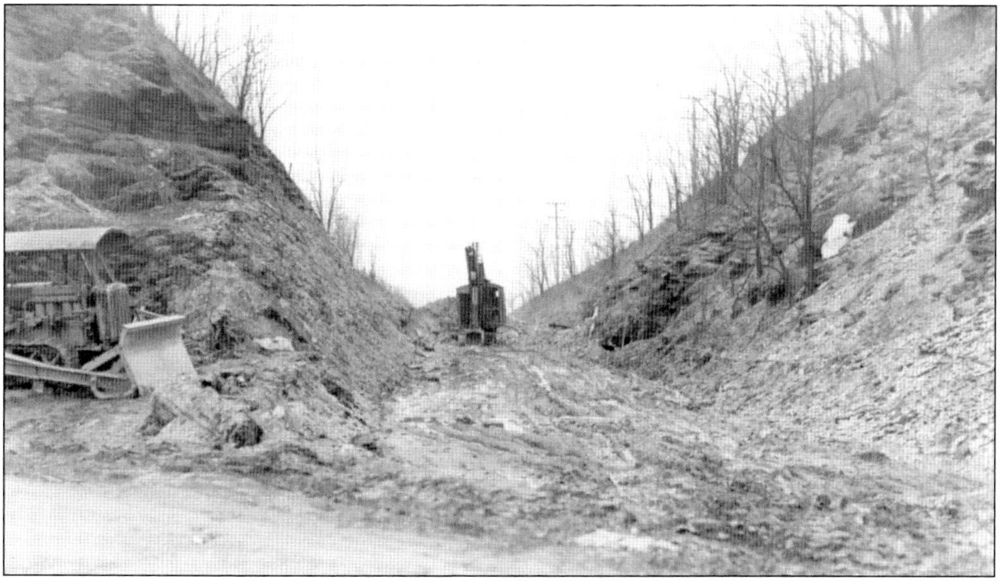

Since the days of Dettmar Basse, traffic crossing the Connoquenessing Creek had to make an immediate left turn on what is now Madison Drive, then proceed around Allen's Hill to Ellwood. The first cut through the hill was made in 1908 for the Harmony Short Line. The line continued to Fombell, Ellwood, and New Castle. After it was discontinued in 1931, the cut was widened for a two-lane highway. The Bassenheim mansion was near this location, as Dr. Warren Wilson played in the ruins as a youth, but no ruins remain today. The photograph below is the Short Line Wilson's Bridge near the former Wilson farm, now the location of the airport. After 1938, the route carried automobile traffic along Route 588, across the creek on the narrow one-lane bridge, and motorists had to take turns crossing it. (Above, Beth Wilson; below, Larry Parisi.)

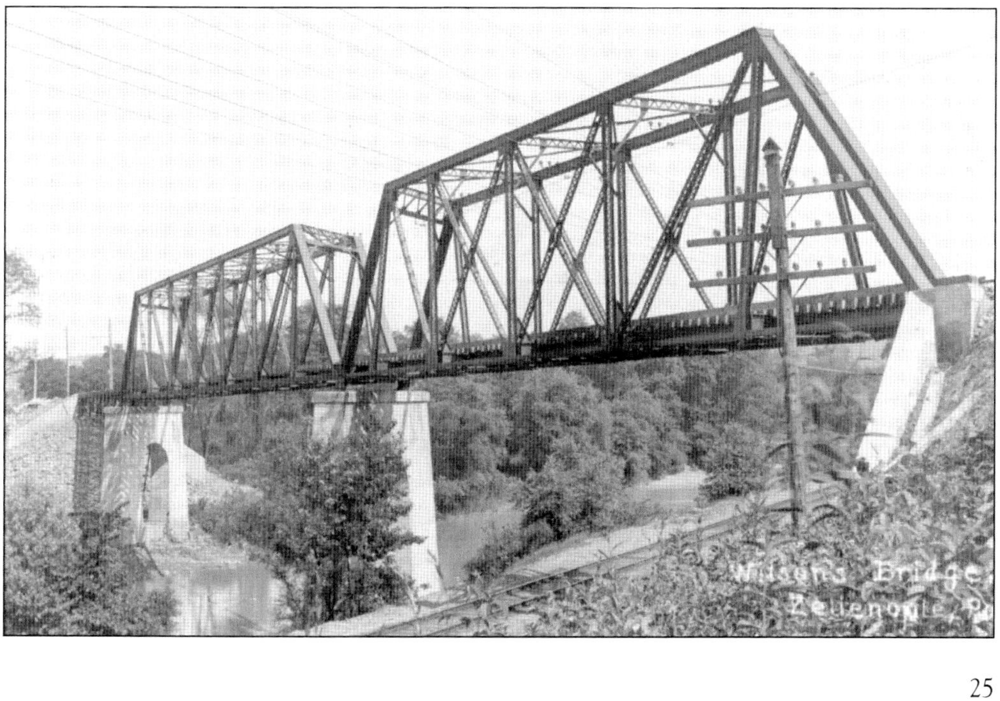

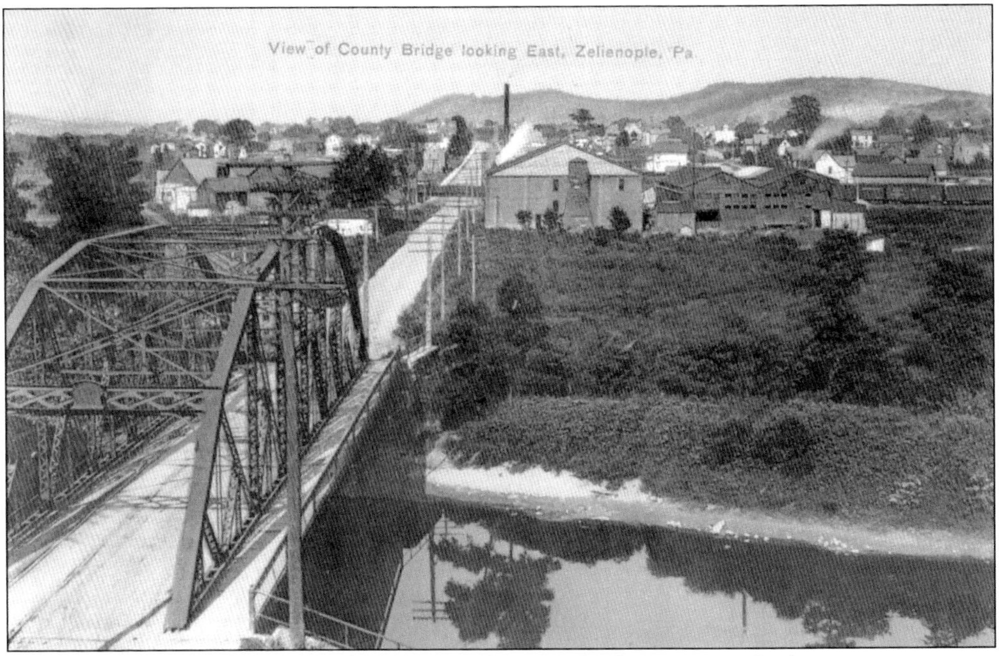

This interesting postcard shows the New Castle Street Bridge in a view looking east into town. Notice the bridge has the Harmony Short Line tracks on the far left and a roadway in the middle. Starting in 1908, the Short Line cars went straight through the Allen's Hill cut, while automobile traffic went to the right and around the hill to Ellwood and New Castle. (Larry Parisi.)

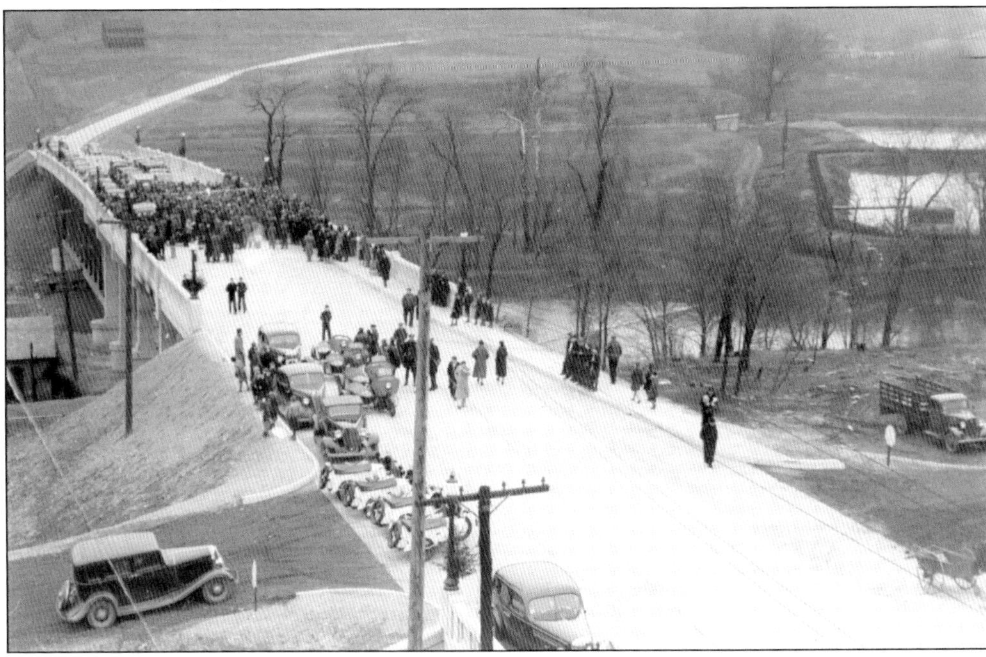

In 1936, there was a big event in town—the opening of a new bridge across the Connoquenessing Creek from Main Street that headed north on Route 19. Prior to this, motorists could either use a ferry service here or go through Harmony. Note the empty farmland to the north and the borough's two new reservoirs, recently completed. The bridge was replaced again in 1989. (ZHS.)

The photograph on the right shows the original town hall and fire department, located at 111 West New Castle Street. The date it was constructed is unknown, but it was replaced in 1931 with the current building shown in the photograph below. This new building cost $35,000, and a bronze plaque inside identifies the 1931 council members Seaton, Hallstein, Eyles, Blum, Duncan, Frishkorn, Nesbitt, Stokey, and Ziegler. The incorporation of Zelienople Borough was in 1840. Some of the first issues dealt with were road conditions; requiring property boardwalks; dead animal carcasses; geese, pigs, and sheep running loose; outhouse sanitation; and nude swimming in the creek in view of the bridge. It must have been an interesting life in 1840. (Both, ZHS.)

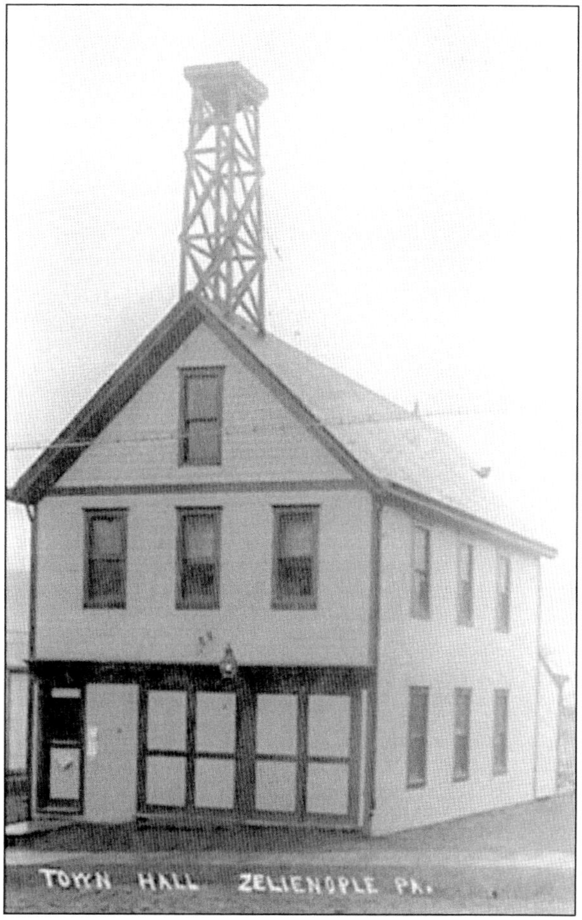

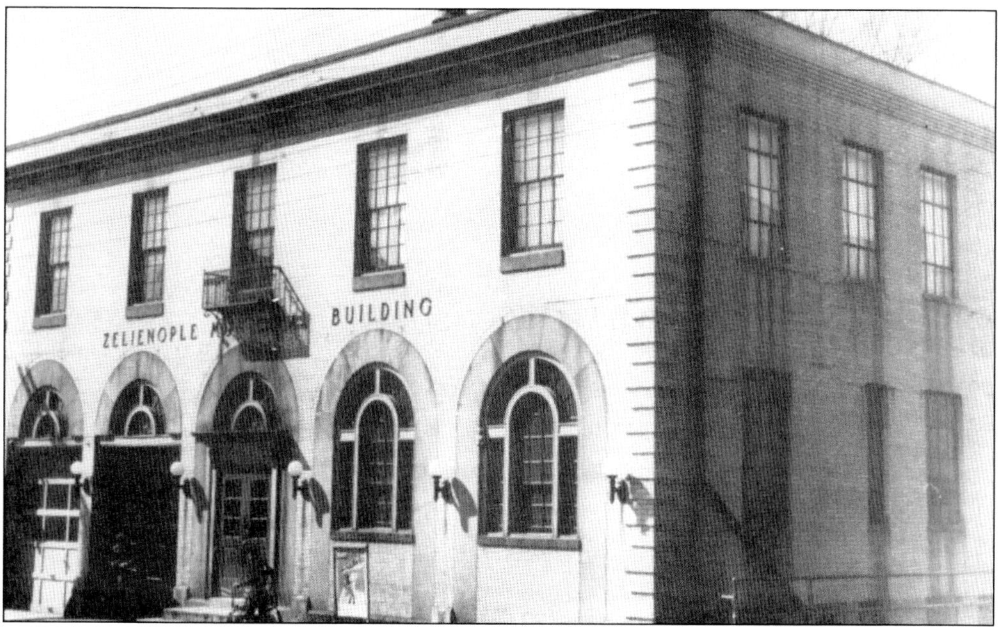

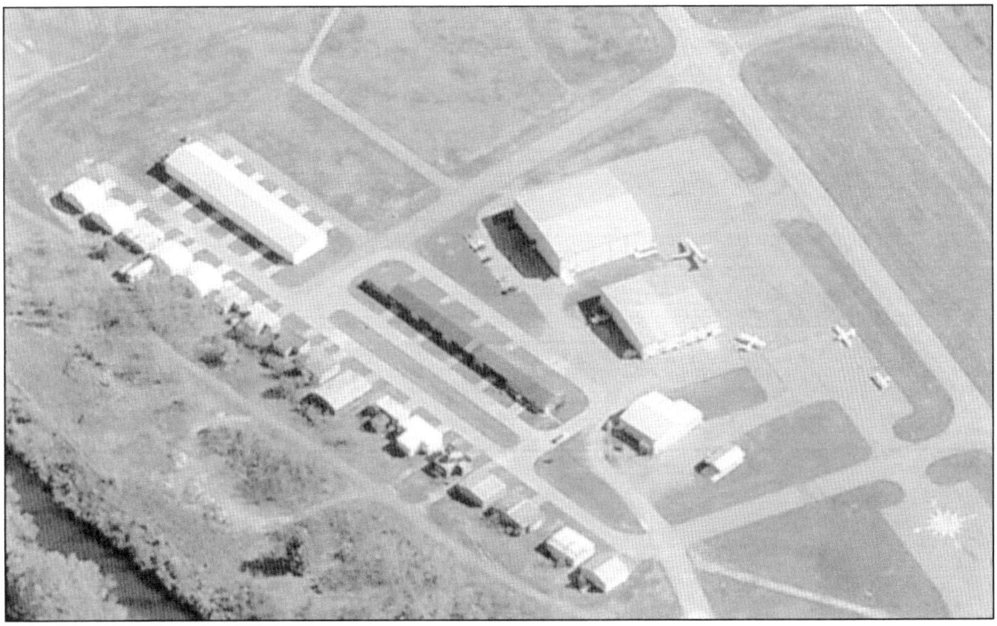

In the 1930s, the Zelienople Airport was constructed on a former strip mine owned by Tasa Coal Company. It was Halstead-Mitchell's private, dirt airstrip until purchased by Zelienople Borough in 1958. The aerial photograph shows the old 1960s garage-type hangers used by local flying enthusiasts. Today, the airport is vastly improved and enlarged with modern hangers, maintenance facilities, and a 5,000-foot paved runway on 300 acres. (Russell Robertson.)

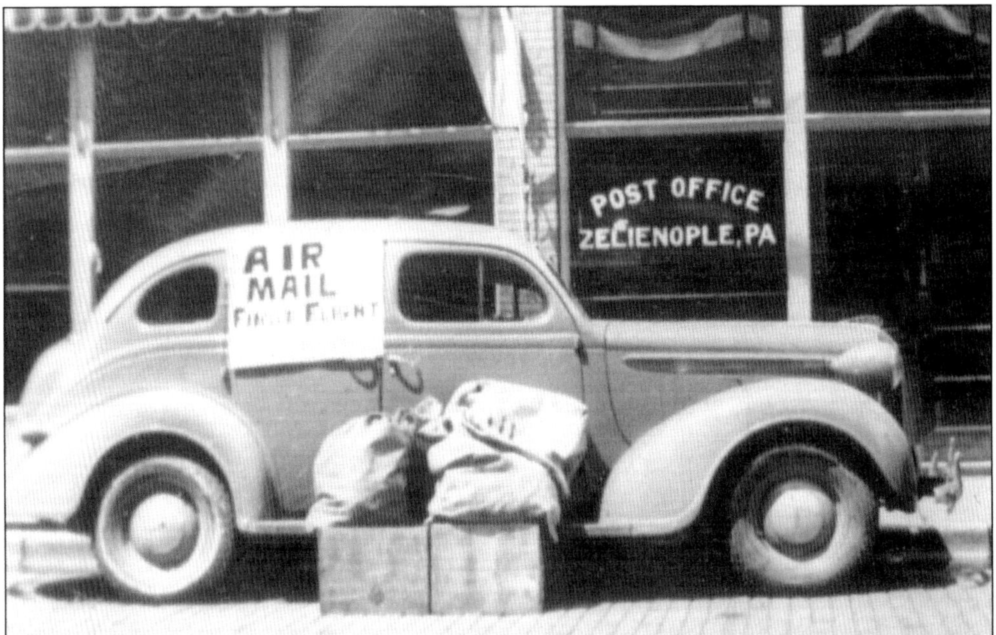

The first official airmail delivery by the US Post Office was made on September 23, 1911, but it took until 1938 for airmail service to reach Zelienople. The "Airmail First Flight" car was photographed outside the post office, located on East New Castle Street behind the Union National Bank, and then driven to the local airport on May 30, 1938, where more photographs were taken. (BZC.)

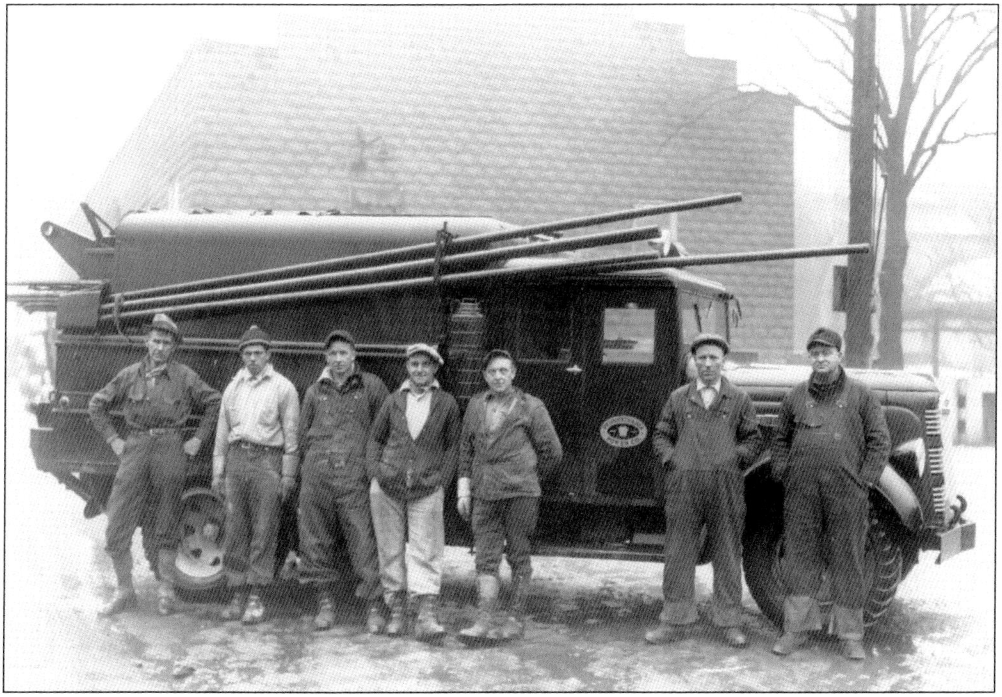

In 1920, Zelienople Borough signed a contract to purchase the poles and wires from the Zelienople Light and Power Company, and a contract with Penn Power for electric current. This photograph from 1937 shows the men who kept the electricity on. In 1956, this building at 201 South Main Street became Roach and Ziegler Interiors, and Penn Power relocated to a large facility on West New Castle Street. (ZHS.)

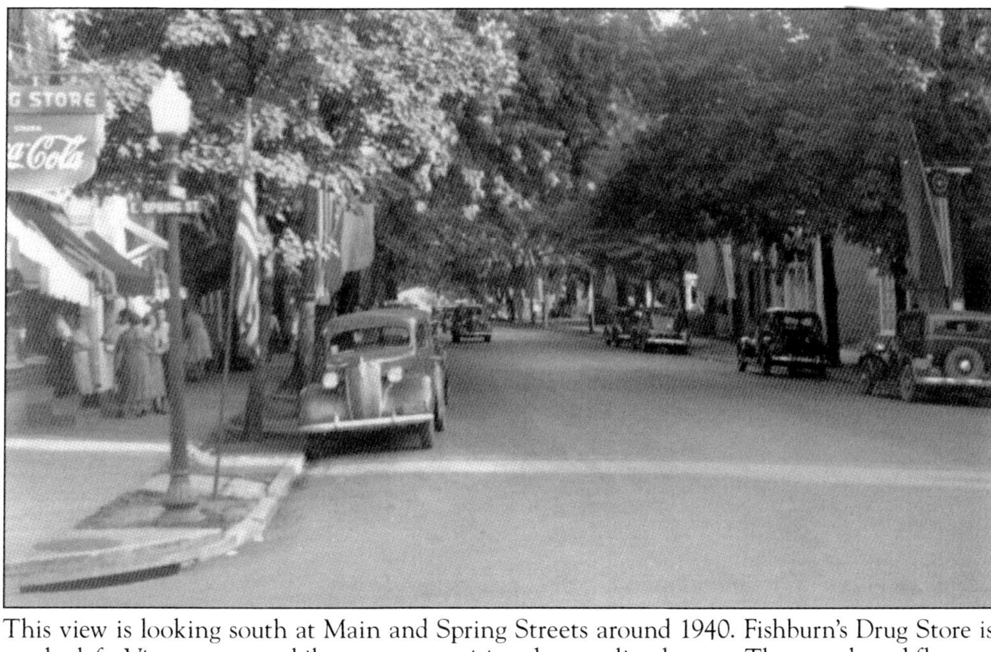

This view is looking south at Main and Spring Streets around 1940. Fishburn's Drug Store is on the left. Vintage automobiles are seen cruising the tree-lined street. The crowds and flags on display would indicate that it is a Memorial Day or the Fourth of July. (ZHS)

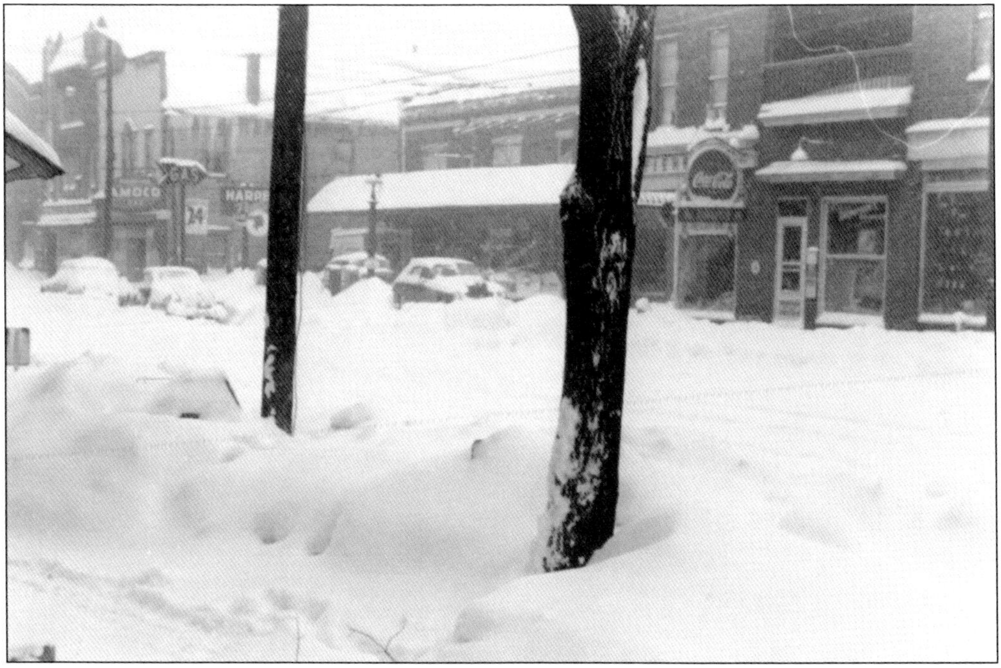

The Great Appalachian Storm of Thanksgiving 1950 moved through the eastern United States, caused significant winds and blizzard conditions, disrupted power to one million, and killed 353 people. Locally, the forecast called for light snow, but the storm dropped over 30 inches of snow, as seen in this Main Street photograph. Everything was at a standstill. Notice that gasoline was selling for 24¢ a gallon at Harper's. (BZC.)

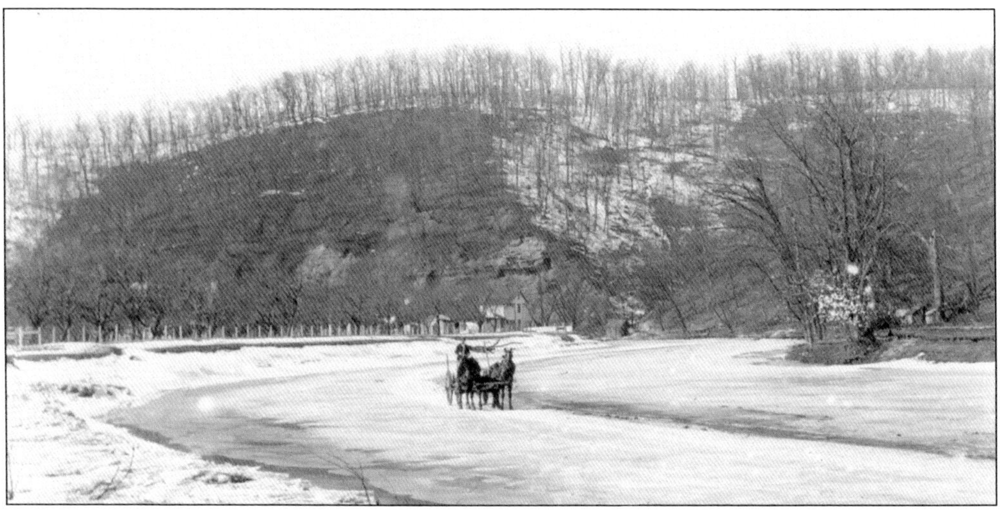

A massive snowstorm in January 1907 did not stop this man from completing his day's work. With all the roads blocked by snow, this man traveled down the center of the frozen Connoquenessing Creek from Cyrus Harper's Feed and Grain Mill, shown in the background. Various grain mills were located here since the time of Dettmar Basse. (ZHS)

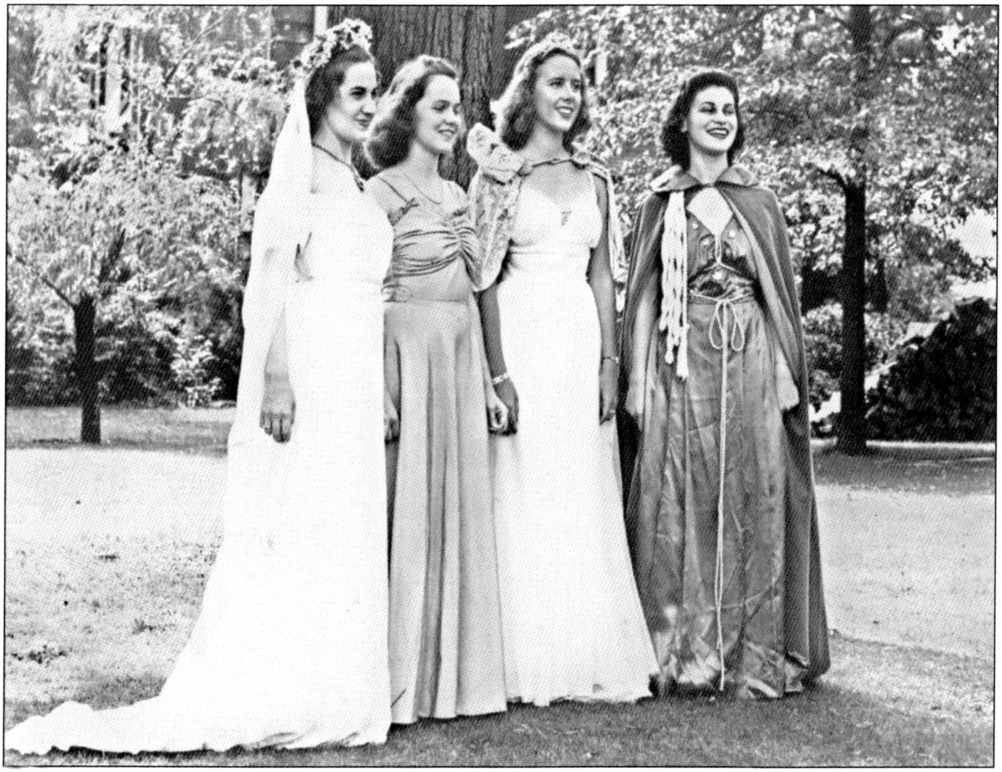

In May 1940, the borough celebrated its centennial with a weekend of festivities, including a parade. The four young ladies representing Zelienople on the Miss Centennial float are, from left to right, Anna Kelly, Amy McKay (Miss Zelienople), Virginia Passavant (queen), and Marjorie Zehner. McKay was a descendant of Christian Buhl, and Passavant was a direct descendant of Zelie Passavant. The photograph below shows some of the other floats in parade, such as those from the Zelia Rebekah Lodge, the Dames of Malta, and the Union National Bank. Zelienople celebrated its 175th anniversary in 2015 with a week full of activities, including a parade featuring grand marshal Amy McKay, age 93. (Both, BZC.)

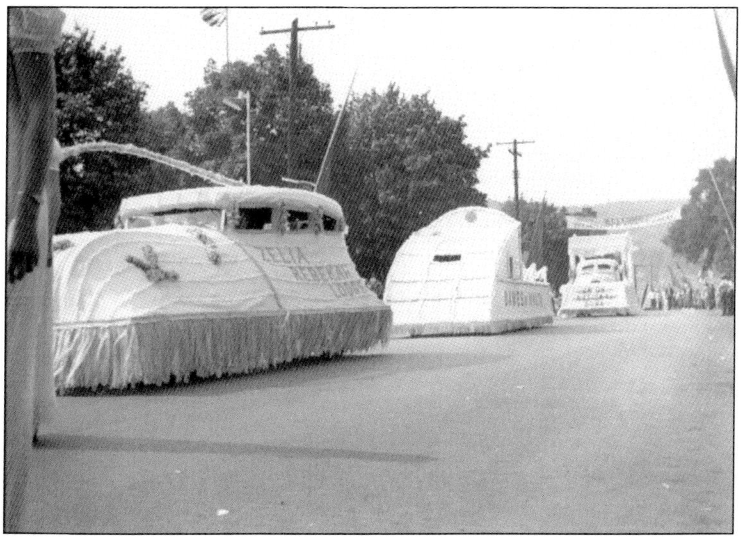

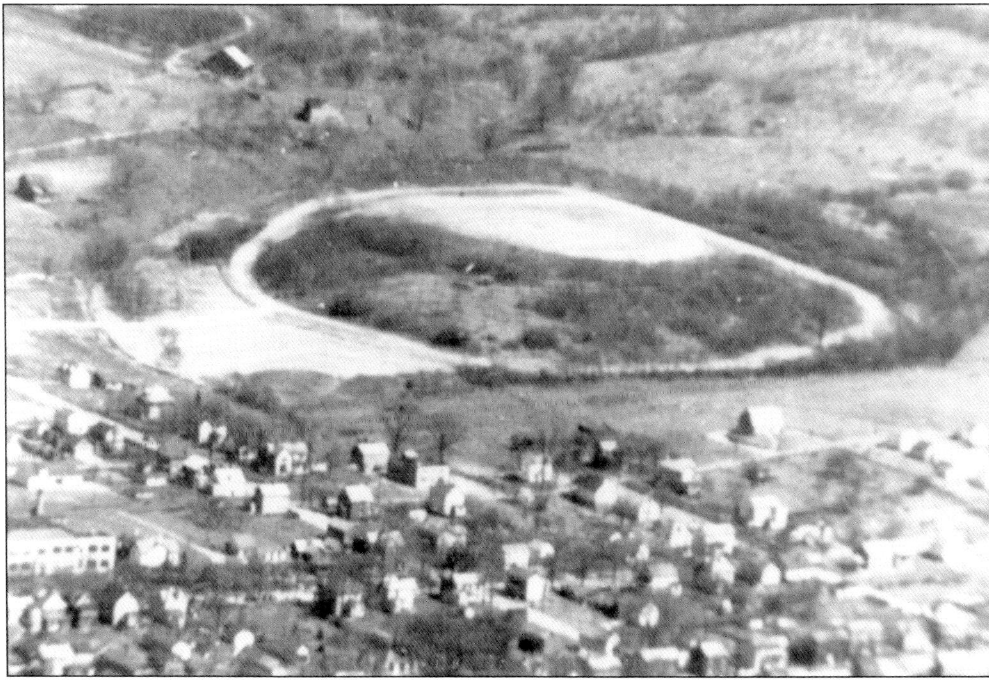

In 1949, a group of astute businessmen contributed $11,500 for land along Beaver Street. Zelienople, Harmony, and Jackson Township all voted to buy the land from the businessmen for that price. The firemen donated swings and slides, the American Legion created the Little League field, and the Lions Club created the larger ball field on the hill; Zelienople Borough added water and electric lines, and the Community Park Association was created. Surrounding the park were the Clark, McClelland, and Hollerman farms, complete with dairy cows. The aerial photograph above shows the park under construction in 1949, and the photograph below shows the filling of the new swimming pool in August 1956. The pool was a major addition to the park and memberships helped pay the costs. Today, the park is the crown jewel of the community. (Both, BZC.)

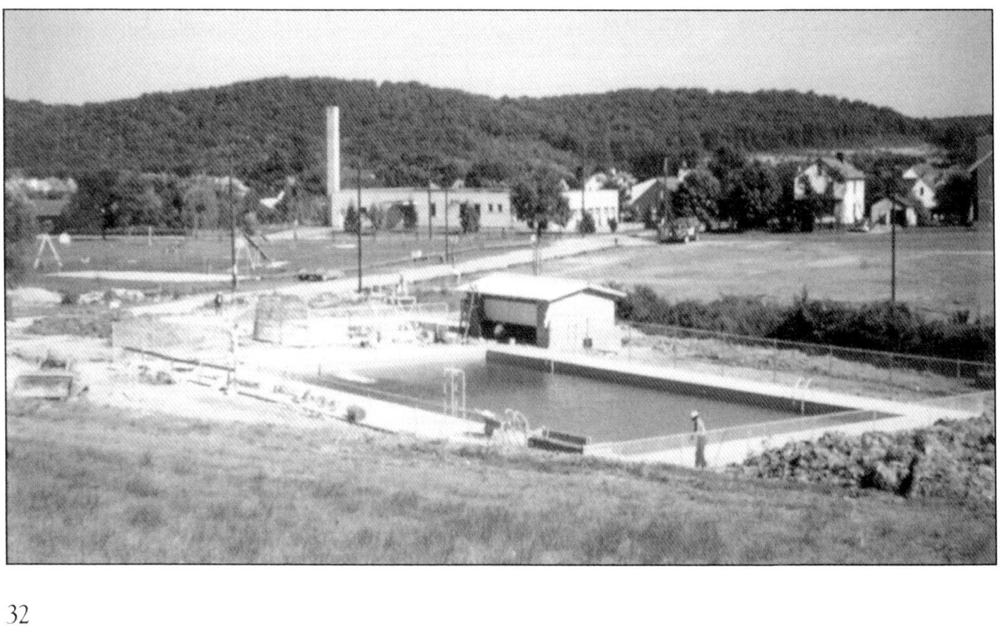

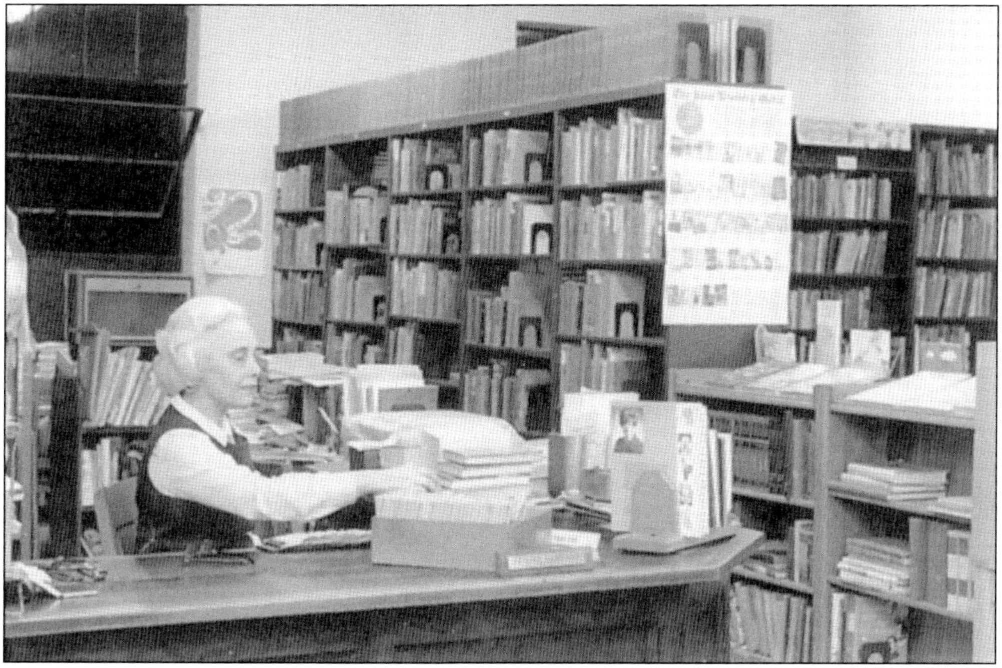

With 74 books, the first town library was organized in the high school building by the Women's Club in 1919. The photograph shows Lenore Lampard working in the library on the second floor of the borough building, where she and the library served the community from 1931 to 1975. In 1975, a new library was built at 227 South High Street on land formerly owned by Charles Passavant Jr. (ZHS.)

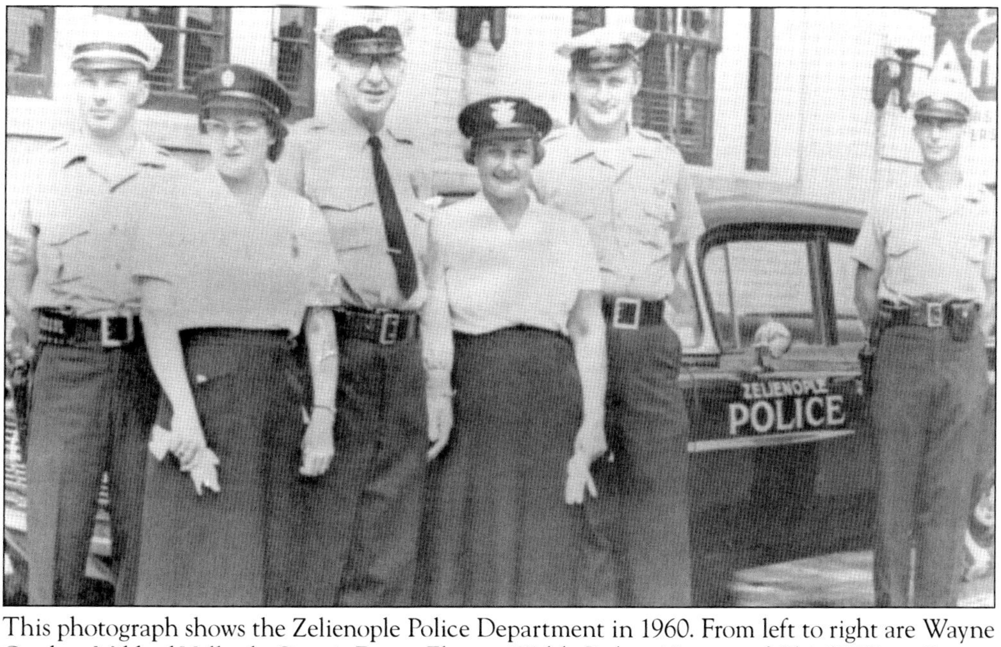

This photograph shows the Zelienople Police Department in 1960. From left to right are Wayne Gordon, Mildred Vollrath, Coonie Evans, Eleanor Walsh, Robert Neese, and Chief William Bozett. Since 1975, the police department has also served nearby Harmony Borough through contracted services. It still operates from the original 1931 borough building. (ZHS.)

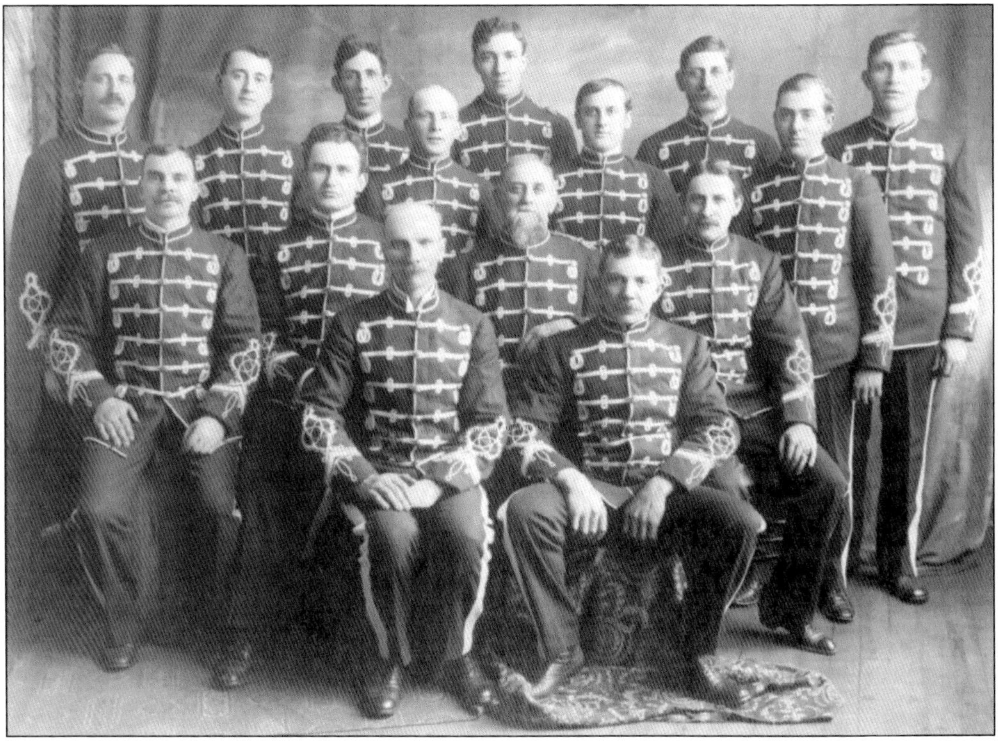

The Zelienople Volunteer Fire Department was organized in 1850. The 1898 photograph above shows firemen smartly dressed in their uniforms. The most disastrous fire in Zelienople history occurred on December 27, 1902. Near the hour of midnight, the cry of "fire" filled the air. The Hildebrand Bakery and Lauten Meat Market in the Kline Building were ablaze. The fire in this wooden building quickly spread to the adjacent structures, including the Amelia Kline residence, John Allen residence, Bastian Hardware, and the Grand Central Hotel. Everything was a total loss, as the fire was almost beyond the capabilities of the horse-drawn equipment. The department later purchased the first motorized equipment in Butler County—a 1919 Ford Model T fire truck. Today, the department is equipped with the latest training and modern equipment. The photograph below shows the volunteers in 1940. (Both, ZHS.)

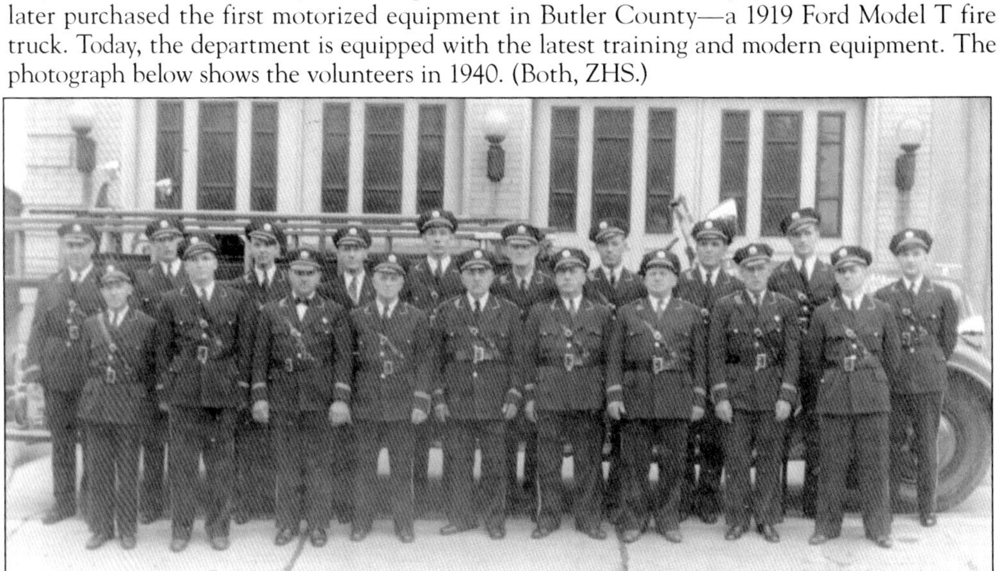

Three

Building Schools and Churches

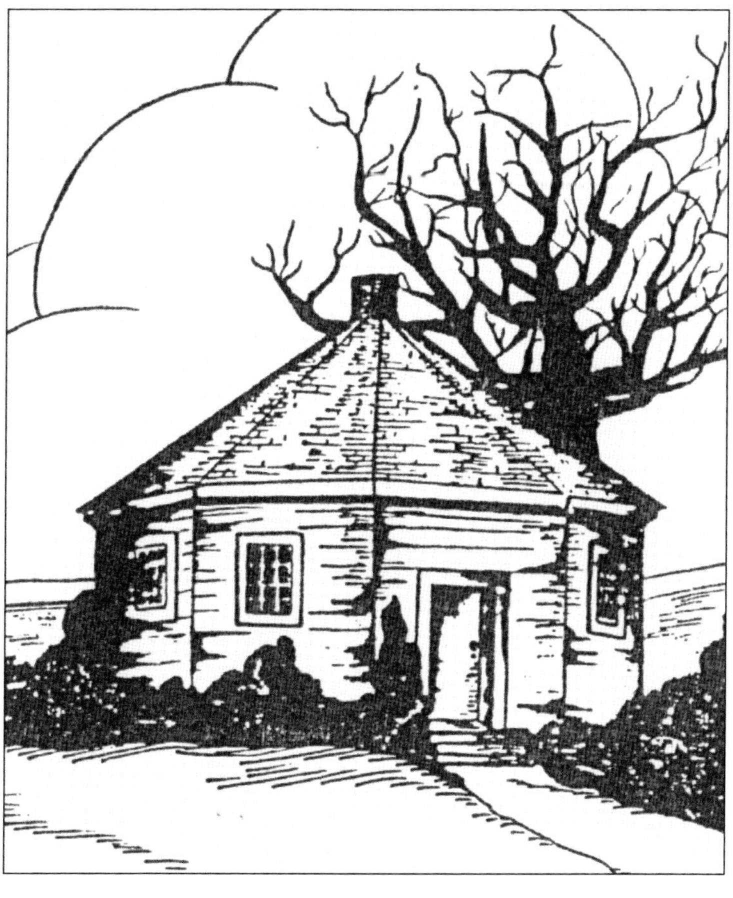

In 1810, pioneer settlers of Zelienople decided to build a schoolhouse at Main and Mill Streets (now Main Street and Grandview Avenue). Land was deeded by Dettmar Basse and bricks from his brickyard were used to construct an octagonal building. The teacher stood in the middle and conducted classes while the students were seated on plain wooded benches, the young in front and older in rear. This school was funded by the town. (ZHS.)

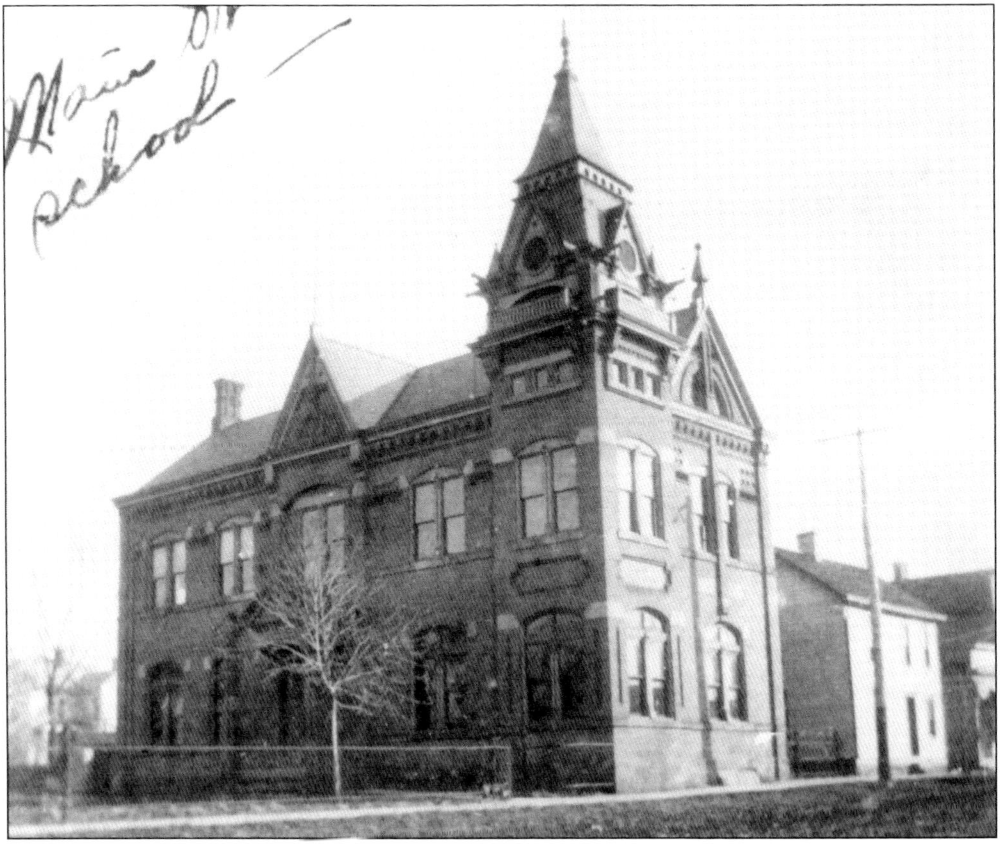

Almost no one remembers this early view of the Zelienople Public School when it was built in 1884 at the corner of Main and Mill Streets. It originally consisted of only four rooms of elementary school students. John E. Kocher was both principal and teacher, working with other certified teachers who graduated from two-year normal schools. A normal school trained teachers to establish teaching standards, or "norms," hence the name. The photograph below shows one of the elementary classes from the early 1900s. Kocher is on the far right. (Both, ZHS.)

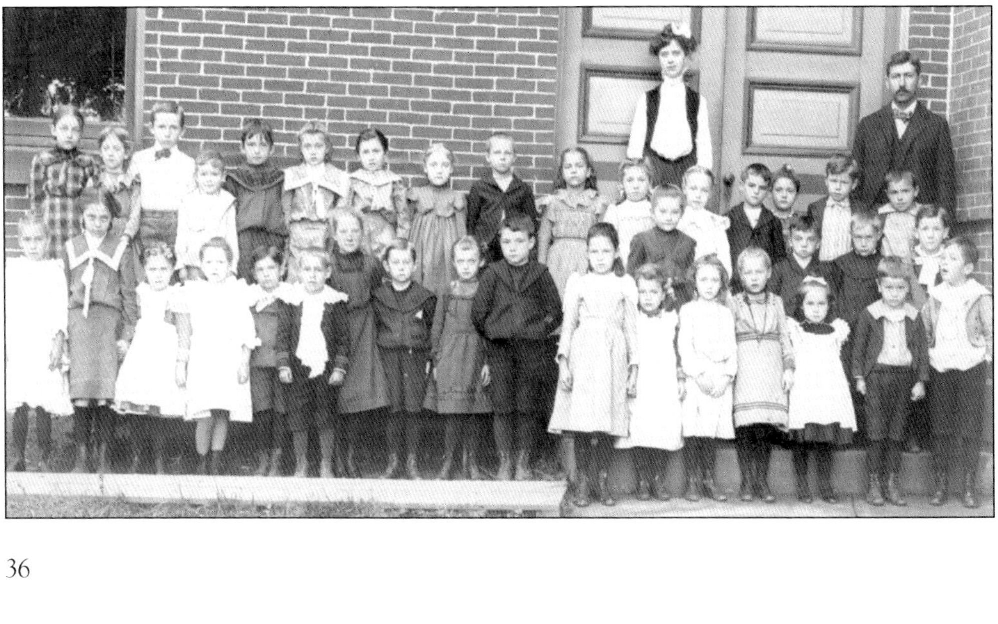

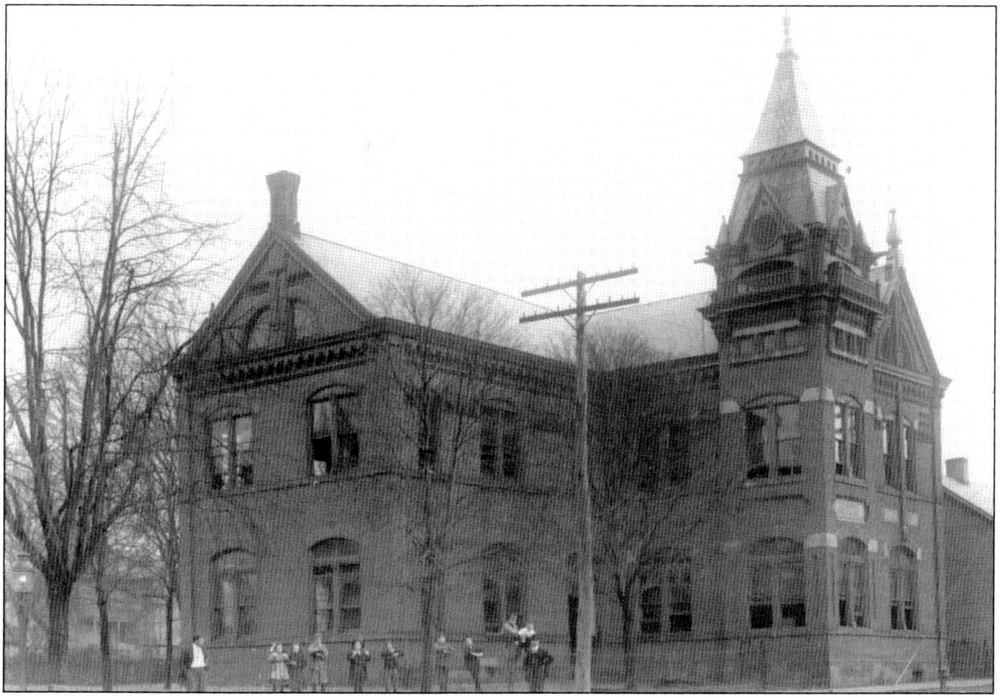

In 1896, principal John Kocher established the first high school in this building. It proved to be so successful that the following year, the building had to be enlarged, as can be seen in the photograph above. The first high school class of seven students graduated in 1899. Both elementary and secondary classes were taught in this building until 1909, when a new high school was erected. This school was still used as an elementary school until 1956, when a new elementary school was constructed near the community park. Unfortunately, this brick building was demolished in 1960 to make way for a community parking lot. The photograph below shows a 1920 elementary class. (Both, Sharon Shanks.)

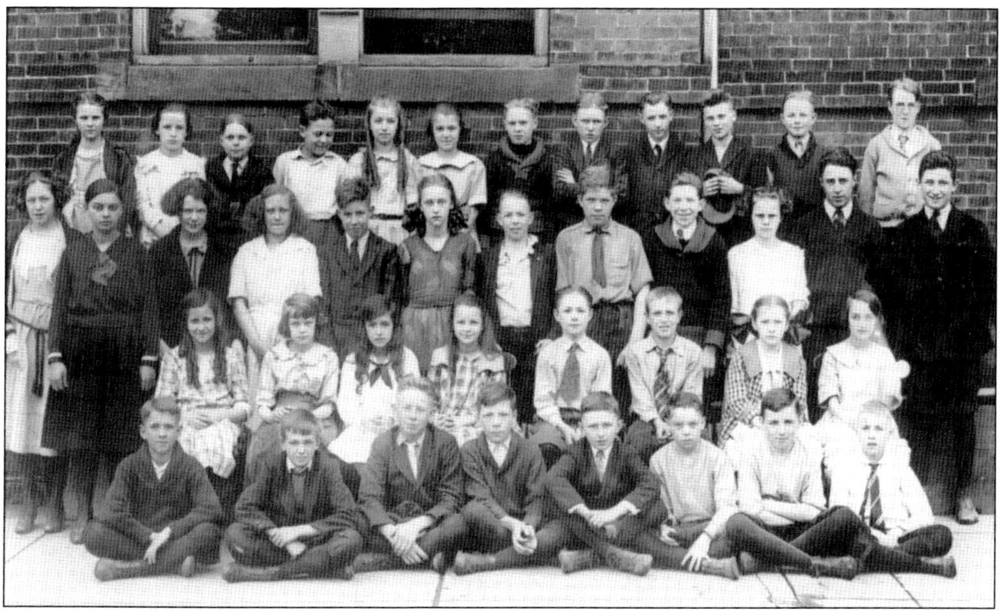

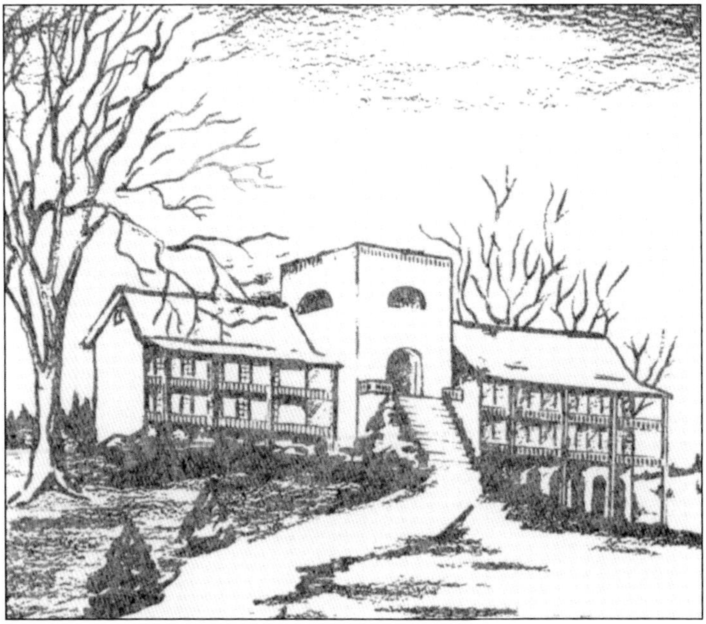

In 1825, the Presbyterian Church opened the Bassenheim Manual Training School in the vacated home of Dettmar Basse. The school accepted young men like Henry Foster, brother of composer Stephen Foster, and William A. Passavant, son of Zelie. They worked the fields for their tuition, room, and board. The school closed in 1836 when the Bassenheim property was sold to Joseph Allen. Today, it is called Allen's Hill. (ZHS.)

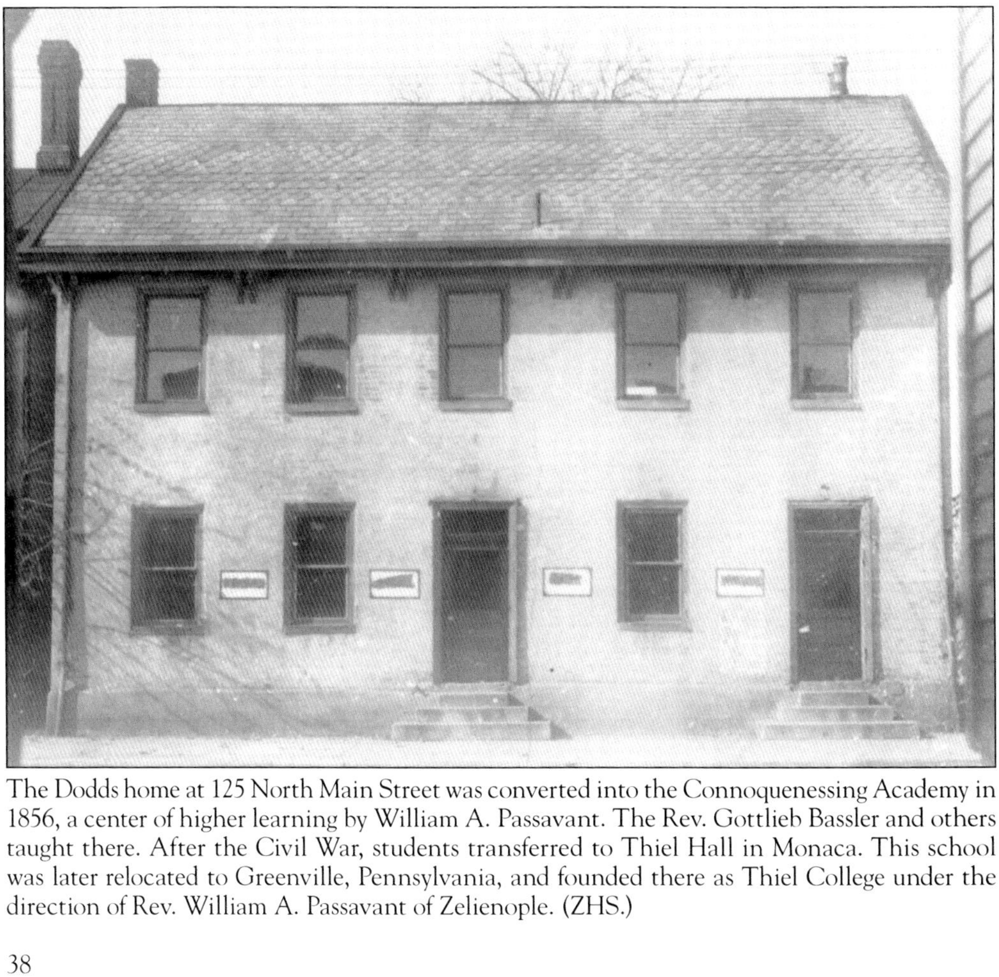

The Dodds home at 125 North Main Street was converted into the Connoquenessing Academy in 1856, a center of higher learning by William A. Passavant. The Rev. Gottlieb Bassler and others taught there. After the Civil War, students transferred to Thiel Hall in Monaca. This school was later relocated to Greenville, Pennsylvania, and founded there as Thiel College under the direction of Rev. William A. Passavant of Zelienople. (ZHS.)

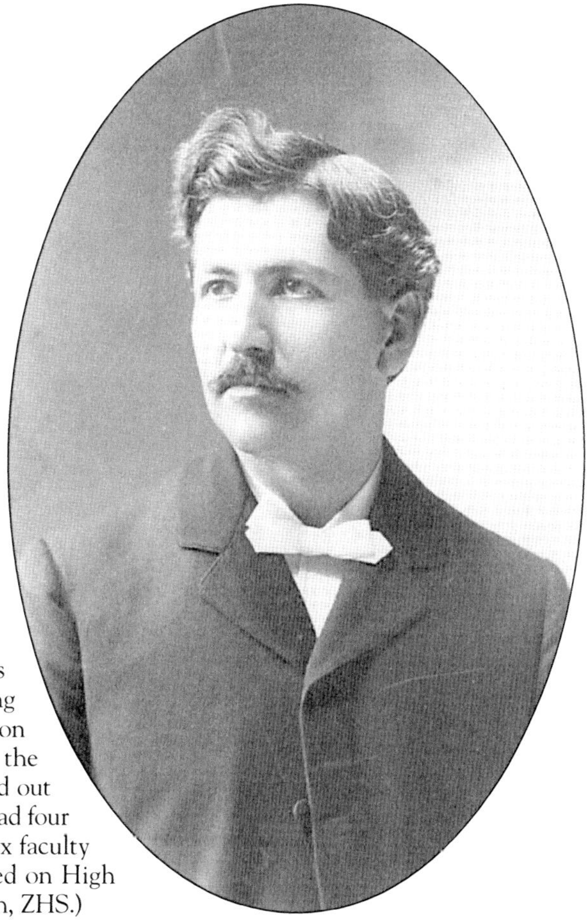

John E. Kocher (right) was born on a farm north of Zelienople in 1870. After graduating from Slippery Rock State Normal School in 1895, Kocher founded a three-year high school in the public school building on Main Street in 1896. The first graduating class in 1899 only had seven students. Because of the success in his program and increased enrollment, a separate building was needed. In 1909, Zelienople High School was built by J.J. Fogel & Sons at a cost of $12,000. Ground was broken in May 1909, the school building completed in March 1910, and a dedication held on April 7, 1910. Visitors' day was the following day, and half the town turned out to tour the building. The school only had four rooms, seating 45 pupils in each, and six faculty members. The new high school located on High Street is pictured (below) in 1911. (Both, ZHS.)

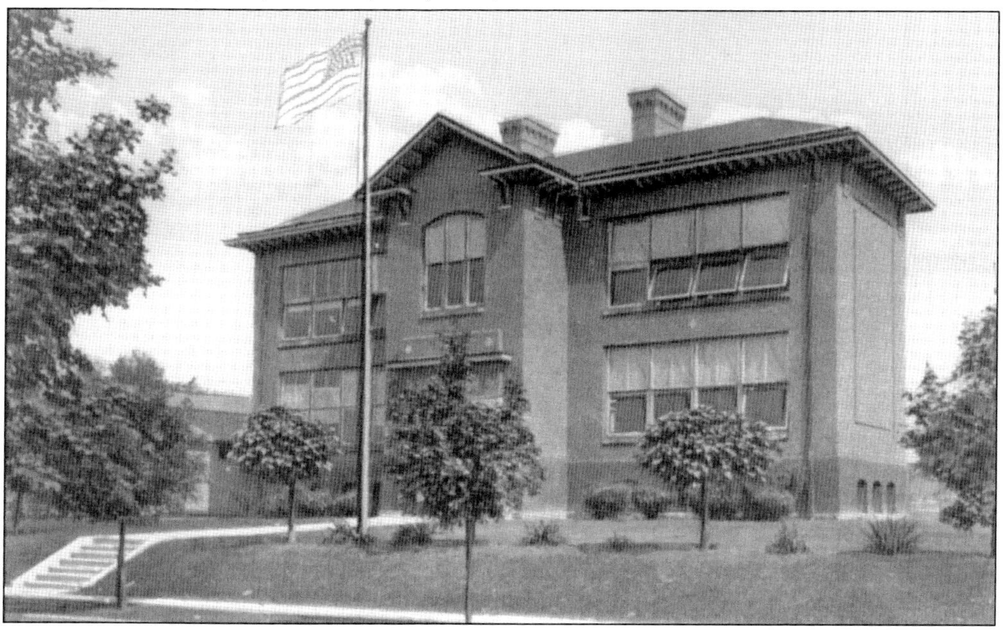

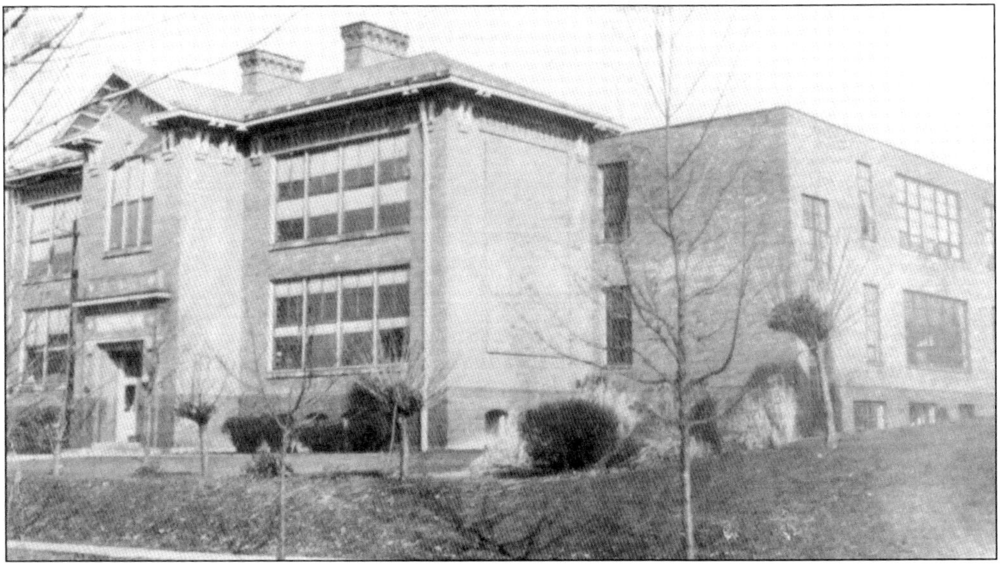

In April 1925, a bond issue for $85,000 was approved for expansion of the high school. It added the gymnasium, dining hall, and four classrooms on the south side of the building. The photograph above shows the 1926 addition to the growing school. The photograph below is a good view of the interior of the gymnasium and seating for assemblies. This photograph shows the 1930 basketball team that played under coach Paul Sager. The addition to the school made it possible to offer band, orchestra, glee clubs, and school plays. (Both, ZHS.)

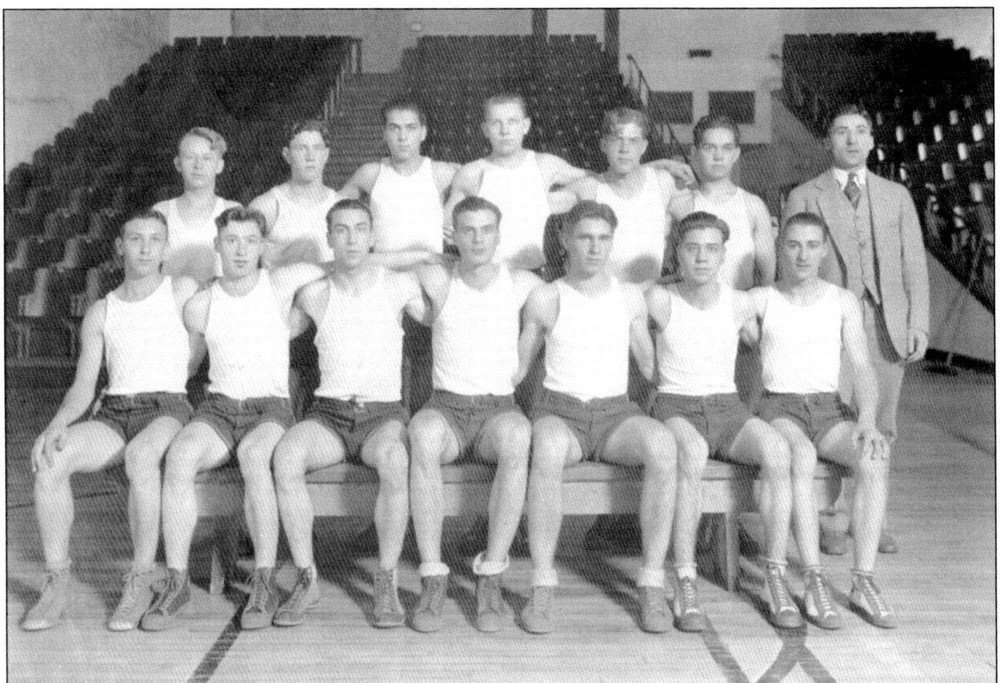

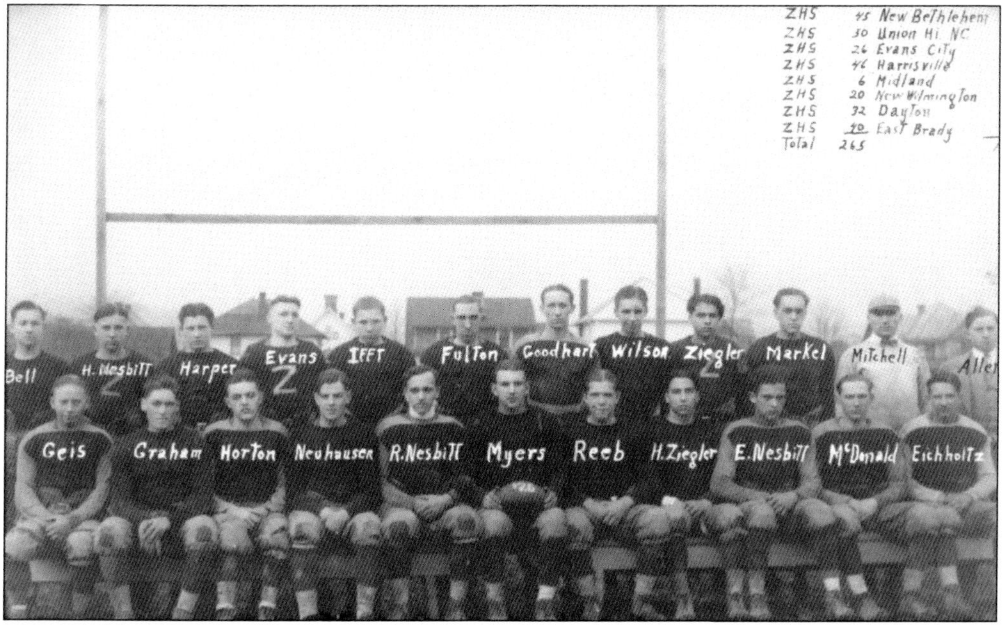

In 1935, the high school was enlarged again, adding typing, mathematics, and chemistry rooms. In 1940, the final enlargement provided rooms for biology, home economics, a library, industrial arts, and the portable music building. The Varner home next door was also purchased for use as departments for art and special education. The 180-pupil capacity of the original building had been increased to a student body of 600, allowing grades 7–12 to attend here. The photograph above shows the 1927 football team with its record in the upper right corner. The photograph below shows the seventh and eighth graders from 1935. (Both, ZHS.)

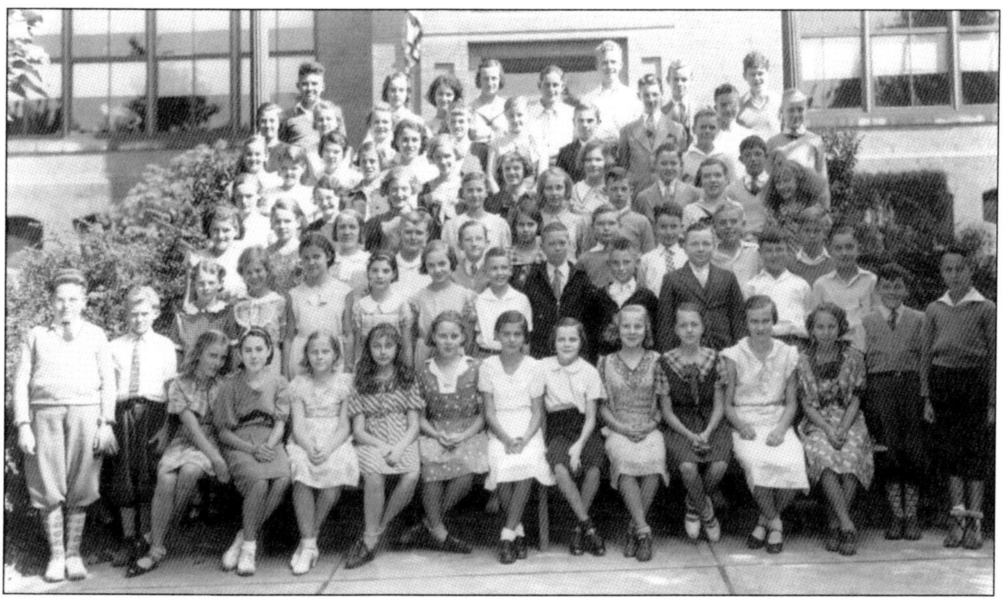

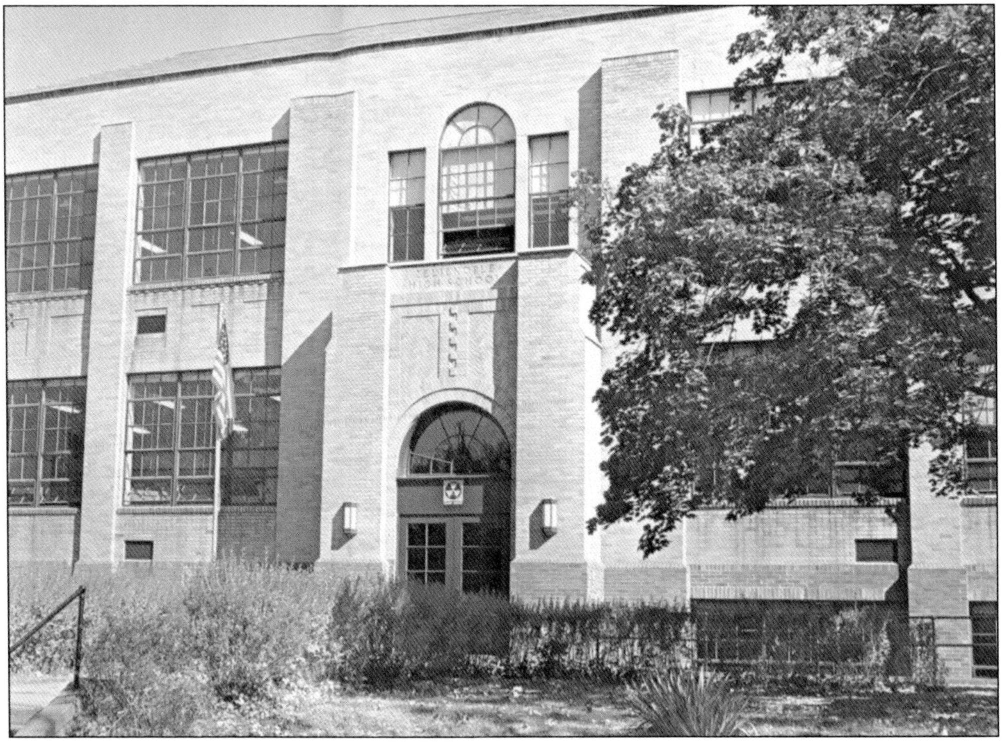

Zelienople High School was used for grades 8–12 until the last graduating class of 100 students in 1964, of which this author was a member. At that time, Zelienople and Evans City schools merged into the Seneca Valley School District, which included all of Cranberry, Forward, Jackson, and Lancaster townships. A new high school for grades 9–12 was built east of Harmony on the former Peter Nesbitt farm of 58 acres. The first year of operation, 1964–1965, was not pleasant for the students, as the new facility was not fully completed. The photograph above is probably the last official photograph of the high school printed in the 1964 *Zelie Ann* yearbook. The photograph below shows the gymnasium/auditorium where teachers "Red" Bender and "Ma" Morgan taught physical education and where many exciting basketball games were played. (Both, ZHS.)

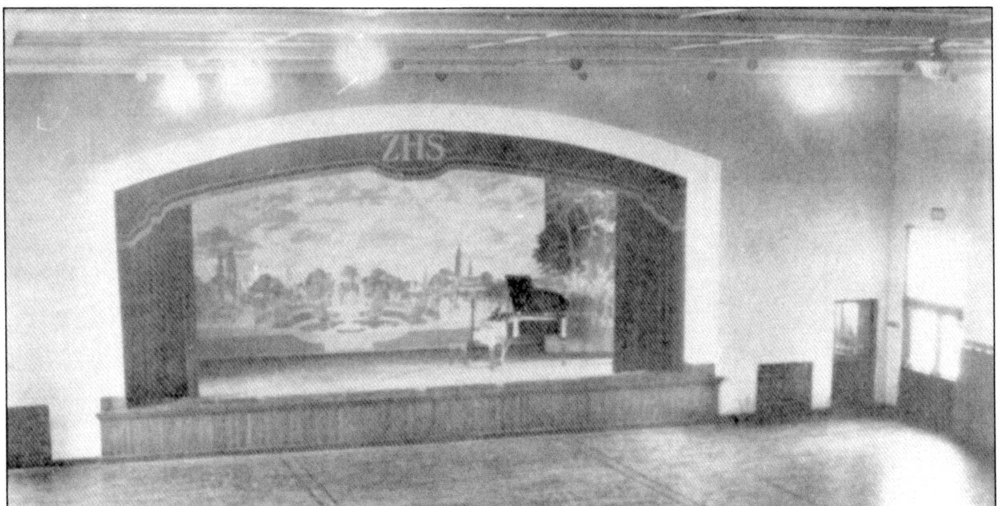

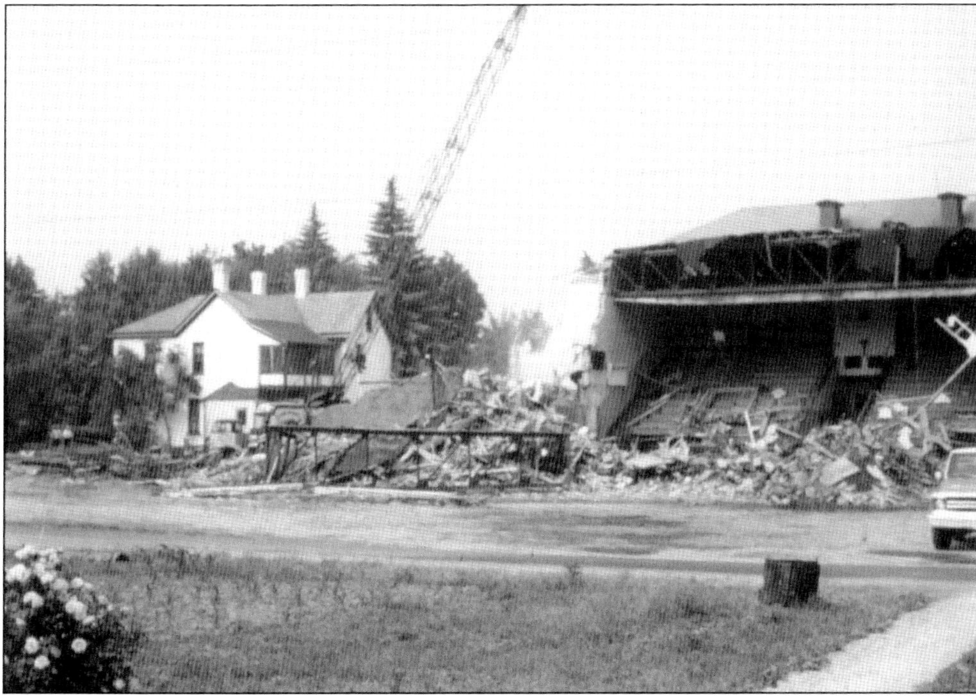

Zelienople High School continued to be used as a sixth grade for the entire school district until 1968, when the old Evans City High School was remodeled and used for that purpose. It was a sad day for the whole town in 1970 when the wrecking ball and demolition equipment showed up. Just about everyone in town had family members who graduated from this school, which stood proudly at 214 South High Street for over 60 years. These photographs were taken from the rear of the building and show the rear wall removed, revealing the gymnasium and seating. Everything was demolished to make way for Maple Court Senior Housing, which was completed the following year. (Both, BZC.)

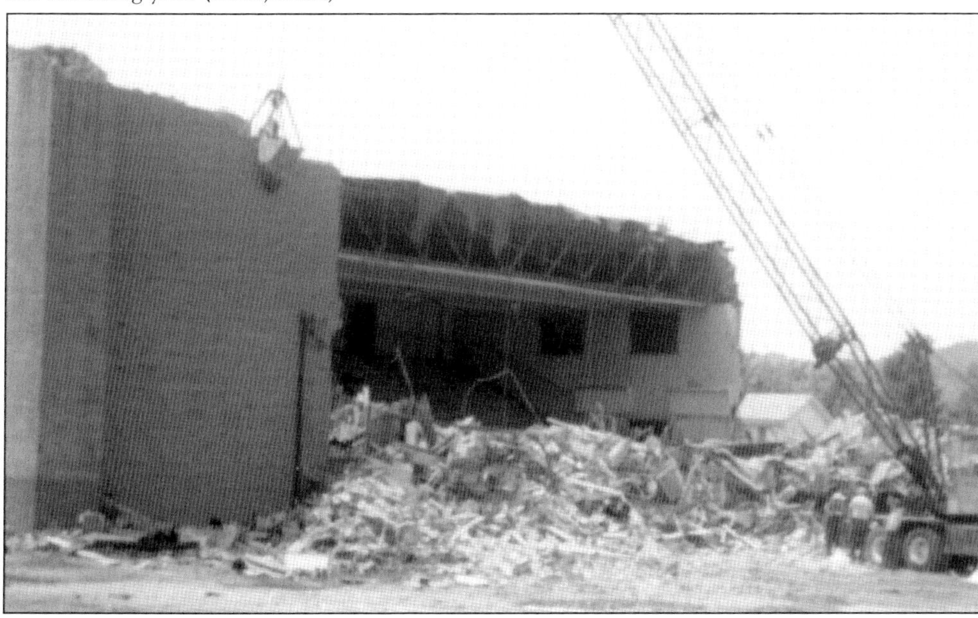

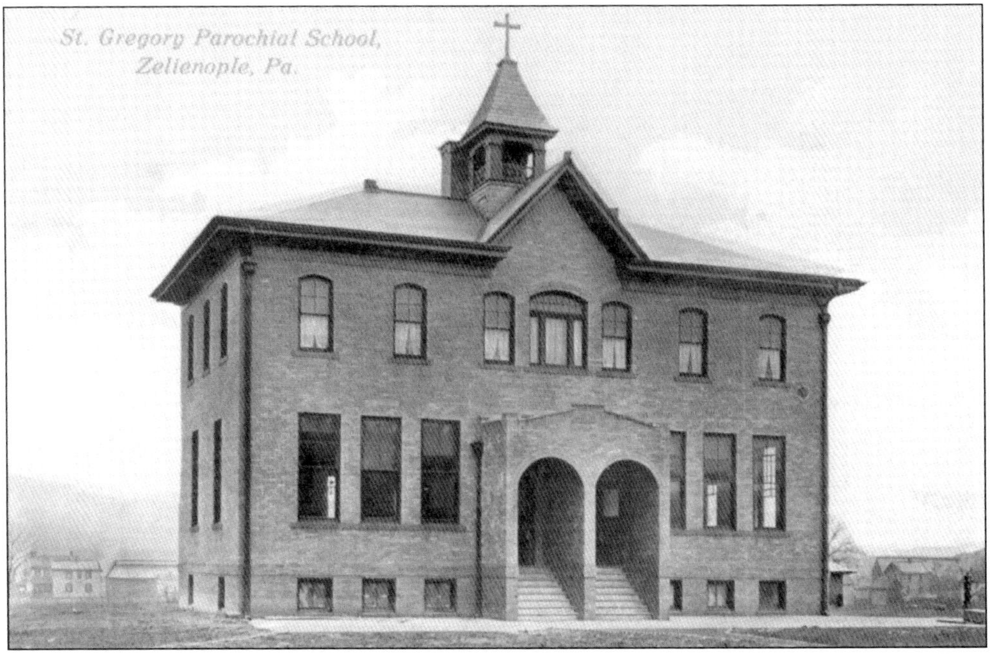

The St. Gregory Parochial School was built in 1911, serving 36 students the first year. Students attended here for elementary grades, and then later attended Zelienople High School. This building has been expanded many times over the years and serves hundreds of students. It is located on the St. Gregory Campus at 115 Pine Street. (ZHS.)

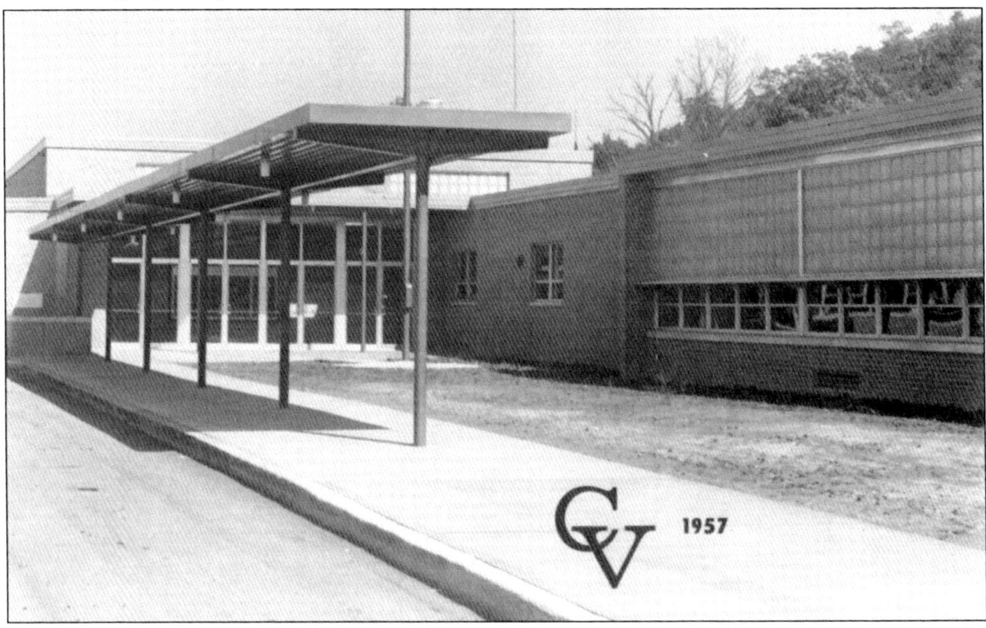

The school district purchased property at the eastern edge of town in 1956 and constructed a new elementary school for grades K–6. The grand opening ceremony was held at the start of classes in September 1957, with local officials, teachers, parents, and students attending. The Connoquenessing Valley Elementary School has been expanded over the years and serves the communities of Harmony and Zelienople. (ZHS.)

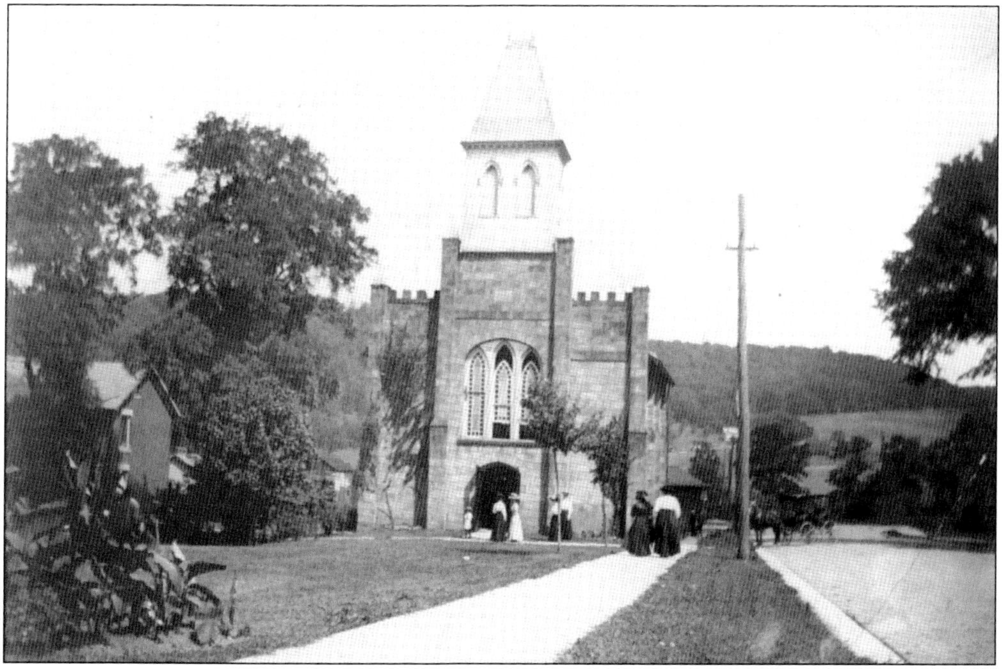

Zelienople's oldest church, St. Paul Lutheran, was organized on September 12, 1821, by a group of early settlers meeting in the home of George Henry Mueller (Benvenue) and led by Bishop Johann C.G. Schweitzerbarth. Schweitzerbarth was the first resident minister of Zelienople, coming here from Germany in 1819. He came to the area at the request of Dettmar Basse, who wanted to establish and build a church in Zelienople. The cornerstone of the church was laid in 1826, and this stone church has stood the weather and the test of time for almost 200 years. The photograph above shows the church on Main Street in the horse-and-buggy days; the photograph below shows attendees of a church picnic around 1912. (Both, ZHS.)

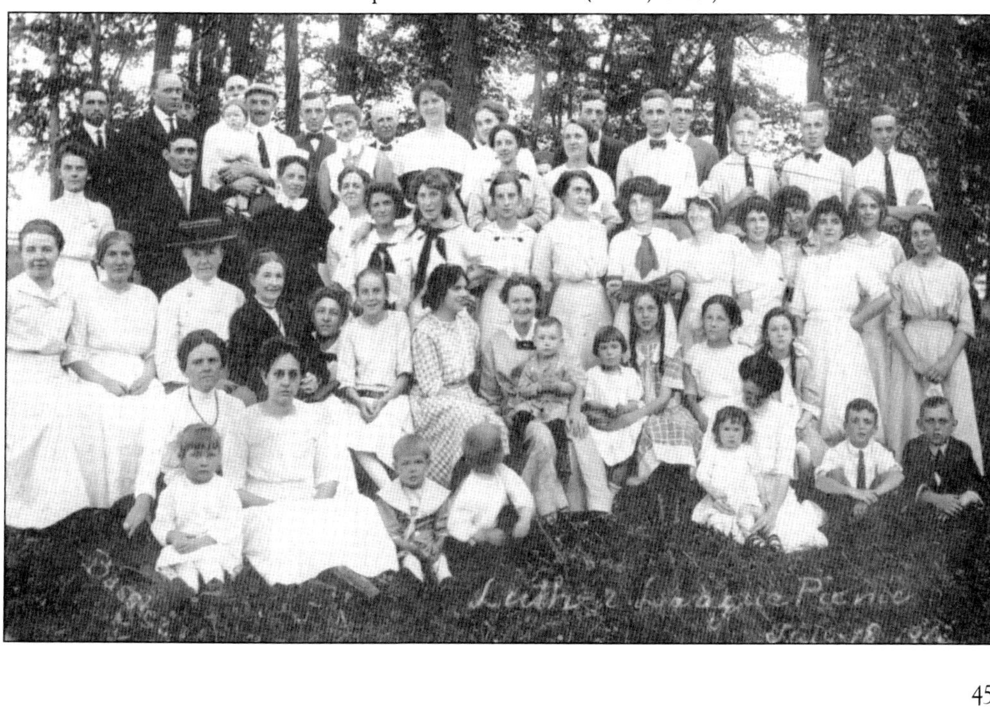

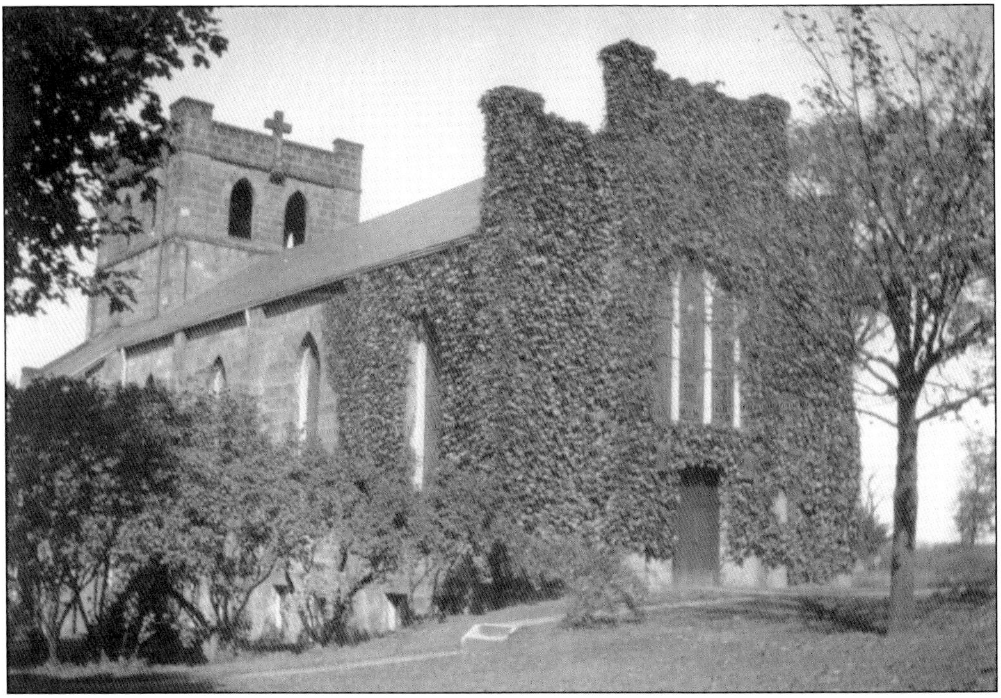

In 1913, St. Paul Lutheran was enlarged, as shown in the photograph above. A new bell tower was added and the interior was remodeled. Henry Buhl Jr. donated the stained-glass Martin Luther window and one of the aisle windows in memory of his grandfather Christian Buhl. Dr. William A. Passavant, the youngest son of Philipp and Zelie Passavant, was baptized and confirmed in this church. Passavant was a renowned Lutheran pastor and founded more than 40 hospitals and institutions throughout the United States. He is regarded by many as the greatest institutional leader that the Lutheran church has ever produced. A plaque in his memory is located in the front of the church. The photograph below shows a gathering of the ladies of the church in 1940. (Both, ZHS.)

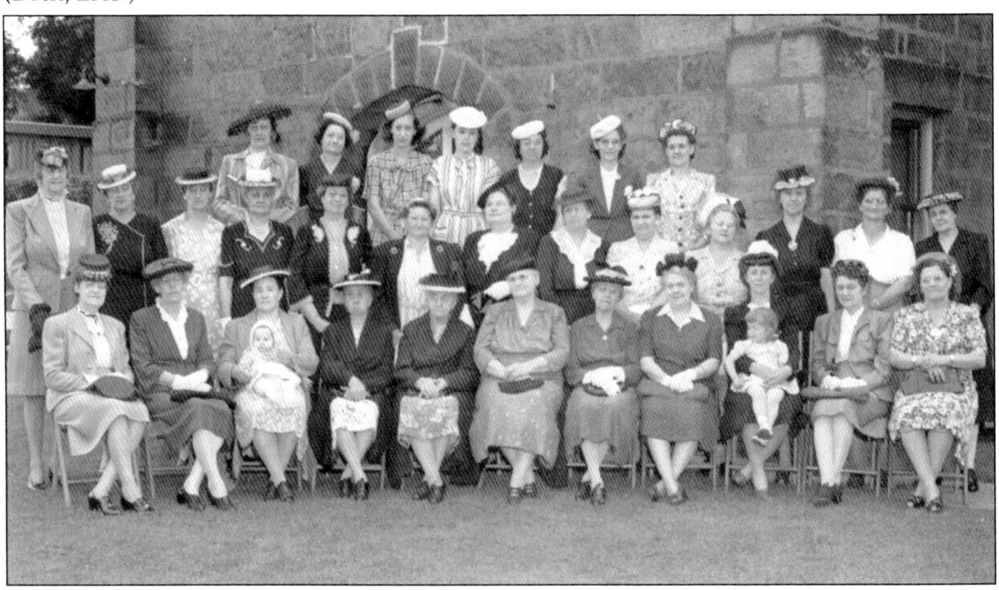

Because the people of Zelienople shared a common German heritage, the St. Paul Lutheran sermons were in the German tongue. As other immigrants joined the community, they requested that the sermons be delivered in English. St. Paul's bishop, Johann C.G. Schweitzerbarth, called Rev. Gottlieb Bassler to fill this need. The English Evangelical Lutheran Church of Zelienople was then organized in 1843, and a small stone church was built for that congregation. As shown in the photograph on the right, the 1883 church that was built lasted until 1905, at which time the beautiful stone church shown below was constructed on Grandview Avenue. In 2011, the two churches combined under the leadership of one pastor. (Both, ZHS.)

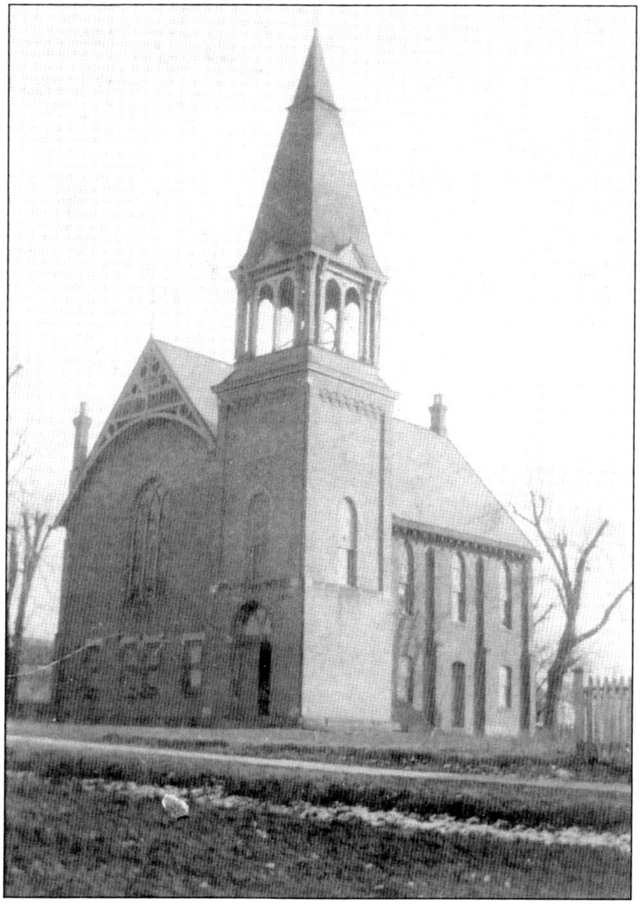

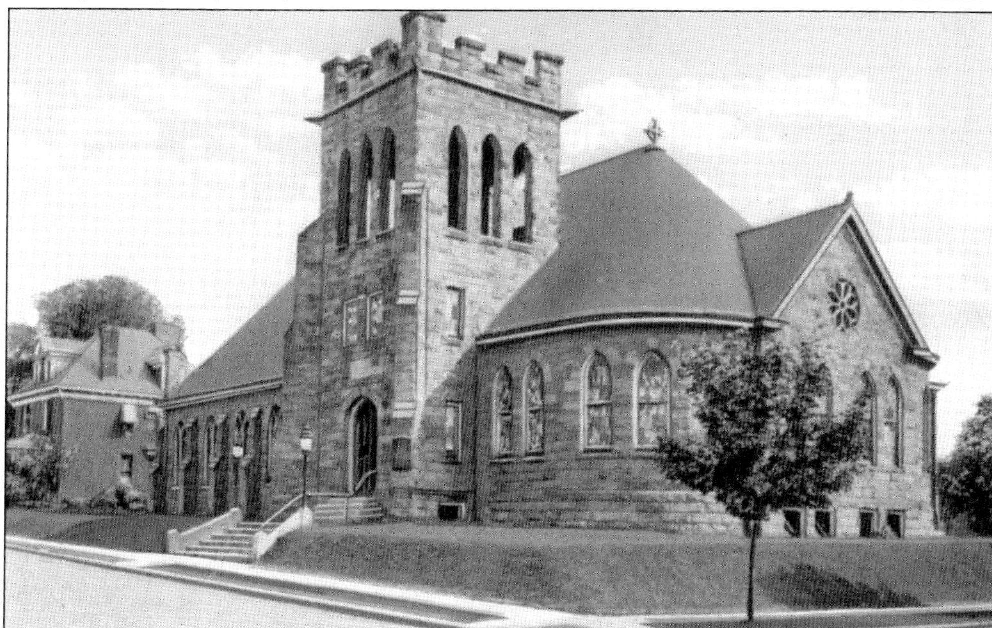

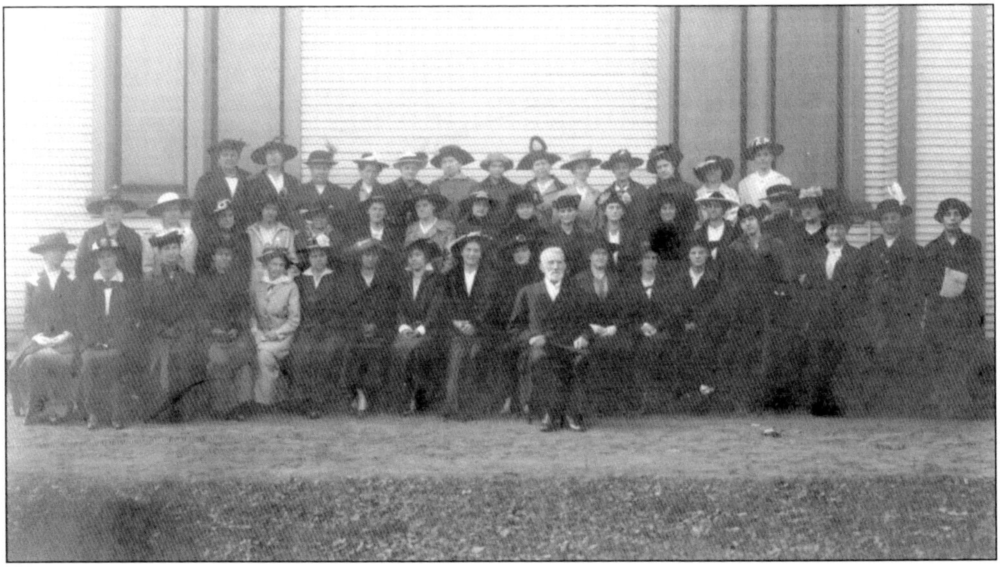

Located on Grandview Avenue, St. Peter's Reformed Church traces its origin to November 14, 1858, when 40 families formed the German Evangelical Protestant United Congregation under the leadership of Rev. Ernest F. Winter (1813–1884). Reverend Winter founded 12 churches in the local area and was the pastor at St. Peter's for 22 years. The congregation first met in the English Presbyterian Church, but erected its own wooden church in 1861 at a cost of $3,000. These photographs are of the original church with the minister and congregation gathered outside around 1910. In 1927, the wooden church was replaced with the current brick one, enlarged in 2005. Church offices are located in the adjoining house on Grandview Avenue. (Both, ZHS.)

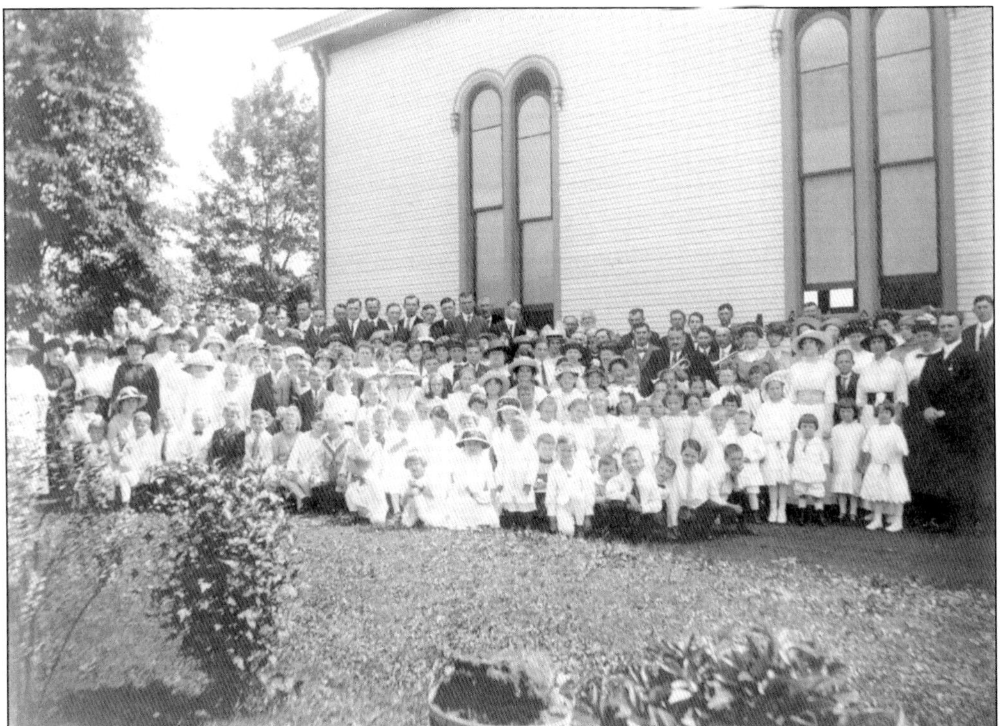

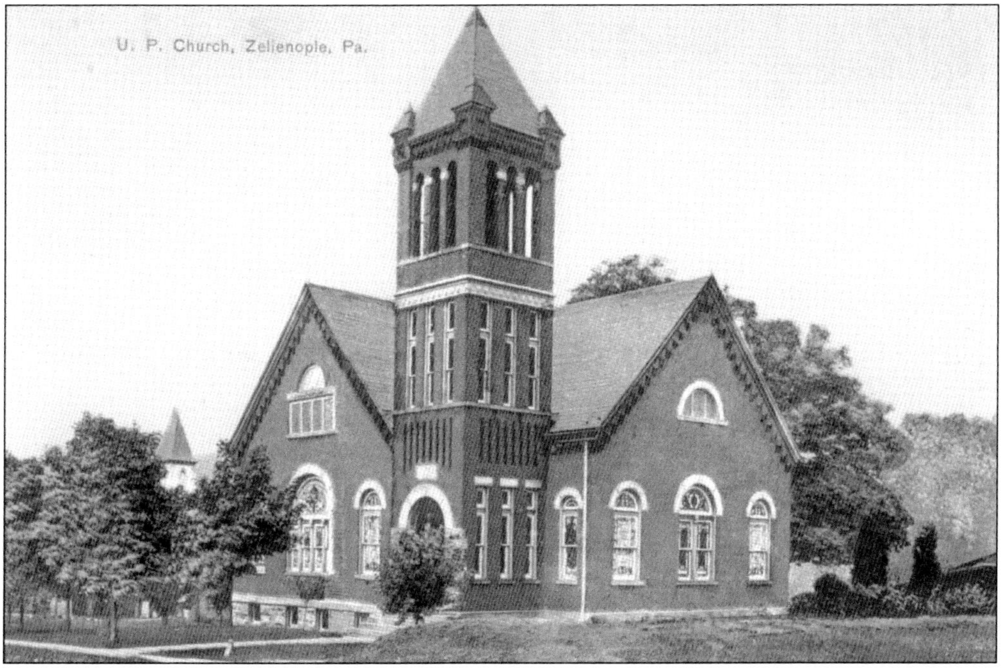

The Park United Presbyterian Church congregation initially met with 25 members in 1895 in a store on Main Street. Even with few members, the church managed to erect a building in 1897, which still stands today on Grandview Avenue. In 1910, the church suffered a major fire, but was rebuilt. In 2014, a runaway truck caused serious damage to the church sanctuary, but repair plans are underway. (ZHS.)

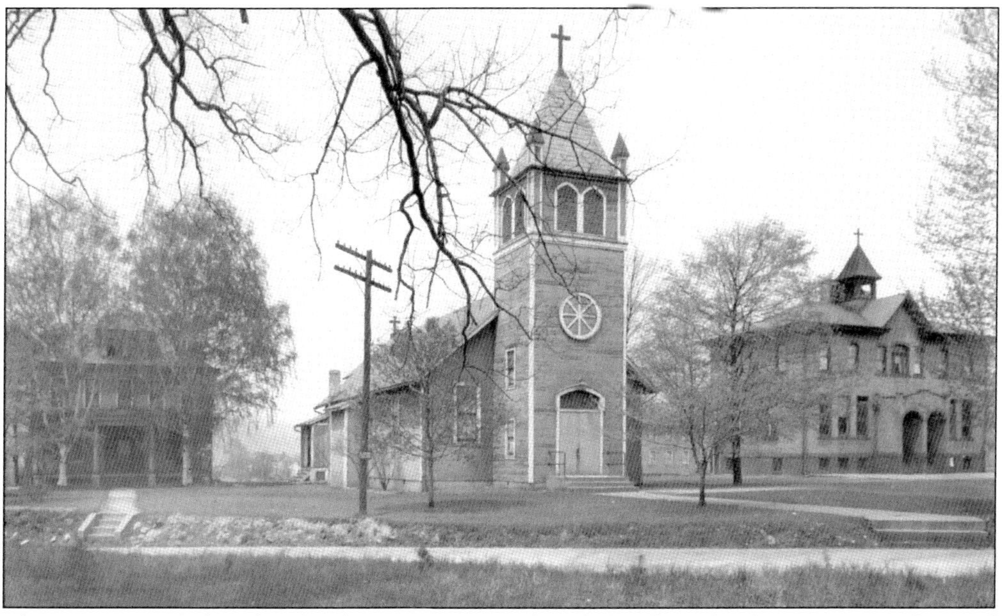

The Roman Catholic Church of St. Gregory was founded with 70 families in 1906 and named for St. Gregory, the bishop of Constantinople. The church was built on the Zelienople Extension Plan of lots, and land was donated by the Zelienople Land Company. In 1908, the rectory was built; in 1911, the parochial school was built on the campus located on Pine Street. (ZHS.)

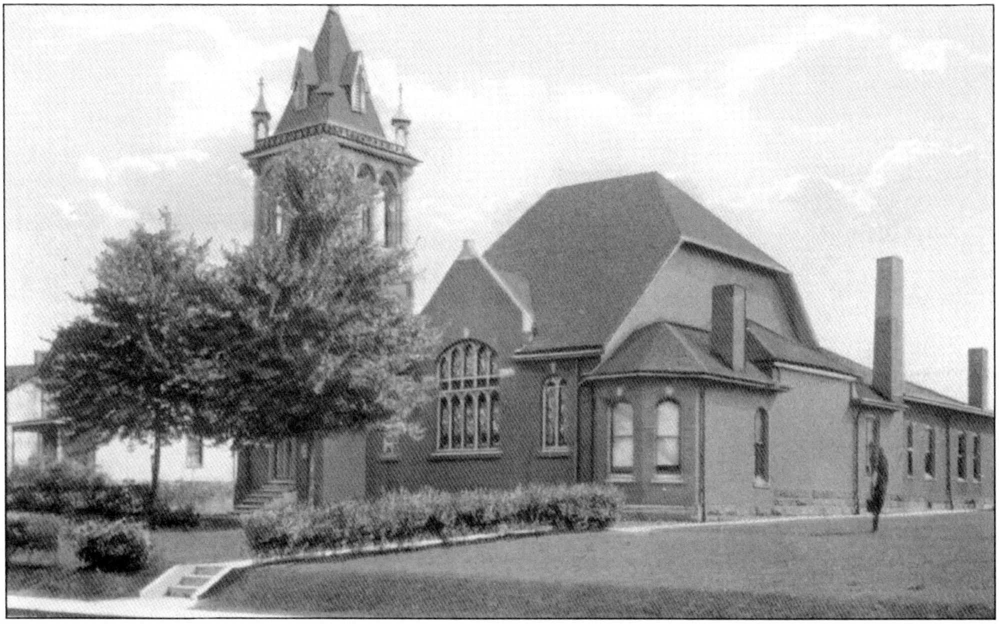

In the early 1800s, the predominantly German Lutheran community had only a few Scottish Presbyterian settlers. In 1845, they founded the Calvin Presbyterian Church under the leadership of Reverend Leake. The nine founding members included Robert Bolton, John Covert, William Covert, R.E. Hays, Dr. L. Lusk, Frederick Pearce, J.S. Welsh, Thomas Wilson, and Joseph Wilson, who was killed in the Civil War. The members met in a local school building until a small church was built in the 1850s; it is still used as a fellowship room within the current building on Grandview Avenue. The photograph above shows the present church that was built in 1901, and the Bassler photograph below is of a men's church group in 1912. (Both, ZHS.)

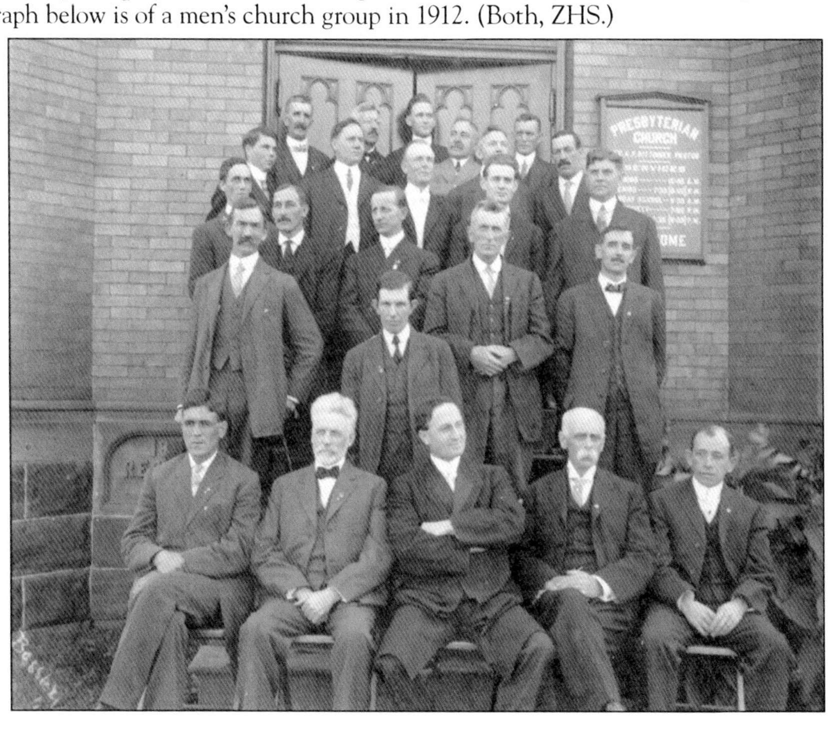

Four

MAIN STREET MERCHANTS

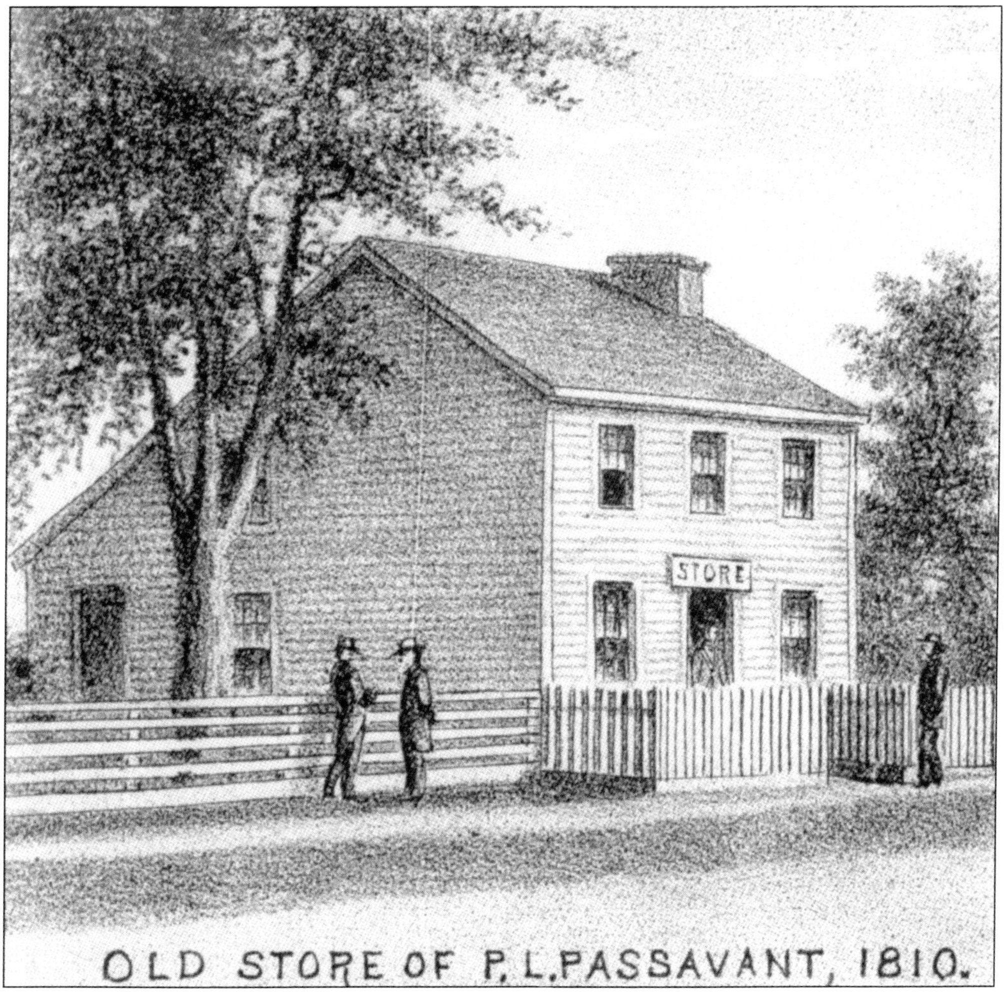

The first store in Zelienople was built in 1807 by Philipp Passavant, who became the town's first merchant. Located at 239 South Main Street, it was built with logs and the second floor was used as the residence of Philipp and Zelie Passavant. This sketch represents the store that was located to the right of the current Passavant House. (ZHS.)

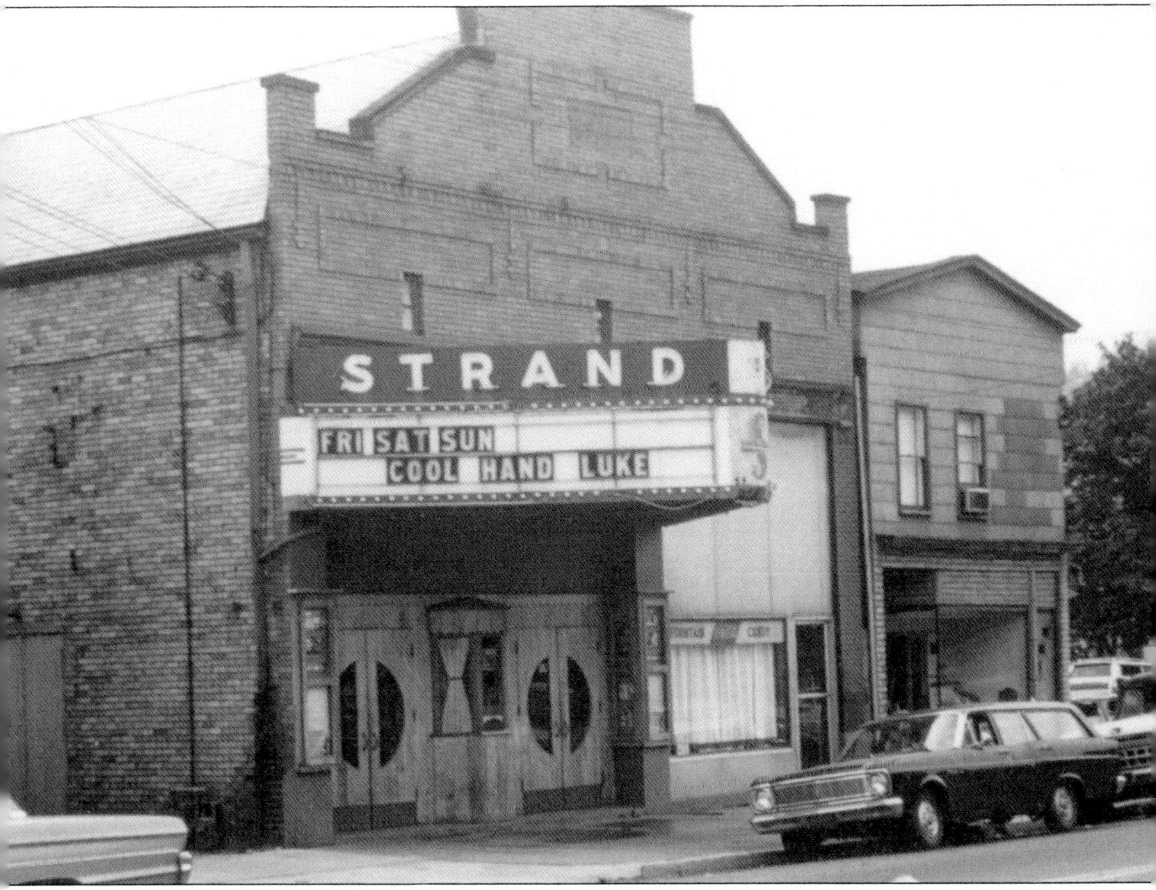

On the west side of Main Street, the Strand Theater was constructed and managed by Joseph and Rosalie Sapienza in 1914. Joseph originally wanted to build a fruit market, but the local banker convinced him that the town really needed a theater. So two-thirds of the structure was dedicated to the theater and one-third for the fruit market. The Strand featured silent films with live piano accompaniment as well as vaudeville-style shows on its small stage. In 1939, the Strand underwent a major renovation and the fruit market was moved across the street to a new building. During the 1950s–1960s, the Strand was owned by the Thomas family; and during the 1970s–1980s, it was owned by the Nalevanko family. The 1968 photograph shows the current movie and refreshment area to the right, which was originally the fruit market. The first building to the right was originally the tin shop of Frederick Frishkorn, later Casey's Bakery and Paul's Sports, but the Strand plans to expand into this building for a larger stage area. Further right was the Dodds home, which was razed for a gas station and convenience store. One of the last movies shown at the theater was *Top Gun*, released in 1986. Afterwards, the theater sat vacant for years until the Strand Theater Initiative was created in 2001. Through private and public financial support, the group purchased the Strand in 2002 and completed a full renovation, including changing the seating 90 degrees. In July 2009, Debbie Reynolds was the star of the grand reopening, talking and showing clips from her long career in Hollywood. The Strand has become the jewel of Main Street, with movies, shows, and concerts for all ages and interests. (ZHS.)

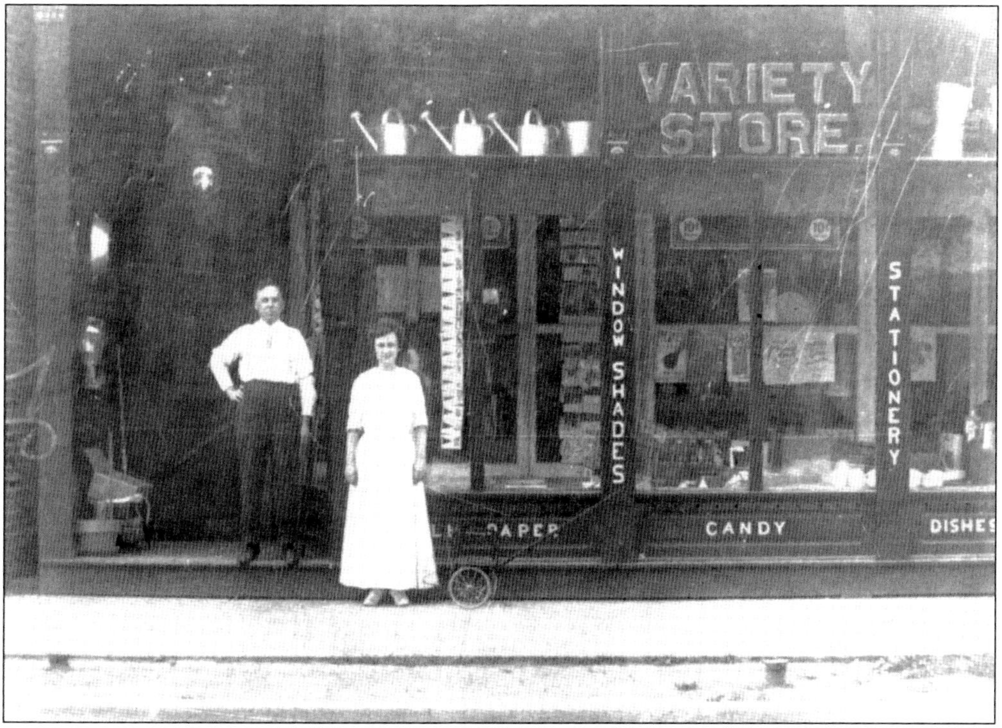

The Variety Store at 111 North Main Street was first opened by Harry McKim and later by Anna Heberling. It offered a variety of home merchandise at low prices as well as penny candy. In 1961, this old wooden building was demolished and a new brick building was constructed by Guy Alfonso at a cost of $75,000. It housed Guy's Bar and Grill, State Liquor Store, and Quaker Cleaners. This building can be seen at the far right in the following photograph. (ZHS.)

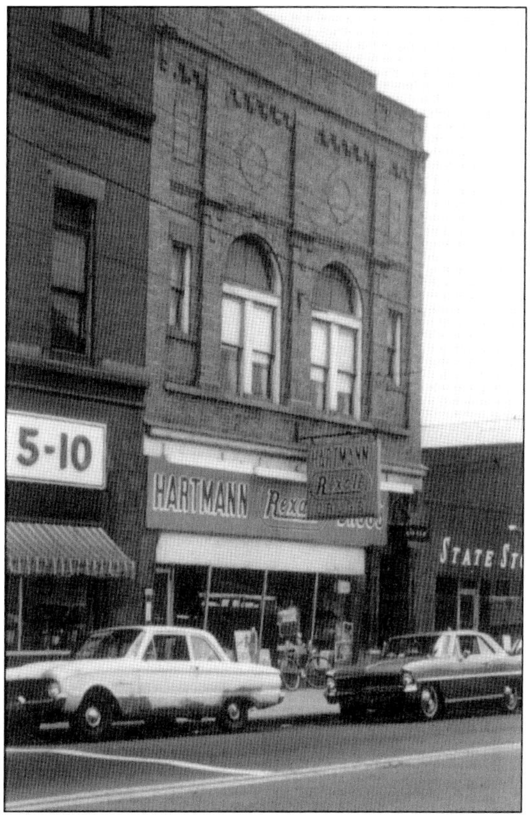

The brick building at 105 North Main Street was erected in 1909 by Alfred Latchaw as a grocery store but became a series of drugstores, including Sitler, Yockey, Craig, Hartmann, and Rite Aid. Alfred "Doc" Hartmann operated his drugstore from 1951 to 1973, with an old-fashioned soda bar that was enjoyed by many. He sold live colored baby chicks in the front window every Easter. (Eric Sipes.)

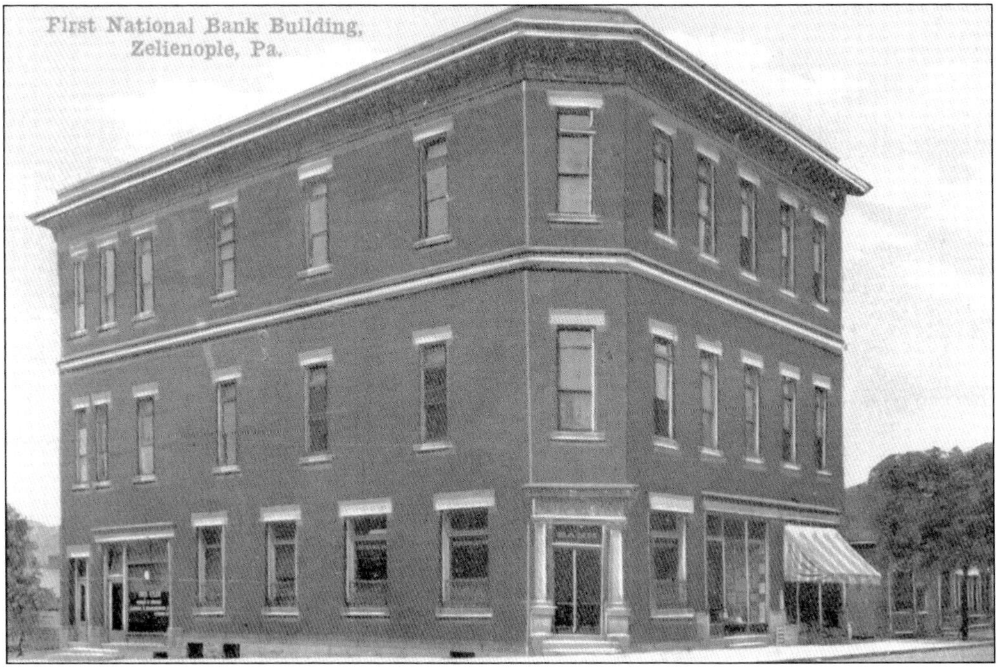

The 1872 home of Frank Wallace, wagonmaker and wheelwright, was located at 101 North Main Street, but it was demolished in 1902 to build First National Bank, which was organized by Charles John David Strohecker (1856–1955). The early postcard above shows the bank entrance within the beveled corner of the building and the Fred Eyles Piano and Organ store at the rear side entrance. Below, this 1920s postcard shows the entrance moved to the front, the building corner squared, and the famous town clock added. After the bank closed, this became a series of stores, including Kroger's Grocery, the popular Ben Franklin 5 & 10 Variety Store, and many others since. On the far left is the old fire department and borough building. (Both, ZHS.)

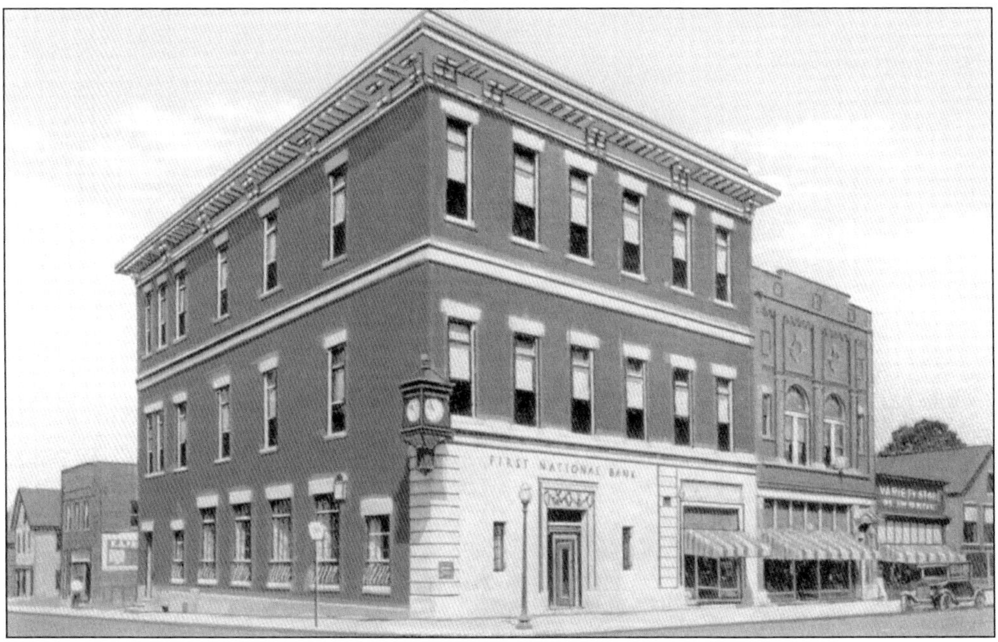

The original bank vault is still located in the basement, but after 100 years, it is no longer operational. When banknotes were first introduced, they were a promise to pay the bearer in gold or silver coins. The photograph shows a First National Bank of Zelienople, series 1929 $20 note, from the same year the stock market crashed. (Author.)

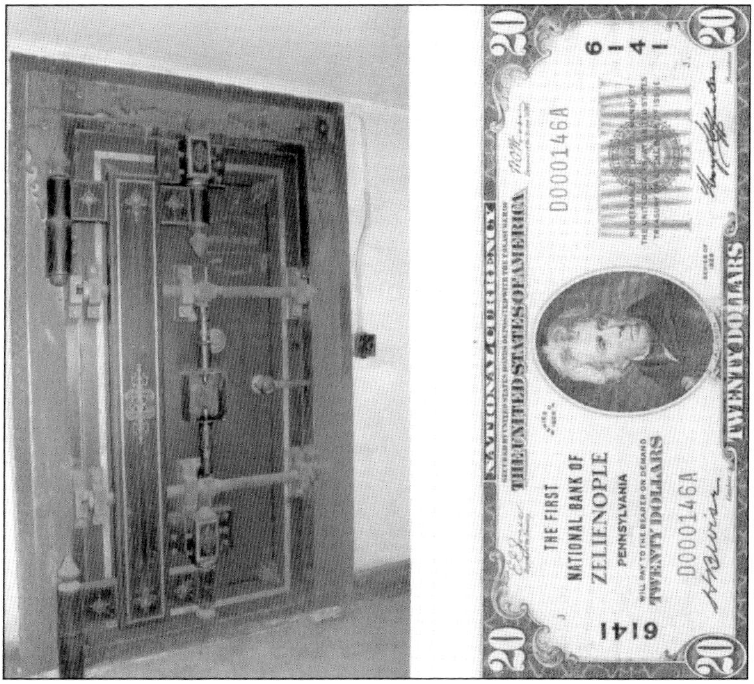

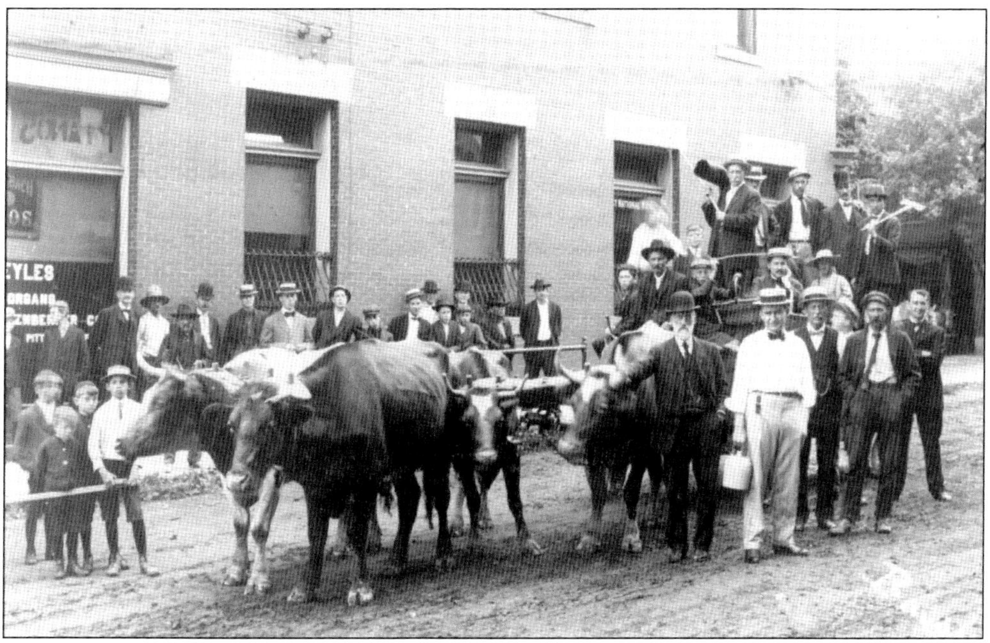

This 1905 photograph is a sight that will not be seen in Zelienople again—cattle at the corner of Main and New Castle Streets. Eyles Piano and many unidentified people are in the background. The men pictured are, from left to right, (directly in front of the wagon) Zenus McMichael, a Mr. Randall, Henry Stokey, unidentified, and Bud Shaw; (standing inside the wagon) Brant Sakey, Dr. Gallagher, Edwin Zehner, and Jack Shaffer with the axe. (BZC.)

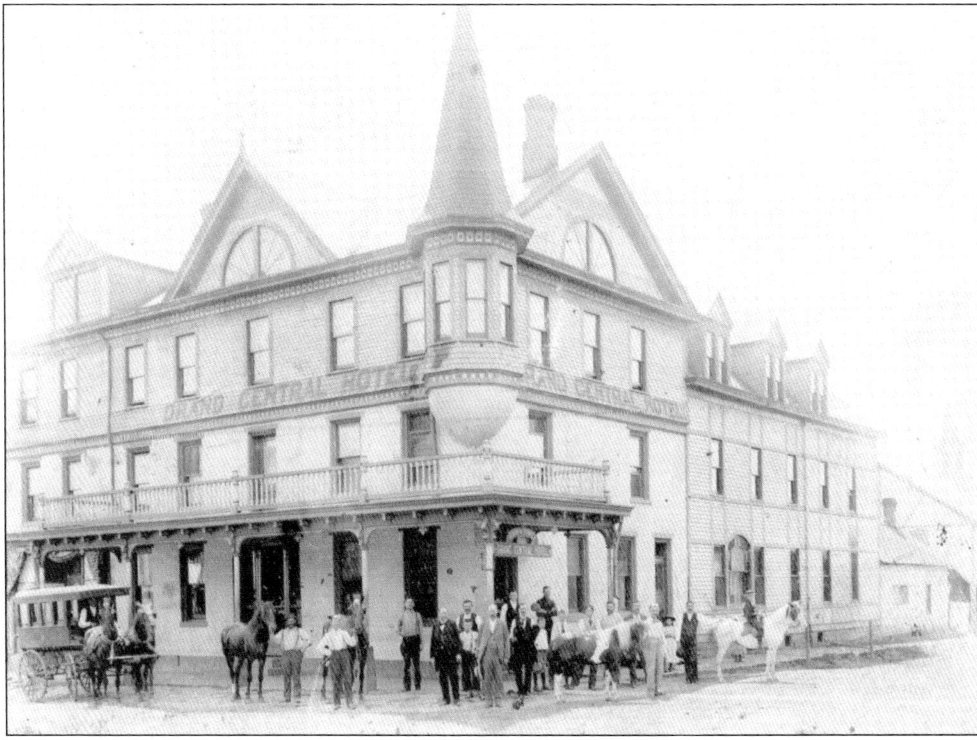

Since 1810, there have been a series of taverns at 105 South Main Street, beginning with Andrew McClure's. During the War of 1812, McClure sympathized with the British and was tarred and feathered by Oliver Perry's militia. In 1820, John Randolph enlarged the building and named it the Cross Keys. In 1859, owner William Bastian renamed it Bastian House. Later, it was operated by Fred Strohecker, and in 1888, Henry Stokey rebuilt it as the Grand Central Hotel, as shown in the rare photograph above. On December 27, 1902, the nearby Hildebrand Bakery caught fire, alighting five other buildings, including the Grand Central Hotel. The photograph below, showing the men building the New Hotel Stokey, is from 1903. Henry Stokey built the hotel essentially as it stands today—a quality brick structure and centerpiece of the town. (Both, ZHS.)

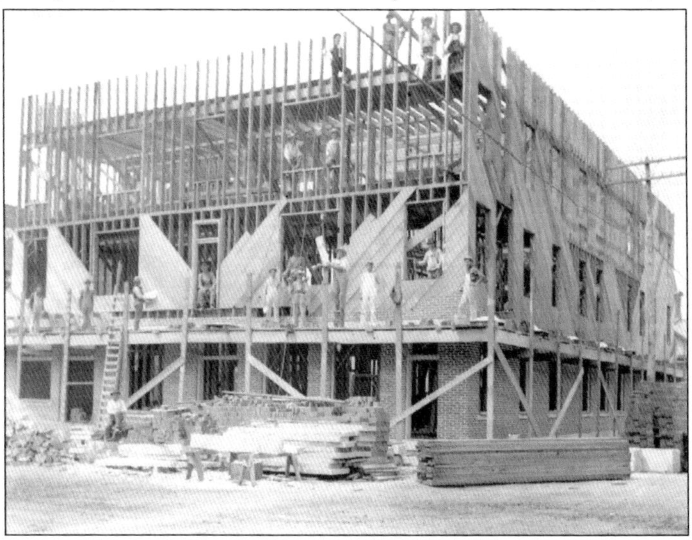

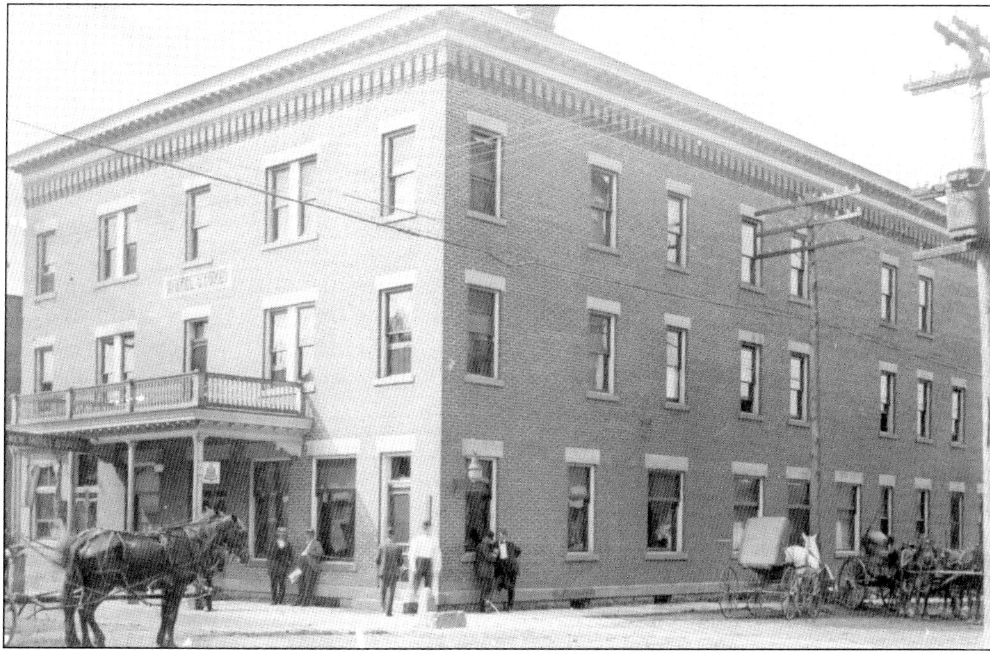

The horse and buggy were still the normal mode of transportation when the photograph above was taken, after the New Hotel Stokey was built and open for business in 1904. In 1924, E.F. Kaufman made a series of improvements and made the Kaufman Hotel one of the most popular on Perry Highway, which runs from Pittsburgh to Erie. In 1944, it was purchased by William Thomas, as shown in the photograph below); in 1974, it was purchased by Ken Pilarski, who renamed it the Kaufman House. Unfortunately, a fire in 2011 caused the closing of the famous hostelry. A consortium of organizations is currently attempting to obtain funding to open the Kaufman House, the best-known landmark of the town. (Both, ZHS.)

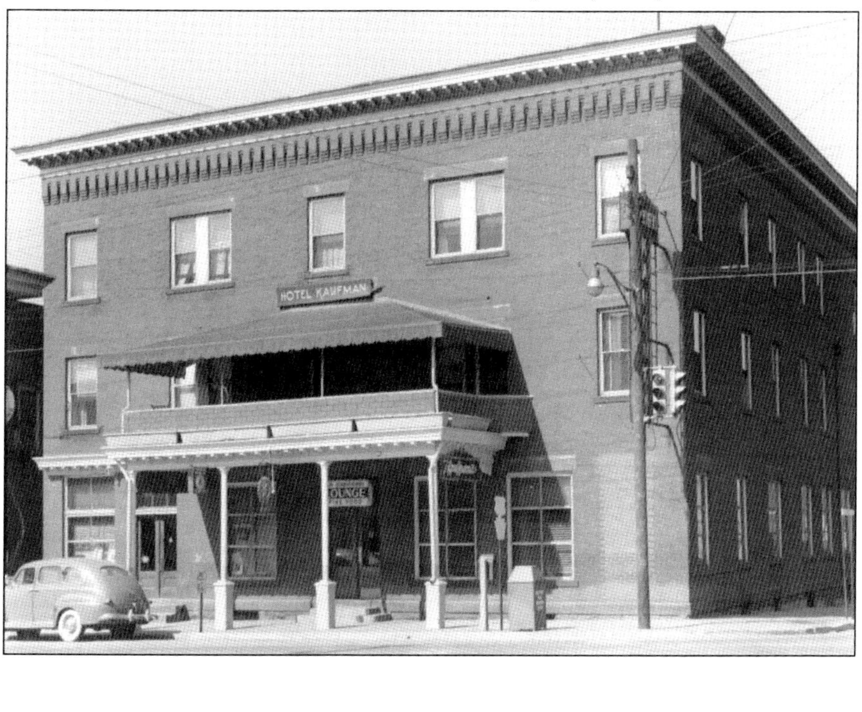

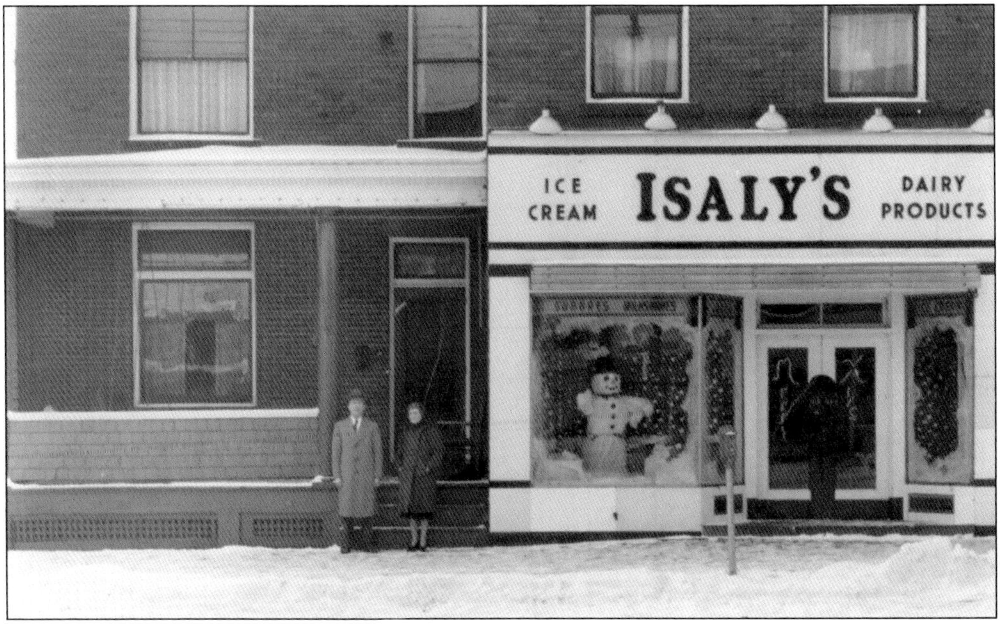

Isaly's, located at 111 South Main, was a favorite hangout of the younger generation. Its famous chipped-chopped ham, a variety of sandwiches, and dairy items were sold here, including the famous Skyscraper ice-cream cone and the Klondike Bar. The photograph above shows owners Dave and Eva Lewis during the 1948 Christmas season. Their residence on the left was later converted into retail space for crafts and gifts. In the photograph below, the staff of Isaly's in 1950 includes, from left to right, Eleanor McWithey, Deloris English, chief cook Pearl Marshal, Elizabeth Boros, Alice Trumble, Phyllis English, Ruth Goehring, Amanda Rich, Tooty Goehring, manager James Meyers, and owner John David Lewis. Isaly's was named for William Isaly, the son of Swiss immigrants to Ohio, but the youngsters of the 1940s said it stood for "I Shall Always Love You Sweetheart." (Both, ZHS.)

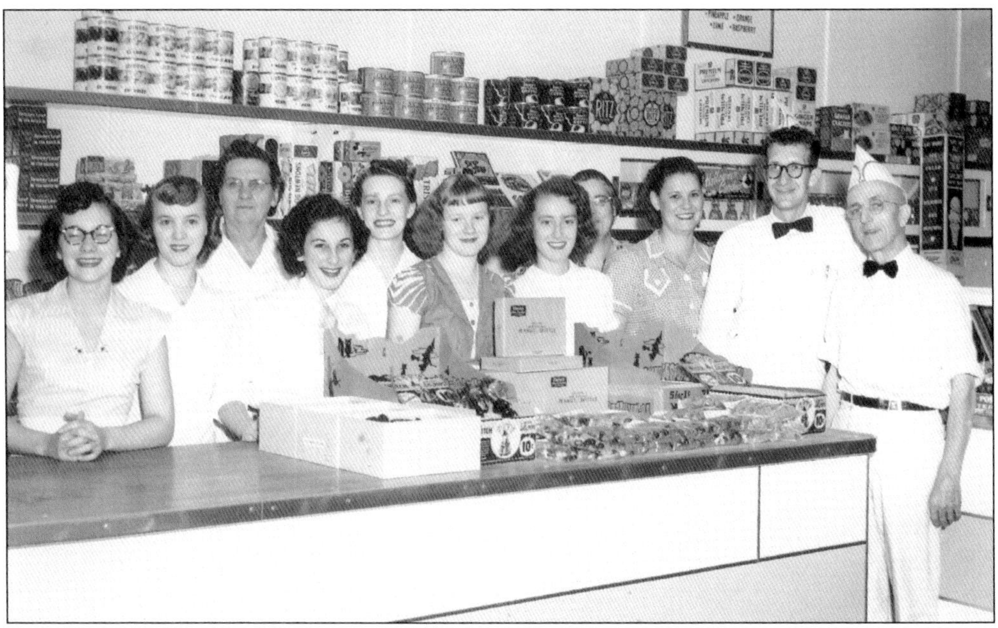

The building to the left of the Kaufman House at 107 South Main Street was originally owned by David Bastian. It was rebuilt after the great fire of 1902 and was used for years as a series of hardware stores, including those owned by Messrs. Bastian, Ohl, White, and Harper. Later, it was Marlene Eppinger's Zelie Ann Shop (as shown in the photograph), and Anna Wright's Children's Shop. Today, it is Joseph Maddalon Jewelers. (ZHS.)

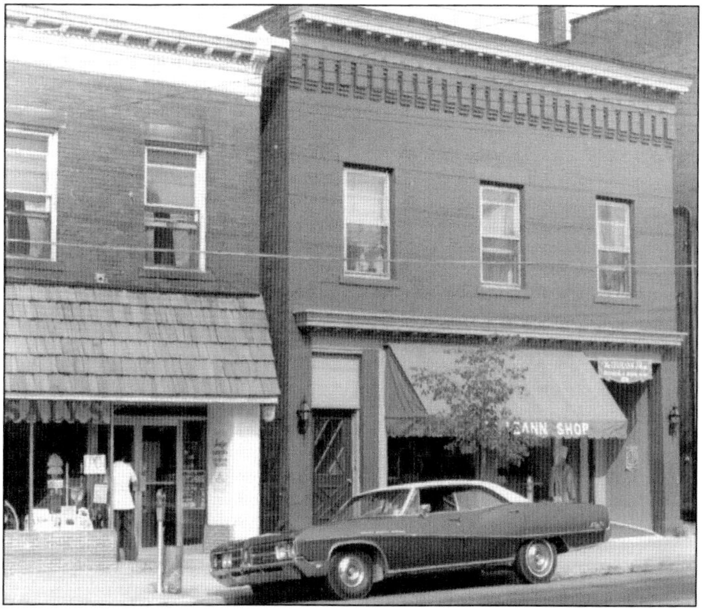

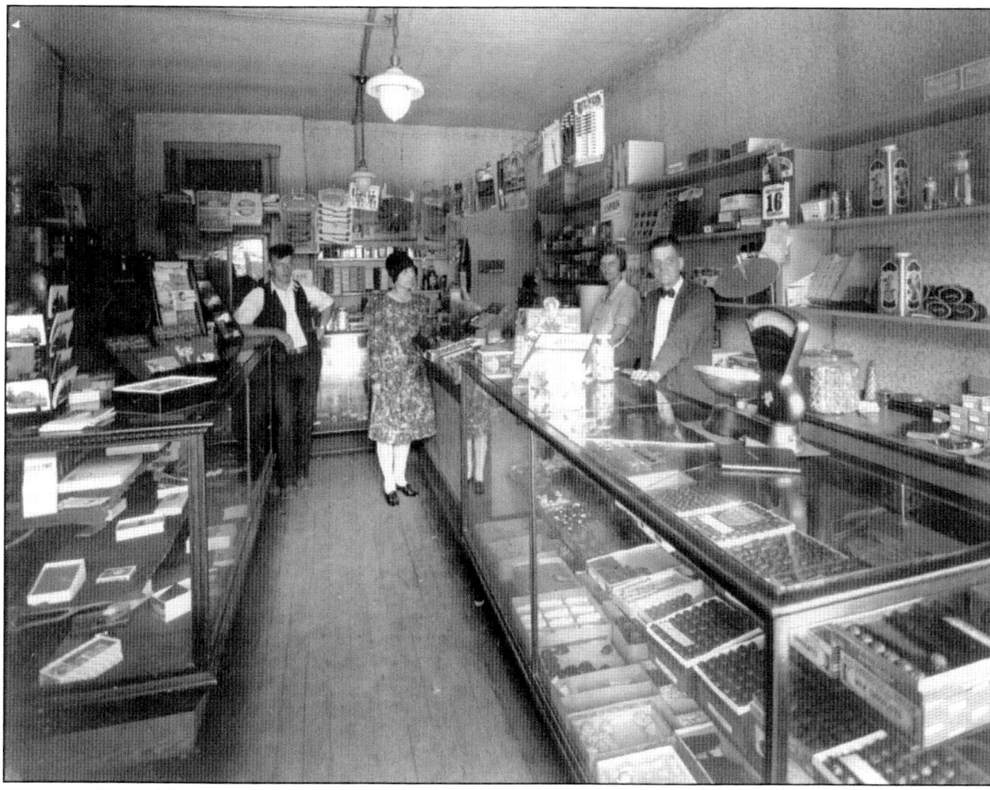

The small building at 117 South Main Street was owned and operated as a newsstand from 1923 to 1931 by Clarence and Winnie McMichael, shown on the right behind the counter. It was sold to Woodberry as a newsstand, to Altha Craig as a gift shop, then to Karl Fisher, who owned Karl's Camera Shop. A series of stores followed until the structure was razed around 2002. (Jack McMichael.)

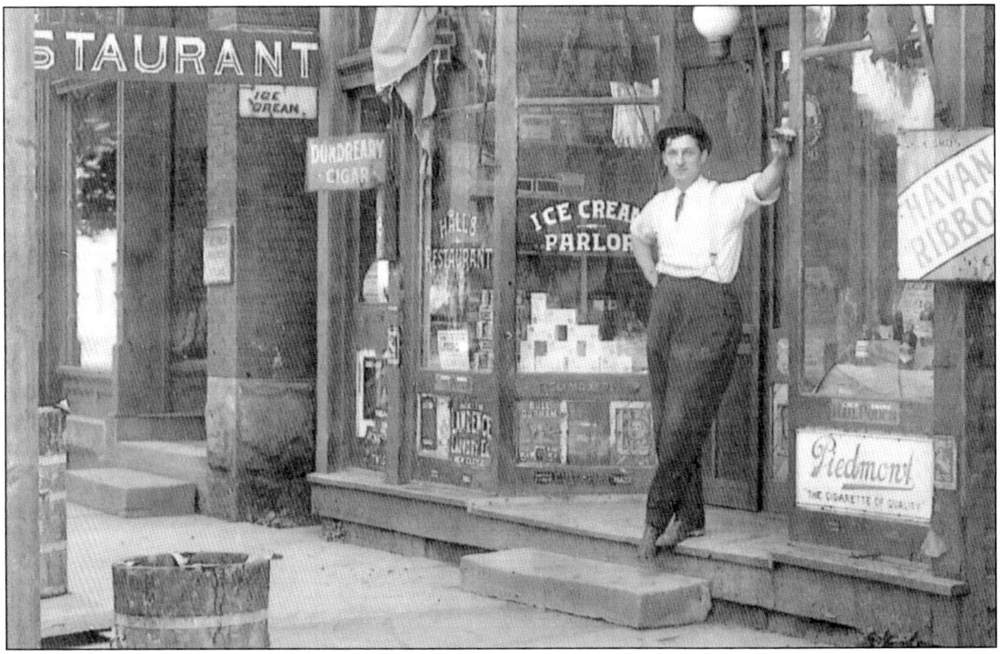

Before the current brick building at 121–125 South Main Street was erected, there were several wooden buildings in this area. One was Casper Bloom's Blacksmith Shop. Another is seen in this photograph, which shows Frank B. Hall standing outside his small restaurant and ice-cream parlor around 1910. He was in business in the area from 1905 to 1916. (Mark Hall.)

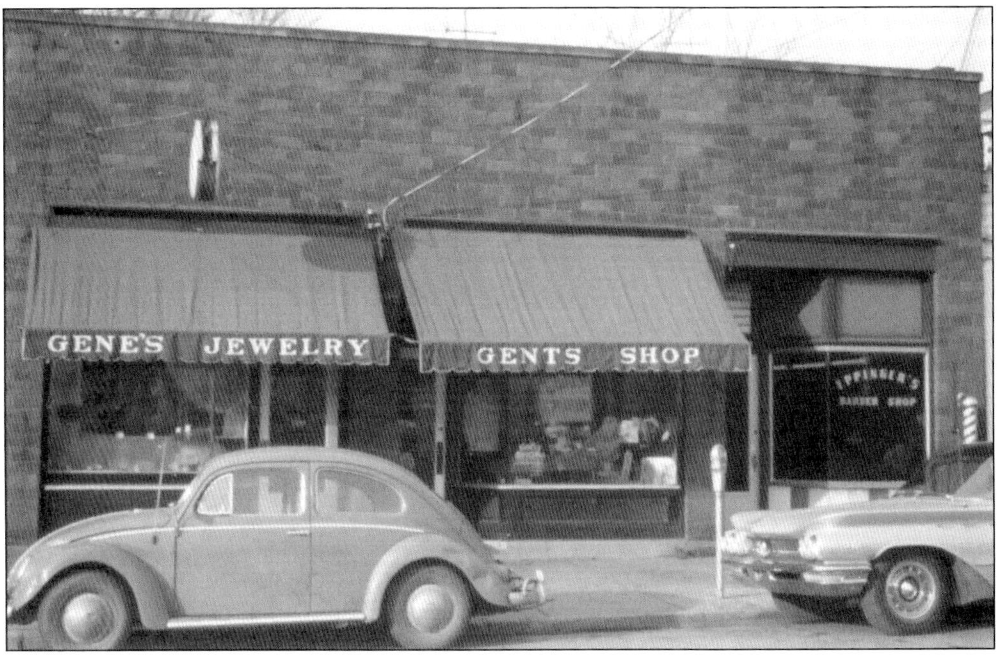

The building at 121–125 South Main Street was constructed around 1950 and has housed many merchants in its three stores over the years. This 1960 photograph shows Gene's Jewelry, which was there for 30 years; the Gents Shop, also in town for 30 years; and Hugh Eppinger's Barber Shop, which trained several young men in the barber trade. (BZC.)

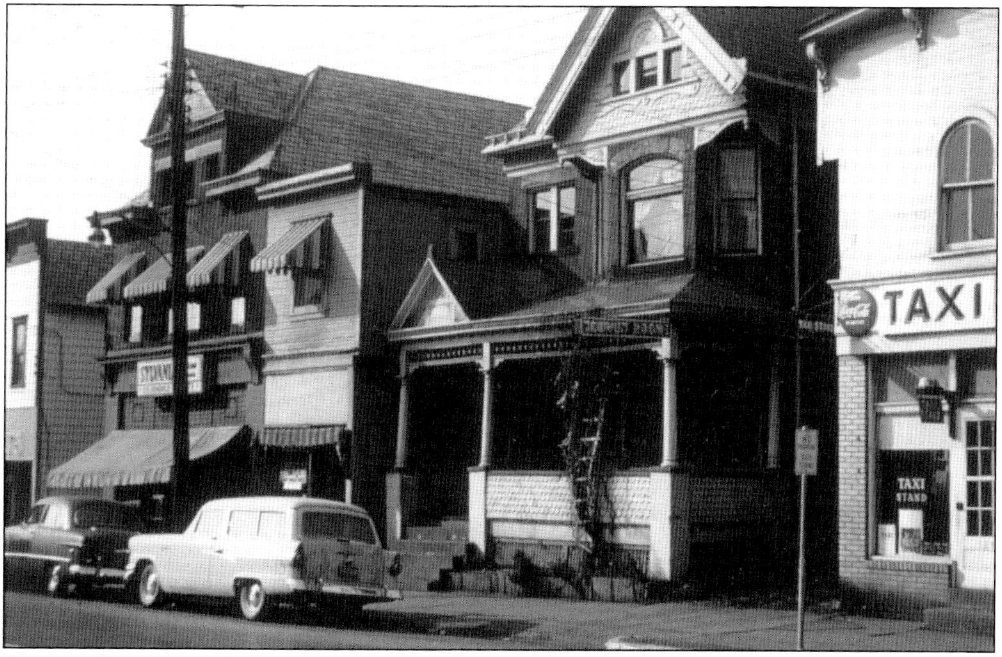

Starting from the right in this 1955 photograph, the building at 127 South Main Street was a general store owned by Conrad Scheel and later by Edwin Meeder. It was replaced by Young's Kitchens. The house at 131 South Main Street was owned by Conrad Scheel; it was later Cullen's Bar and is now Fisher's. Hartmann's Barber Shop was at 133 South Main Street; Stewart's TV was at 135 South Main Street, and it was later Adler's Paint Store for 30 years. (BZC.)

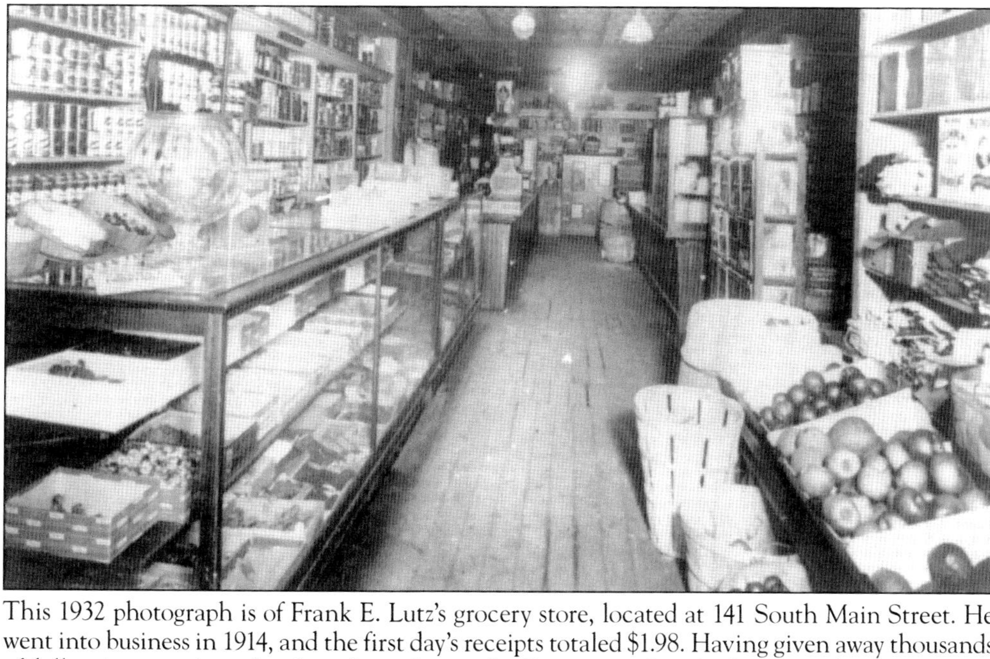

This 1932 photograph is of Frank E. Lutz's grocery store, located at 141 South Main Street. He went into business in 1914, and the first day's receipts totaled $1.98. Having given away thousands of dollars in groceries to local residents during the Depression, Lutz had to close the store in 1941 and became a carpenter. On July 4, 1976, his 97th birthday, Lutz was the honorary grand marshal of the Bicentennial Fourth of July Parade. (May Lutz.)

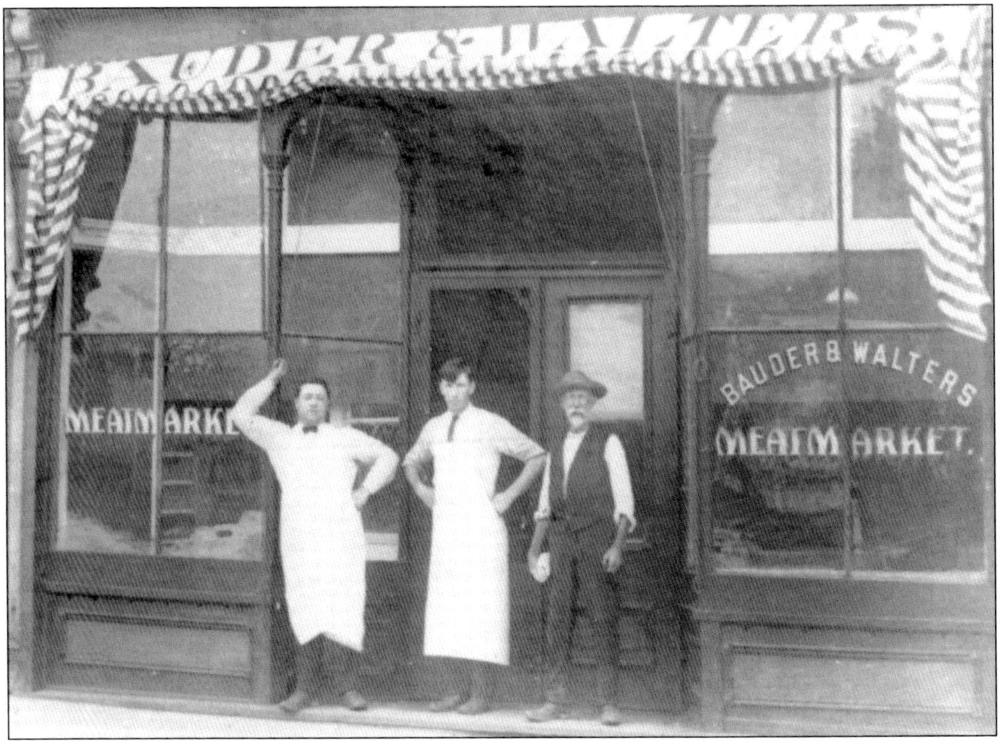

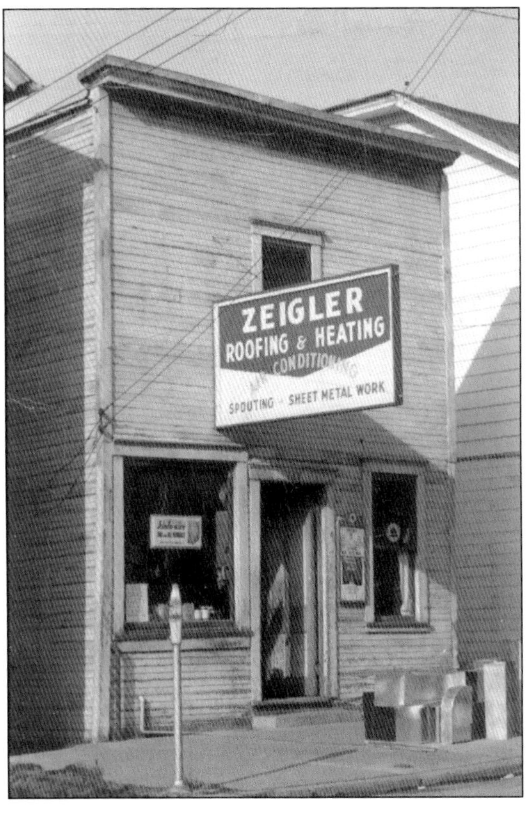

The house at 141 and 143 South Main Street was originally Charles Strohecker's home, but it was later divided and made into stores. This photograph shows the Bauder and Walter's Meat Market, later the Wehr Brothers Meat Market, which was located here for 50 years, from 1920 to 1970. There were many merchants located here over the years, including hair salons, crafts and clothing stores, a newsstand, a florist, and others. (BZC.)

The original location of George Householder's wagon shop, the building at 147 South Main Street, was constructed by Harold Zeigler for his heating and air-conditioning business. In 1969, C.T. McCormick Hardware moved here, updating and expanding into the adjacent building. The Otto Luek home at 155 was purchased by the borough in the 1970s and the site made into a municipal parking lot. (McCormick's Hardware.)

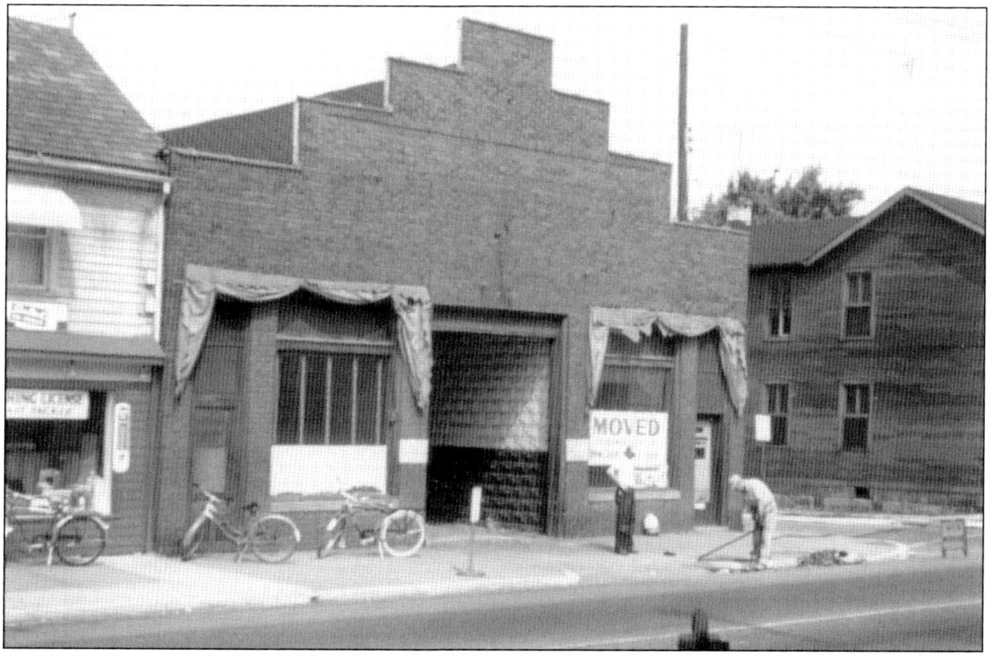

In 1833, John Levis built a log home at the corner of Main and Spring Streets. He was the town's first squire, postmaster, and state senator. Much later, the building at 201 South Main Street was a garage and later the Penn Power building. Shown in the 1956 photograph above, Penn Power is vacating the building. The Otto Luek home is shown at the far right. Roach and Ziegler remodeled the building and moved their furniture and appliances store to this location, as shown in the photograph below. Roach and Ziegler stayed at this location for 58 years, before moving across the street in 2014. This location is now a bridal and formal salon. Fidelity Savings occupied the left portion of this building at 203 South Main Street until it relocated in 1963. (Both, BZC.)

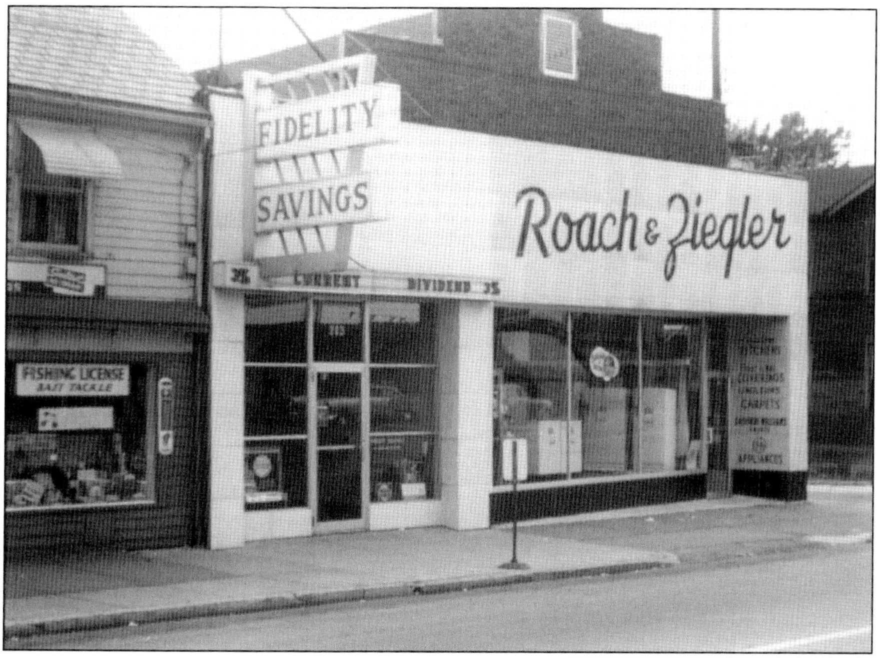

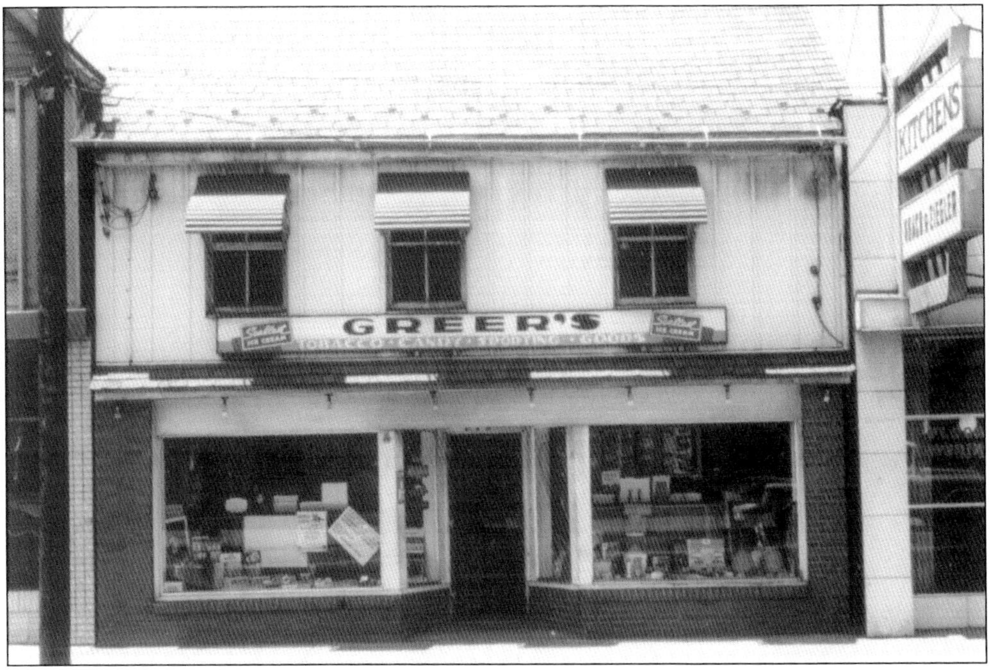

Christian Buhl purchased the log home at 205 South Main Street in 1834 for his daughter Catherine, who married Edward Randolph. Around 1945, James Greer bought the building, remodeled, and opened Greer's Newstand. In 1966, his daughter Jane married Leo Hart, and it became Hart's Newstand. The new owners immediately demolished the old log building shown above, replacing it with the brick structure that stands today. During the days of Pennsylvania blue laws, this was one of the few stores in town open on Sundays. In 1986, it became Benjamin's Pharmacy, and in 1989, it was purchased by Henry Ziegler and renamed the Newstand. Shown on the left in the 1965 photograph below is the K&K Hot Dog Shop at 209 South Main Street. A newer building has since been erected there, serving various businesses. (Both, Henry Ziegler.)

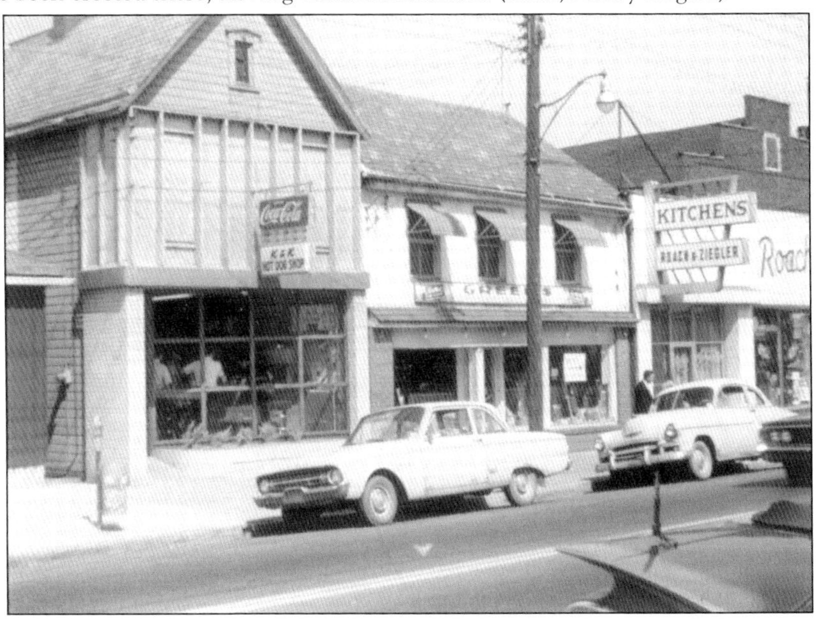

In 1890, Charles Goehring built this home at 215 South Main Street. About 1900, there was a gas leak and major explosion, blowing out every window and scattering bricks and debris out into Main Street. The home was repaired and later used by Dr. Clark Markel for his office. This building was recently updated and is used for offices, providing a good example of how to save historic structures. (ZHS.)

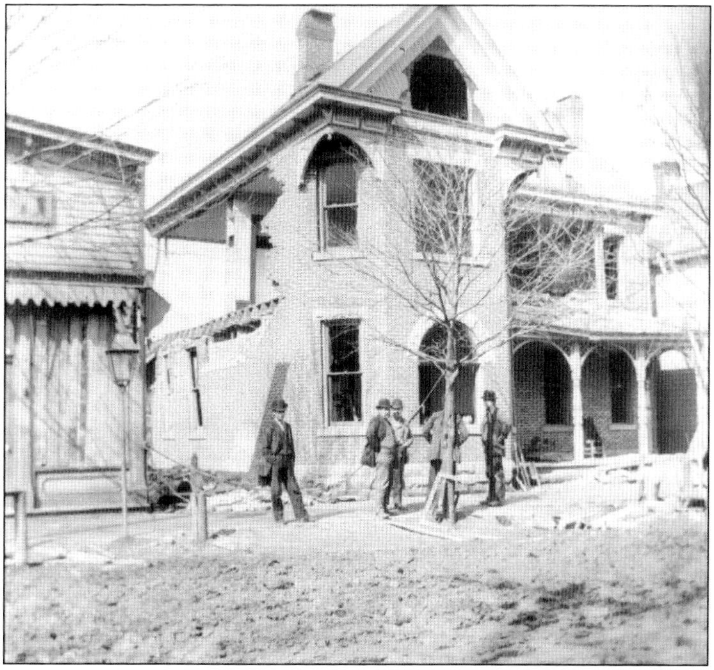

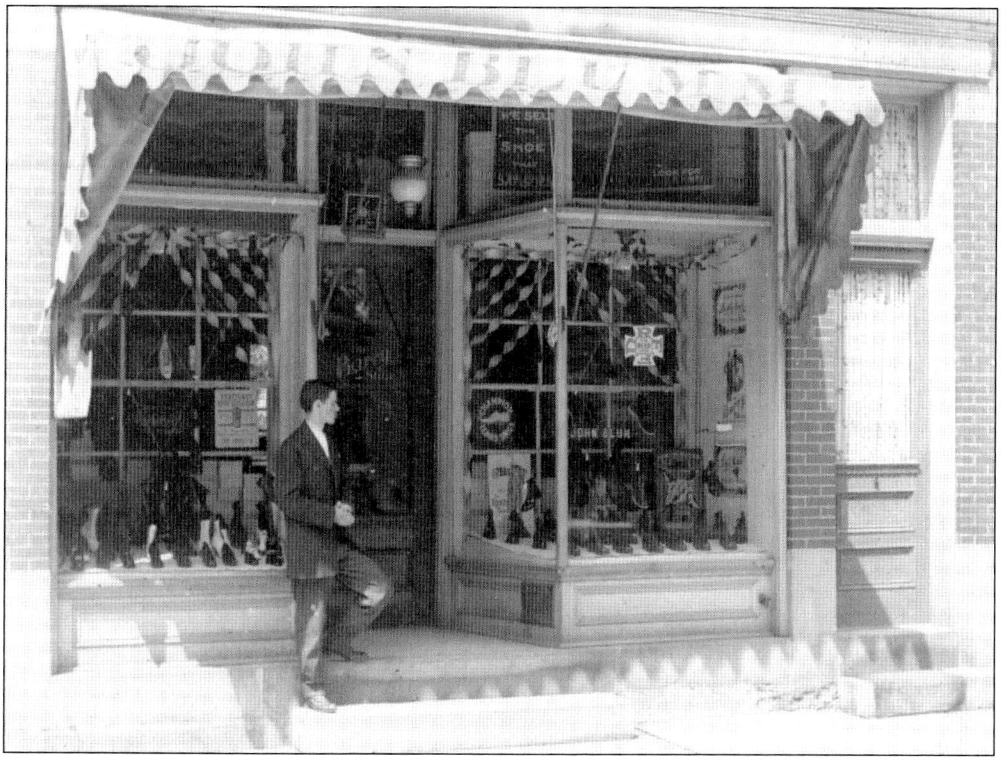

Blum's Shoe Store, located at 219 South Main Street, has had a presence in town since John Blum started his business as a cobbler in 1888. His sons John and Harry carried on and built a new store in 1907 after a fire destroyed the old one. Grandsons Philip and Jack took over in the 1950s, continuing the business until it was sold in 1983. (Gregory Cowell.)

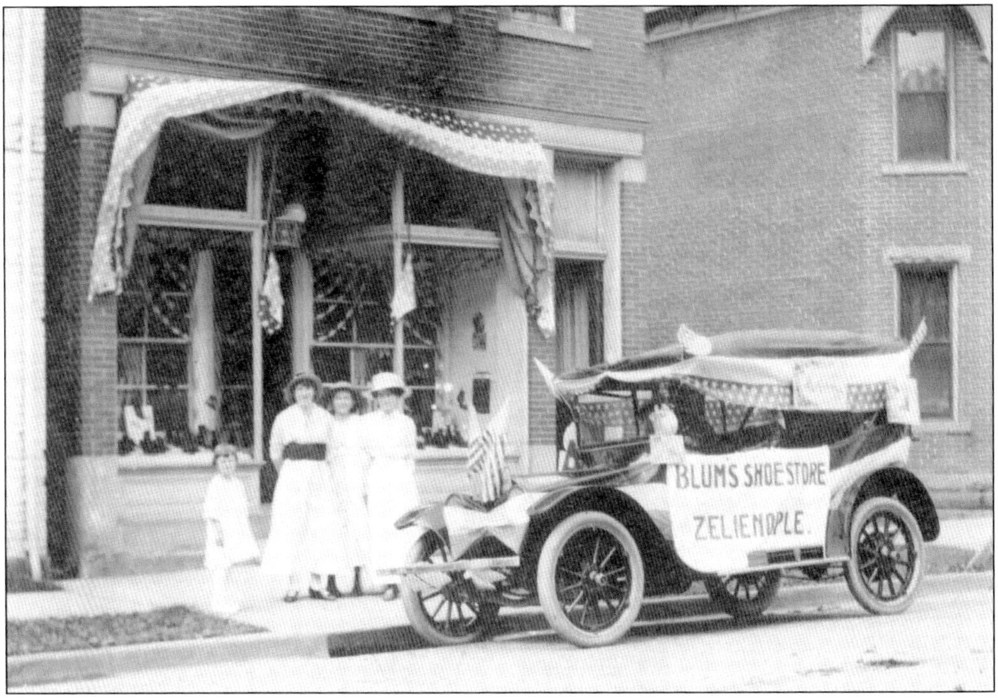

Everyone in town participated in the annual Fourth of July festivities, and Blum's was no exception. This 1920s photograph shows the store in red, white, and blue bunting, the women dressed for the occasion, and their Ford Model T convertible ready to go. Local artist May Lutz painted the interior of the store; the scene has been made into a puzzle by the historical society. (Gregory Cowell.)

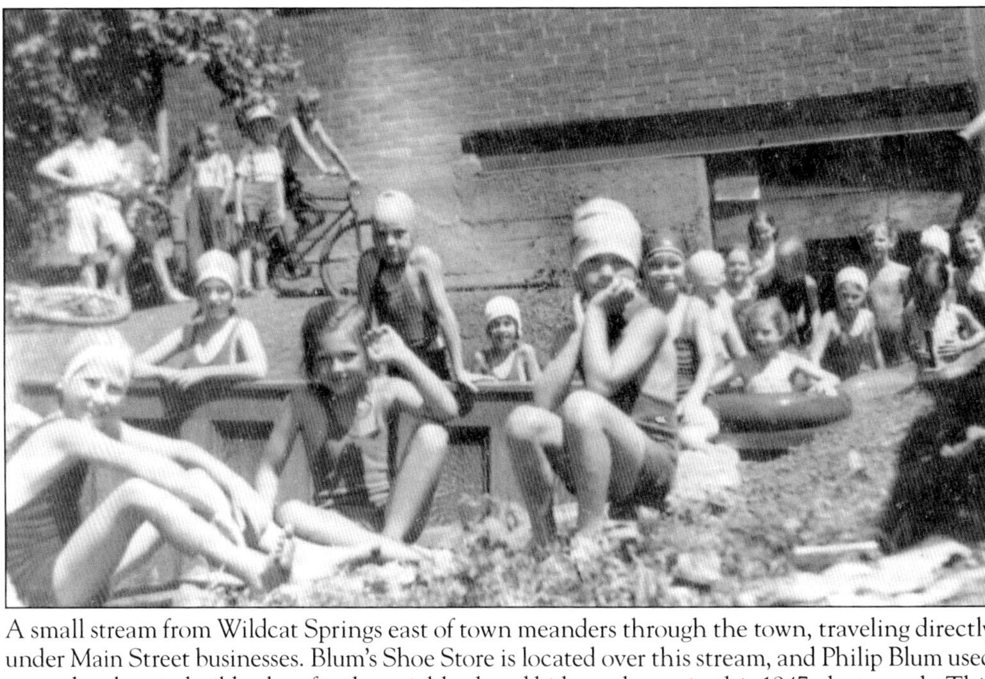

A small stream from Wildcat Springs east of town meanders through the town, traveling directly under Main Street businesses. Blum's Shoe Store is located over this stream, and Philip Blum used a wooden door to build a dam for the neighborhood kids, as shown in this 1947 photograph. This swimming hole entertained many local children who are now senior citizens. (BZC.)

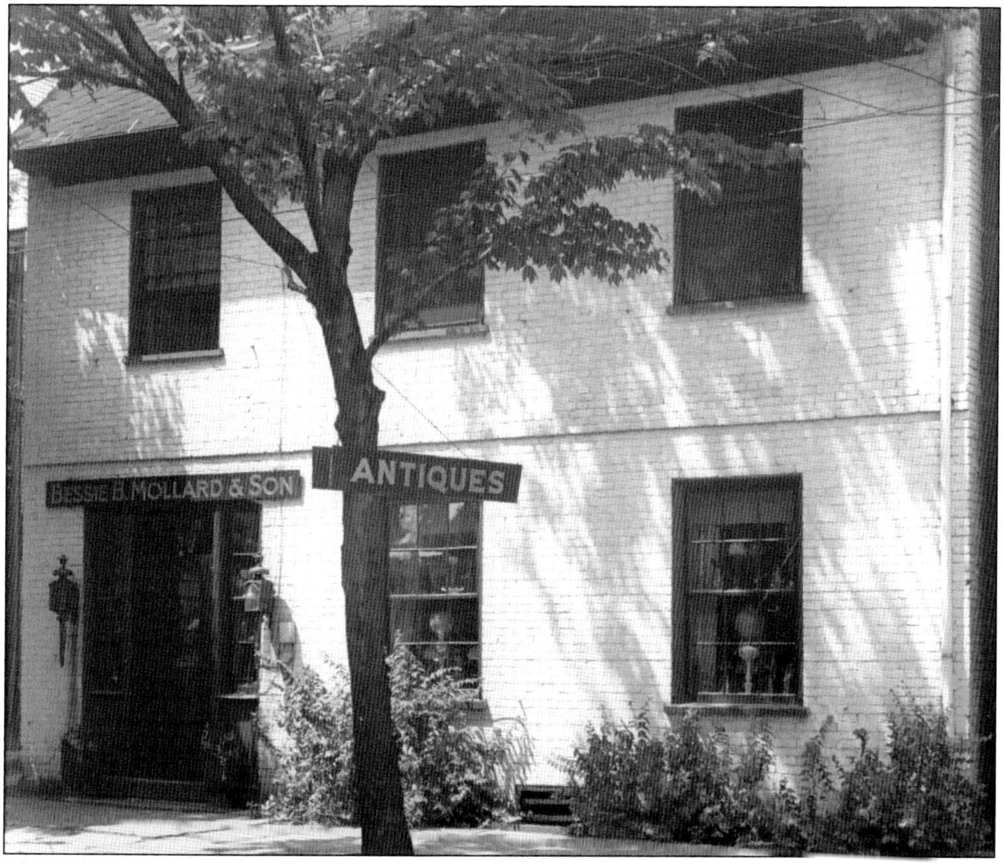

The Buhl House, located at 221 South Main Street, is the oldest home in town. In 1804, Zelienople consisted of two houses, those belonging to Christian Buhl and Daniel Fiedler, who lived in small log cabins near the creek. Buhl was a hatter and furrier, and built the brick house on Main Street in 1805. His grandson Henry Buhl Jr. founded the Boggs and Buhl department store in Pittsburgh. The photograph above shows the Buhl House during the 1960s, when Bessie Mollard and son John Mollard owned an antique shop there. The photograph below is of the early 1800s Buhl carriage house that sits quietly behind the home today. In 1991, the Buhl House was purchased by a Zelienople Historical Society member; one year later, it was gratefully deeded to the society for use as a second museum site. (Both, ZHS.)

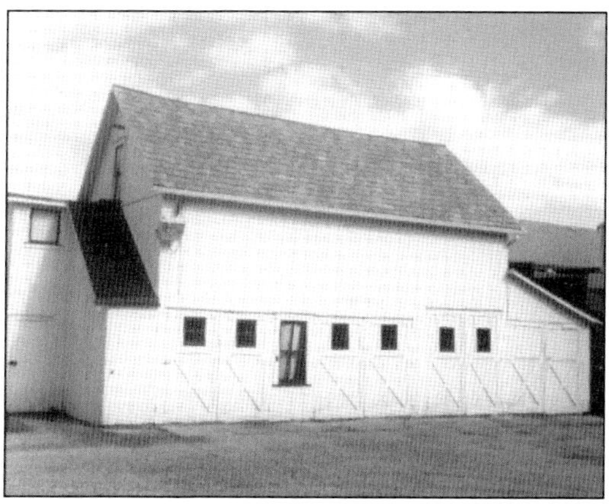

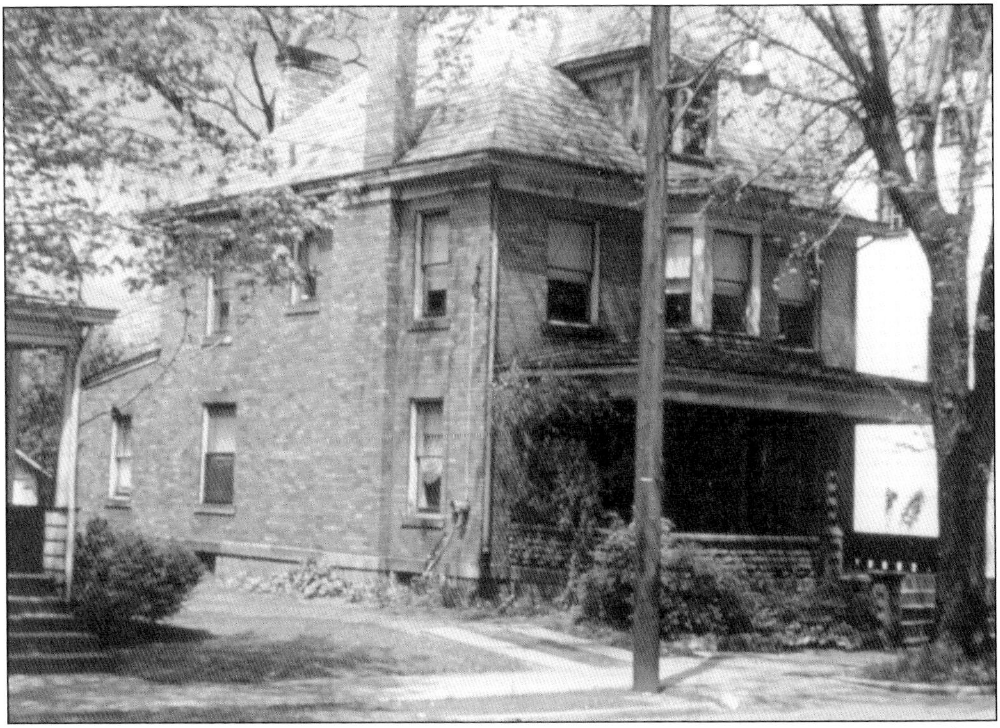

A blacksmith shop was at 223 South Main Street until Gottlieb Zeigler built a brick house there in 1910. In 1946, the Garman C. Murray Agency opened its insurance and real estate office there. In the 1950s, Thomas Murray Sr. and Thomas Murray Jr. joined the firm, later including Patrick Murray, making it a four-generation business. The building has been tastefully expanded to match the existing structure. (BZC.)

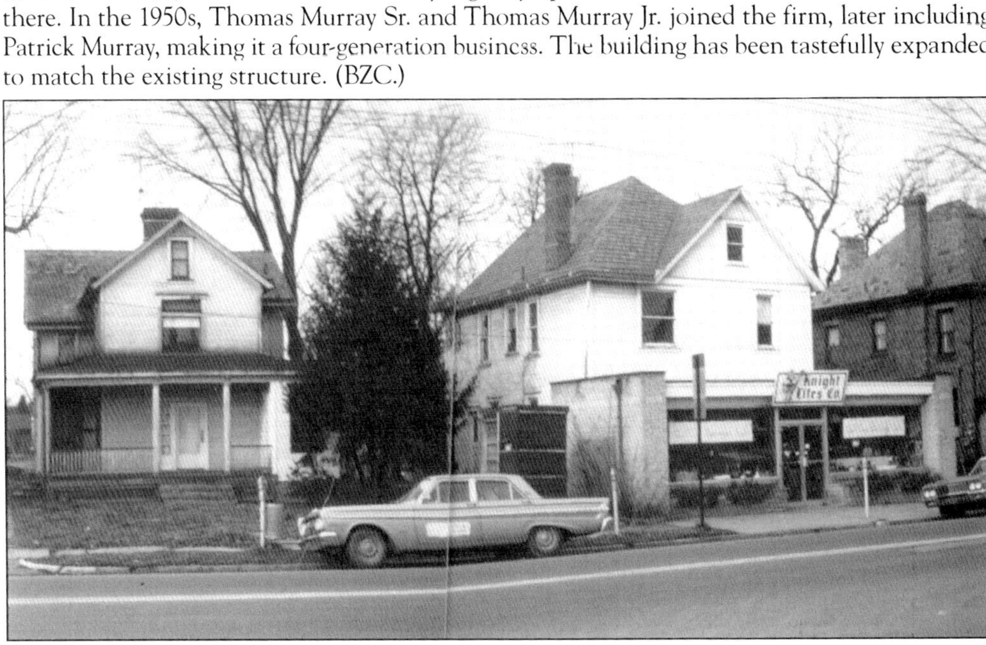

These homes and business at 225 and 229 South Main Street no longer exist. They were demolished in the 1970s for a Gulf Oil station, now the Valero gas and convenience store. In the 1800s, the house at left was the home and blacksmith shop of John Weigel. The house on the right was a dentist office, a taxicab service, and the Knight Lites store, as shown in the photograph. (BZC.)

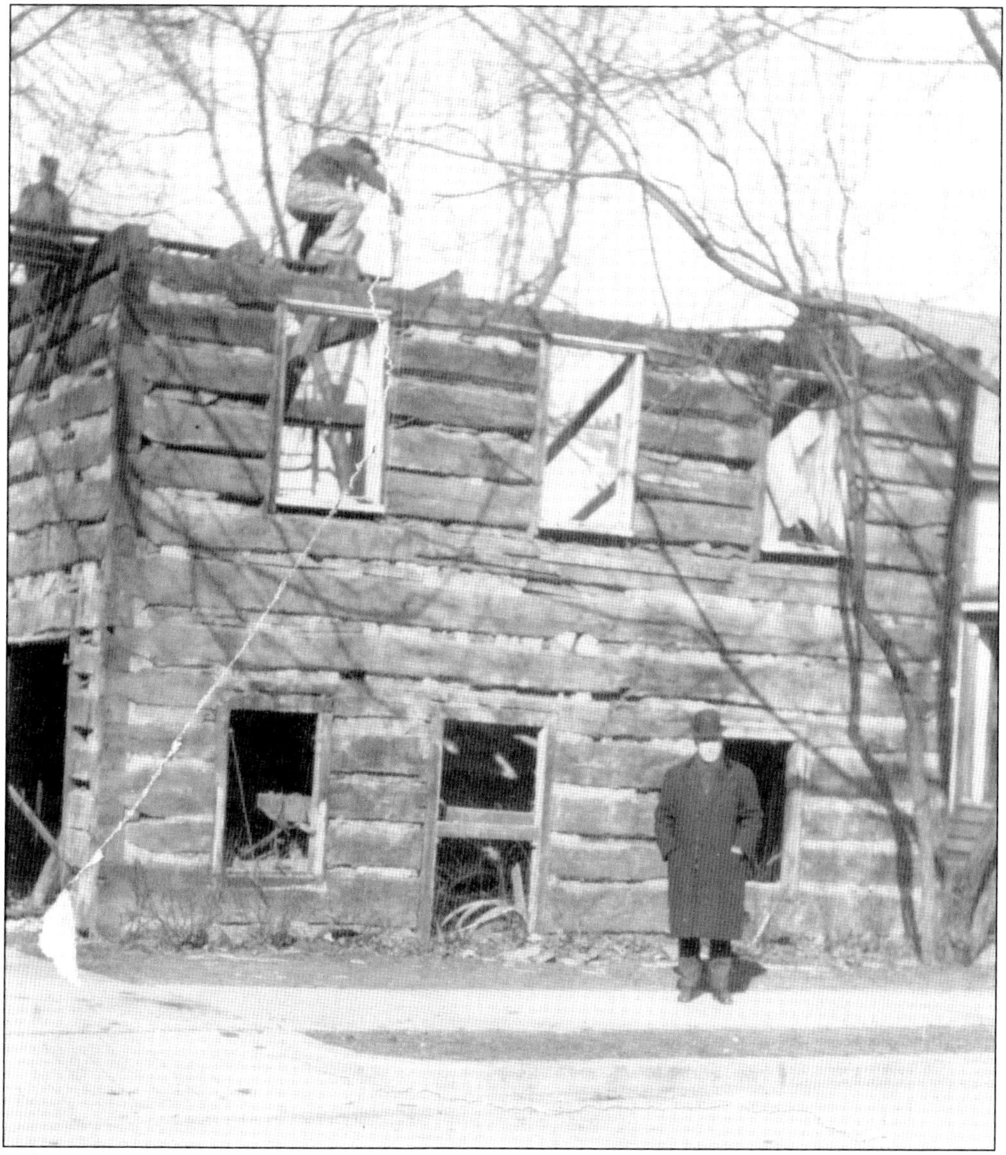

In his 1925 article "Romantic Story of Baron Basse, Founder of Zelienople," Rev. Dettmar Passavant writes that "the razing of the old log house and store on Main Street of Philipp and Zelie Passavant calls for more than passing notice. It was the first house within the known town bounds. We leave this pioneer couple, peacefully sleeping beneath the soughing pines in the hillside graveyard they gave the town, and the 114-year-old log cabin now razed with its records of joys, sorrows, hardships; its still firm and durable timber, fit symbols of the staunch and sturdy virtues of its God-fearing erstwhile inmates, now passes from sight. The memory of the beauty, devotion, self-sacrifice of their lives is forever enshrined in the recollection of their descendants, and treasured by many of the yet-living older townsfolk who knew and loved them." This photograph shows the old store and house at 239 South Main Street being torn down by workmen in 1921, with Rev. Passavant, grandson of Philipp and Zelie, standing in front. It was located at the site of the current Valero car wash. (ZHS.)

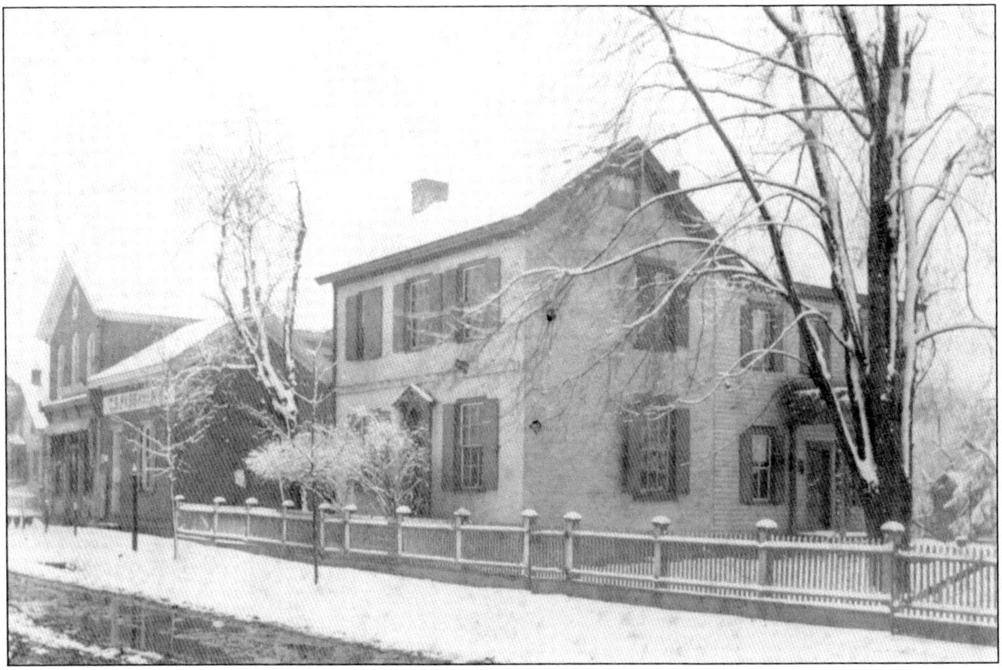

This 1890s photograph shows Philipp and Zelie Passavant's house at 243 South Main Street. To the left of the house is the newer brick Passavant General Store. Charles S. Passavant Sr. and Charles S. Passavant Jr. operated this store until it burned in 1902. Afterwards, the site was a vacant lot until the post office was built there in 1961. (ZHS.)

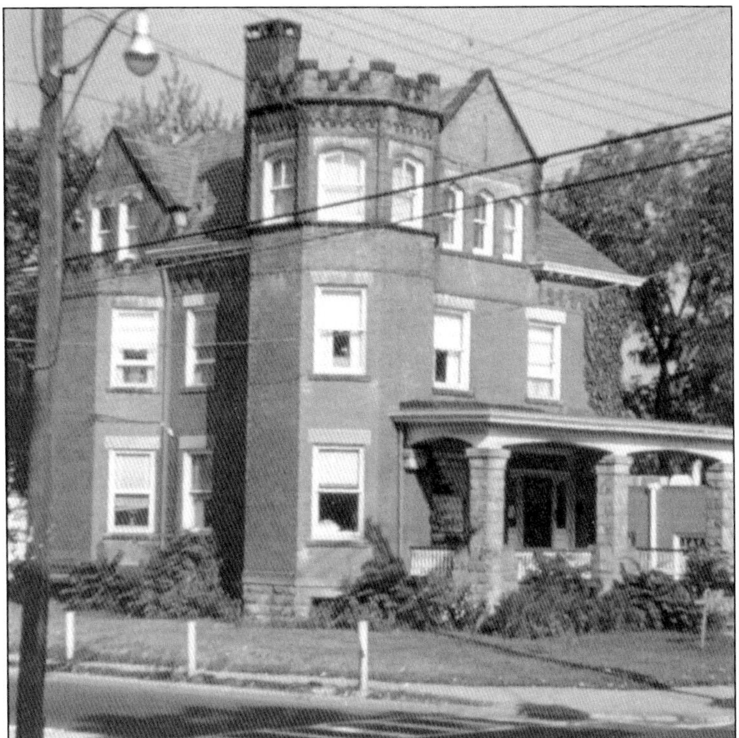

This beautiful home at 251 South Main Street was built in 1901 by C.J.D. Strohecker, the president of Peoples National Bank, who lived to age 99. This home took two years to build, had 14 rooms and 4 fireplaces, and used the best materials, including oak beams. It was sold to Fidelity Savings in 1962 and became a victim of the wrecking ball. Notice the castle-like tower with battlements along the top. (BZC.)

Located at 301 South Main Street was the home of Ulrich Zimmerman, who ran a freight and passenger service until the railroad came to town. Jacob Gudekunst lived there until it was razed for the 7-Eleven store and other convenience stores. This photograph shows Tobias Meeder's family home at 315 South Main Street. In 1960, it was converted into offices by William Kennedy of State Farm Insurance. (BZC.)

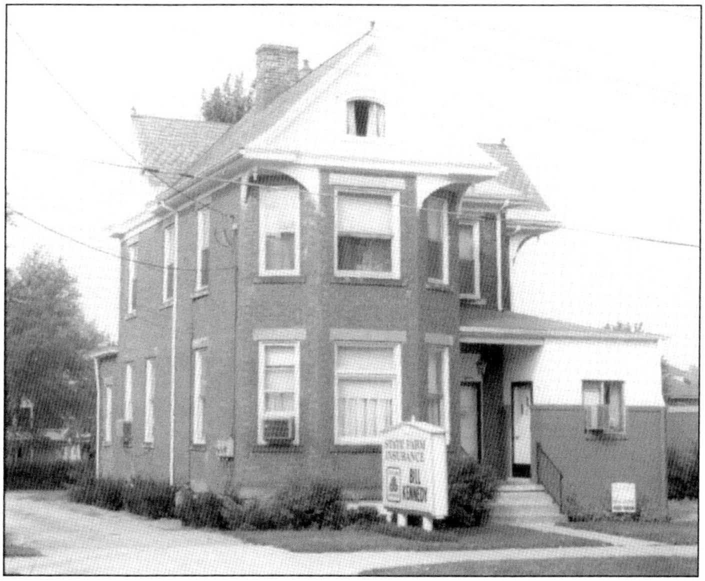

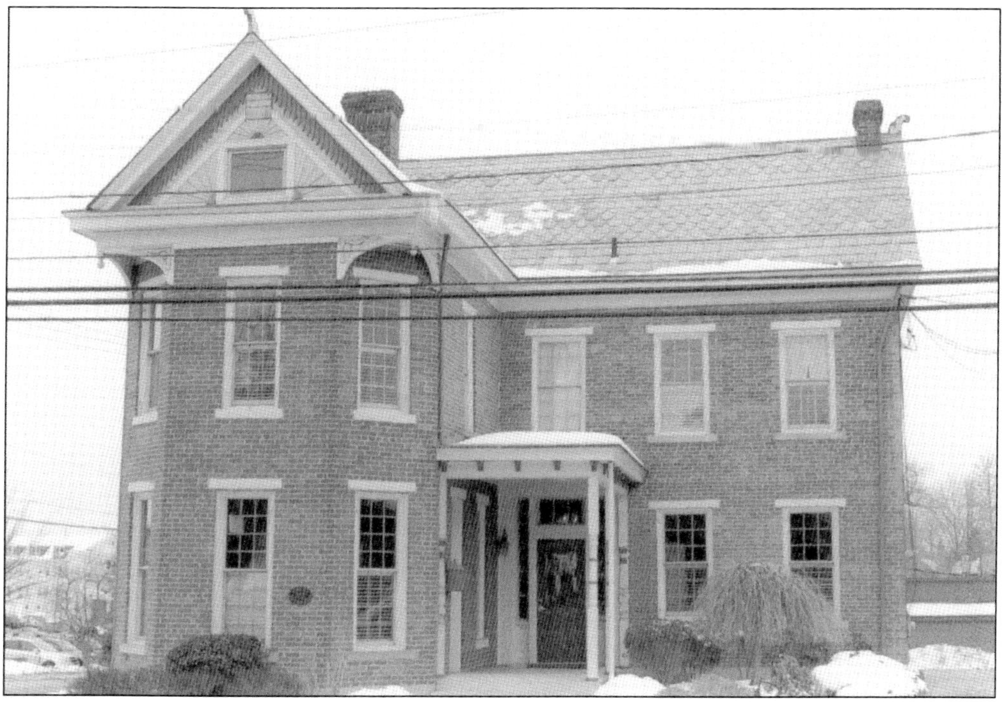

Henry Muntz built this home, located at 323 South Main Street, in 1854. He was the son of George Muntz, who came from Germany in 1804 and owned a farm on Muntz Road, but met his death in 1812 when he was crushed by a falling tree while working at rail-making. The home in the photograph has been renovated by the Camelot Coal Company and is used for its offices. (ZHS.)

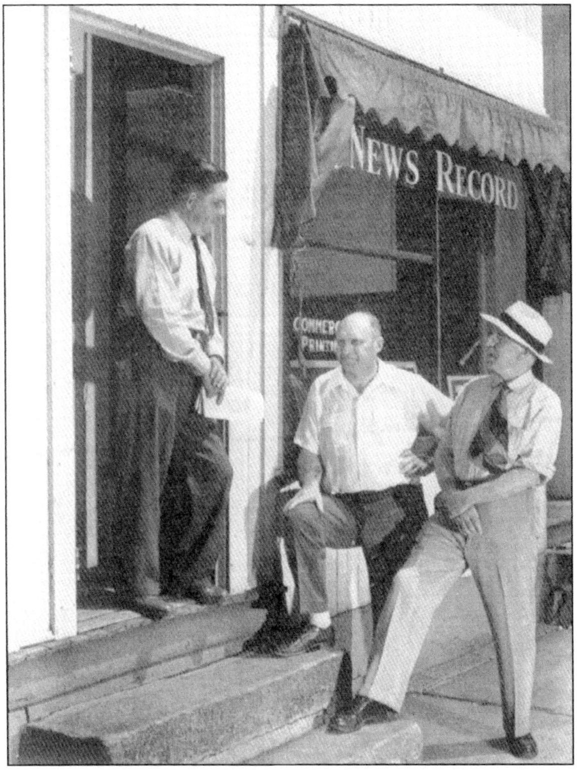

On the east side of Main Street, the building at 126 North Main Street was an early blacksmith shop and the home of Frank Harris. The site was later the home of *Connoquenessing Valley News* (1878–1932), the *News Beacon* (1932–1942), and the *News Record* (1942–1973). This 1960s photograph shows, from left to right, *News Record* editor John E. Rinesmith, chamber of commerce president Kenneth Newcum, and Zelienople mayor Harry Archer. The first newspaper in the borough was the *Zelienople Recorder*. It started publishing in 1847, but was short-lived. (ZHS.)

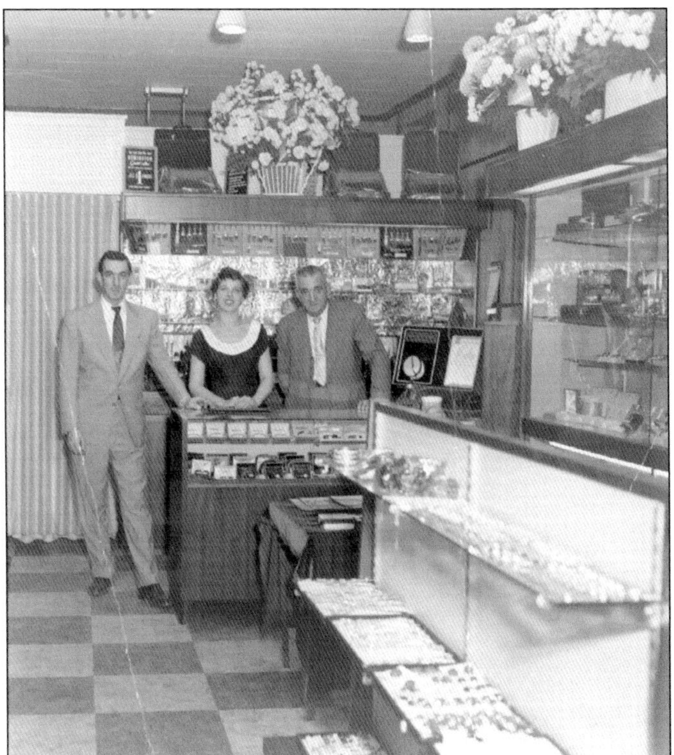

Located at 122 North Main Street was the home of Fred Frishkorn and later William Meyers. In 1947, Andrew Mathew Sr. established Mathew Jewelers here. In the 1950s, his son Andrew Jr. and his wife, Helen, operated the business, followed by the next generation, including Drew, Michelle, and Philip Mathew. This 1955 photograph shows, from left to right, Andrew Jr., Helen, and Andrew Sr. in the original store, which was later expanded and remodeled. (Mathew Jewelers.)

In 1909, the Sapienza family opened a store near Harper's Hardware. In 1914, they opened beside their new Strand Theater, and finally, in 1941, Samuel Sapienza built the store at 118 North Main Street. In 1973, it was operated by Jerry and Darla Sapienza as the first supermarket in the area. The Sapienzas are, from left to right, Leo, Roselia, Tom, Joe, Jim, Tony, and Sam. (Gloria Koch.)

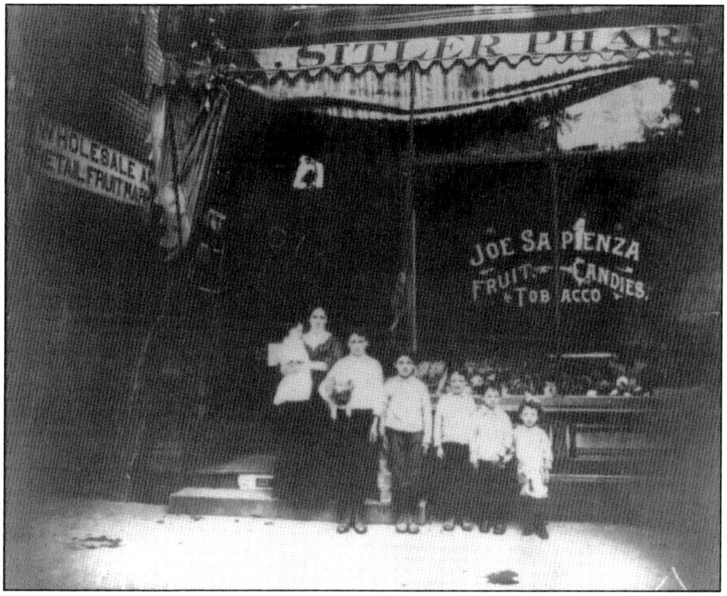

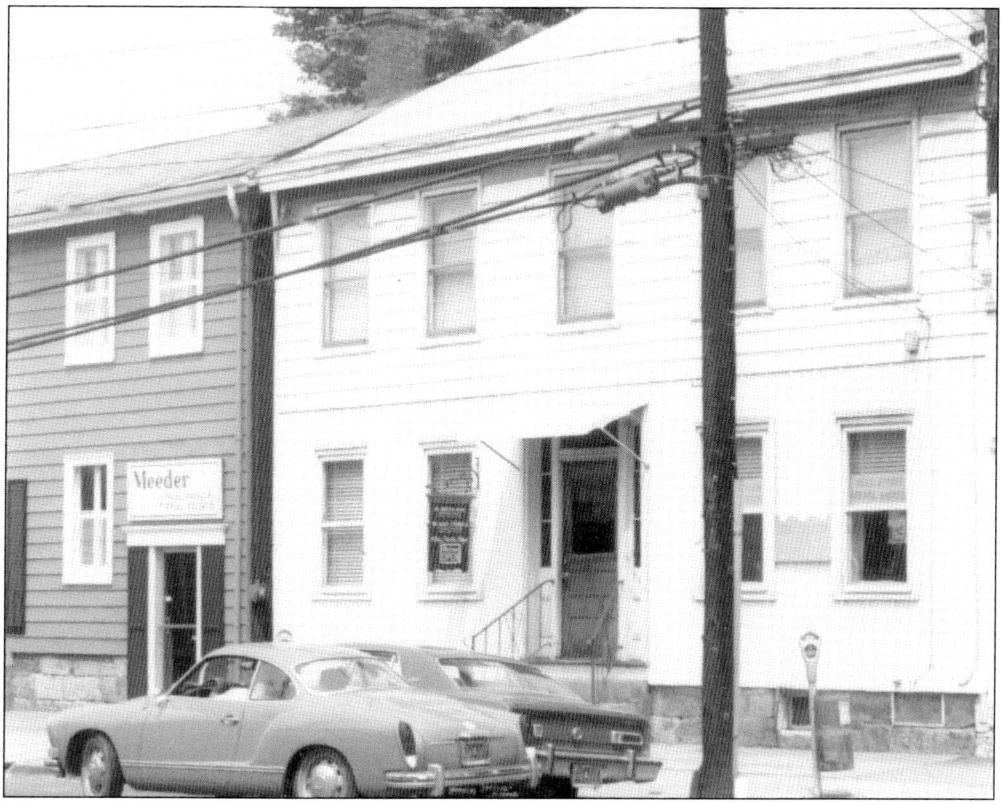

The house on the left at 114 North Main Street was the home of Dr. Amos Lusk; it was later the home and office of Edwin and Ellsworth Meeder Insurance. The house on the right at 110 North Main Street was the home and office of Dr. Burton Kane. Due to eye problems, he switched from dental to optometric school. He was known to give away glasses to children or take garden vegetables in payment for his services. (ZHS.)

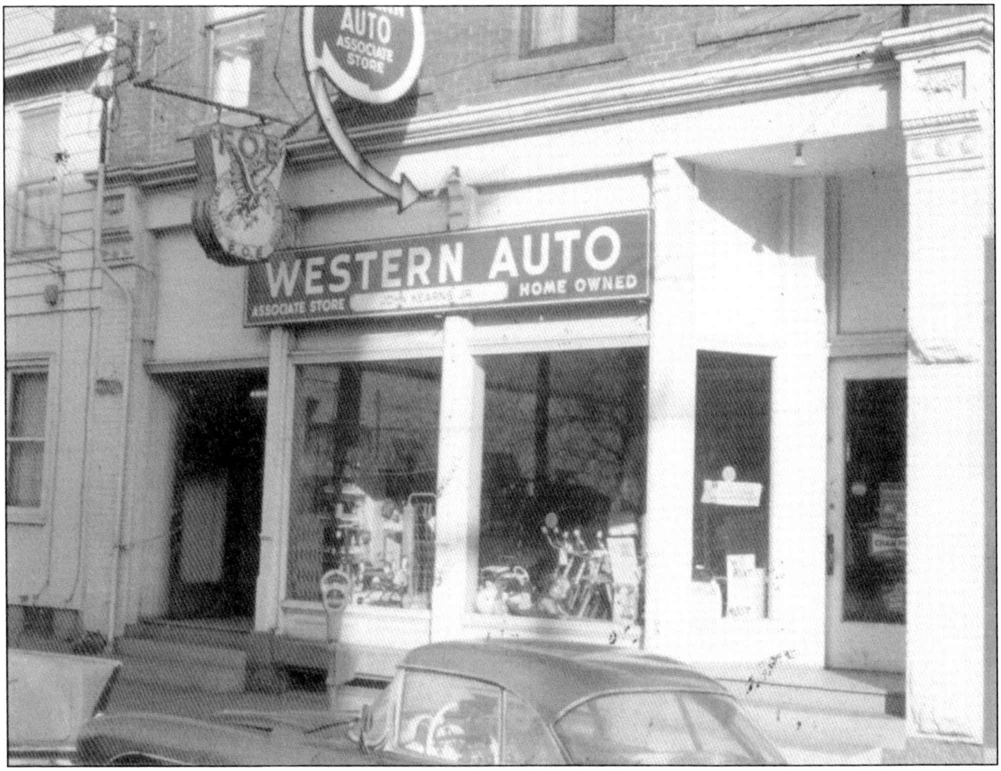

Edwin Zehner erected a three-story brick building at 106 North Main Street in 1896. Zehner was the town undertaker, burying everyone within a 10-mile radius. He and his sons also sold furniture and carpet at this location. In the 1950s, this was the Western Auto Store, as shown in the photograph with appropriate classic cars. It is Andrea's Country Store today. (BZC.)

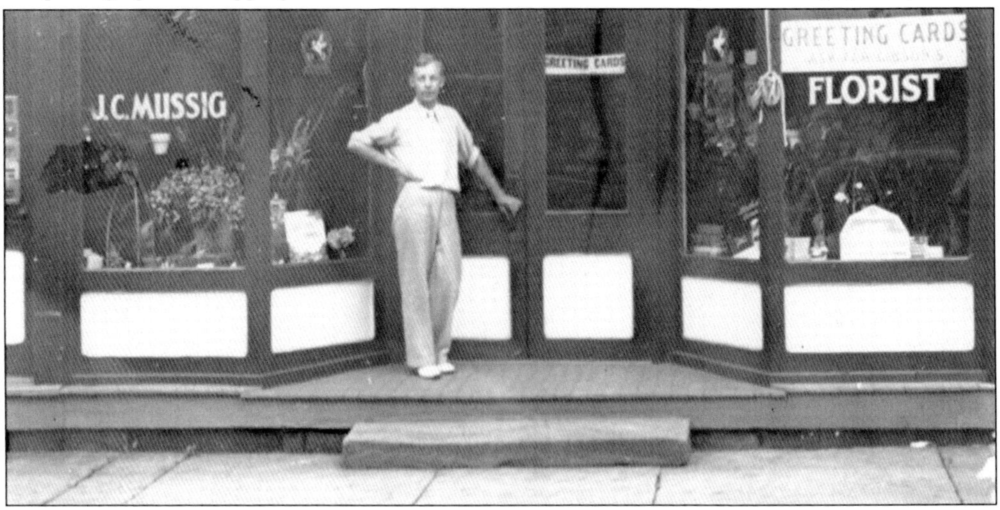

Originally, the building at 104 North Main Street was the home and harness shop of William Wild. In 1932, Julian C. Mussig opened his flower and greeting card shop, as shown in this photograph. In 1950, he constructed a new brick building for Mussig Florist, which is still in business at this location. The business also owns a nursery along the old Perry Highway, just south of town. (Marlene Mussig.)

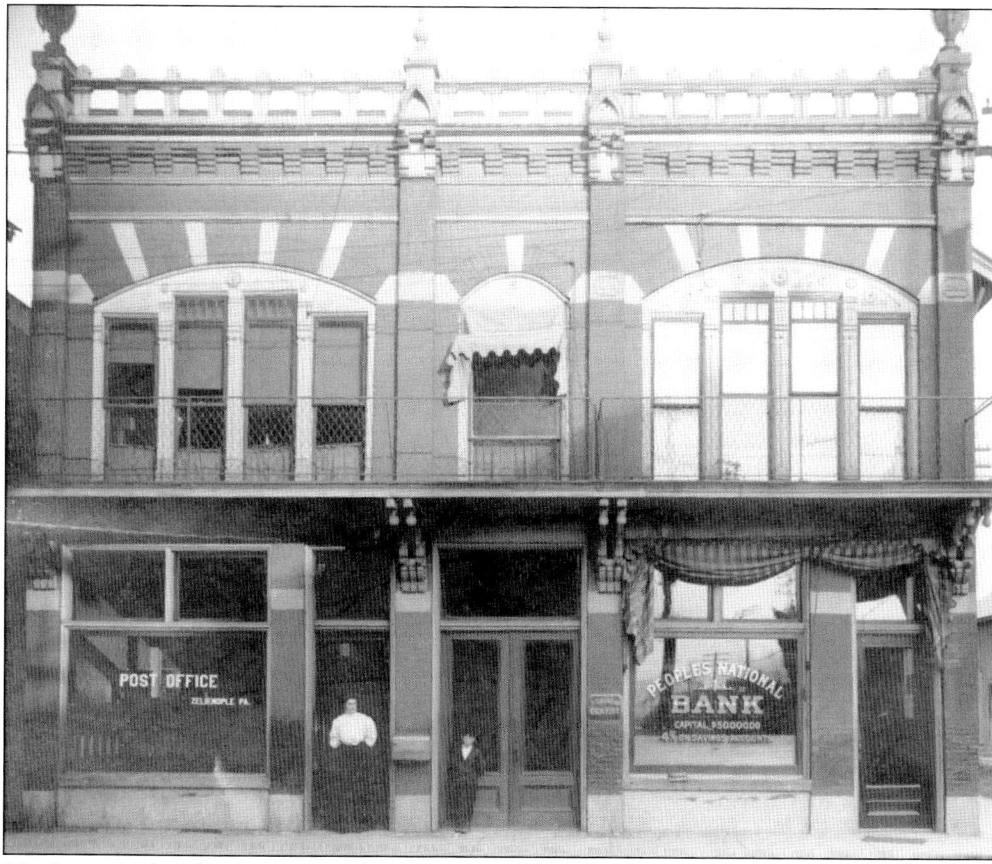

The beautiful building at 100 North Main Street was the jewelry store of Albert Winter. Around 1925, it became the Peoples National Bank and Zelienople Post Office, as seen in the photograph above. In 1934, this building was demolished and the present, more secure one was constructed. This became the Union National Bank with the merger of Peoples Bank and First National Bank. In 1948, it was purchased by Mellon Bank of Pittsburgh, as seen in the 1965 photograph below. Today, it is Citizens Bank. The Huckstein Building in the rear dates back to 1882. The post office was located there from 1934 to 1961. (Both, BZC.)

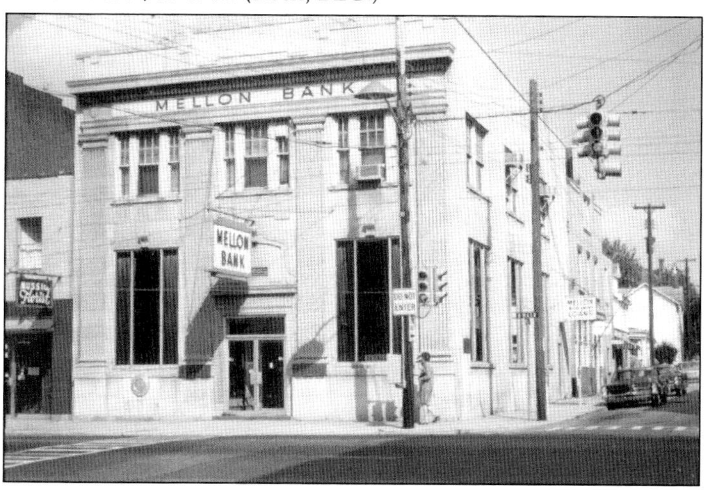

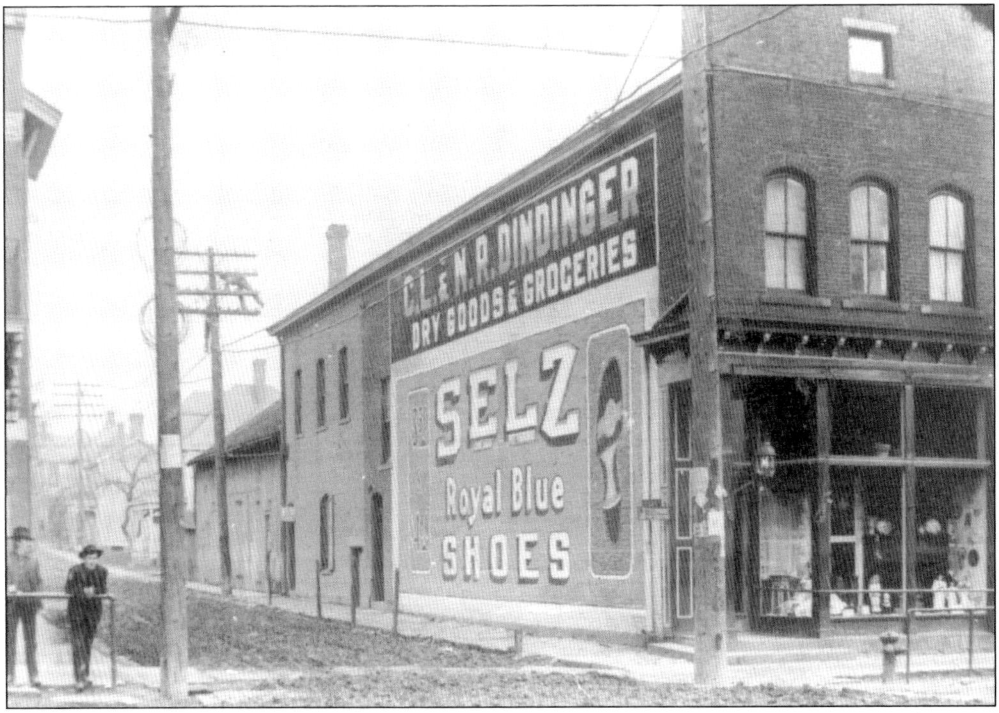

In 1875, John Dindinger built a dry goods and grocery store at 100 South Main Street; the store was later operated by his sons. John served during the Civil War and after as postmaster and in the state legislature. In the 1900 postcard above, there are two telephone workmen balancing on their toes in the background. In 1896, Bell Telephone tried installing poles along Main Street, but the merchants became so upset they cut them down. After service was successfully installed in Harmony, Zelienople merchants changed their minds. The photograph below shows the last manual telephone switchboard operated by Bell Telephone in Pennsylvania. It was located on the second floor of the Mellon Bank Building and was shut down forever at 2:00 a.m. on February 17, 1963. Zelienople then began using the 452 telephone exchange and dial telephones. Customers could now dial a number instead of waiting for an operator to do it for them. (Both, ZHS.)

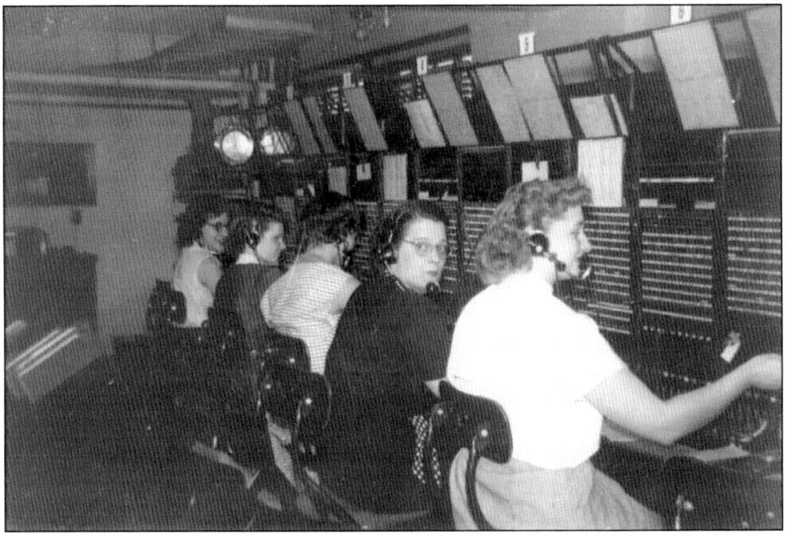

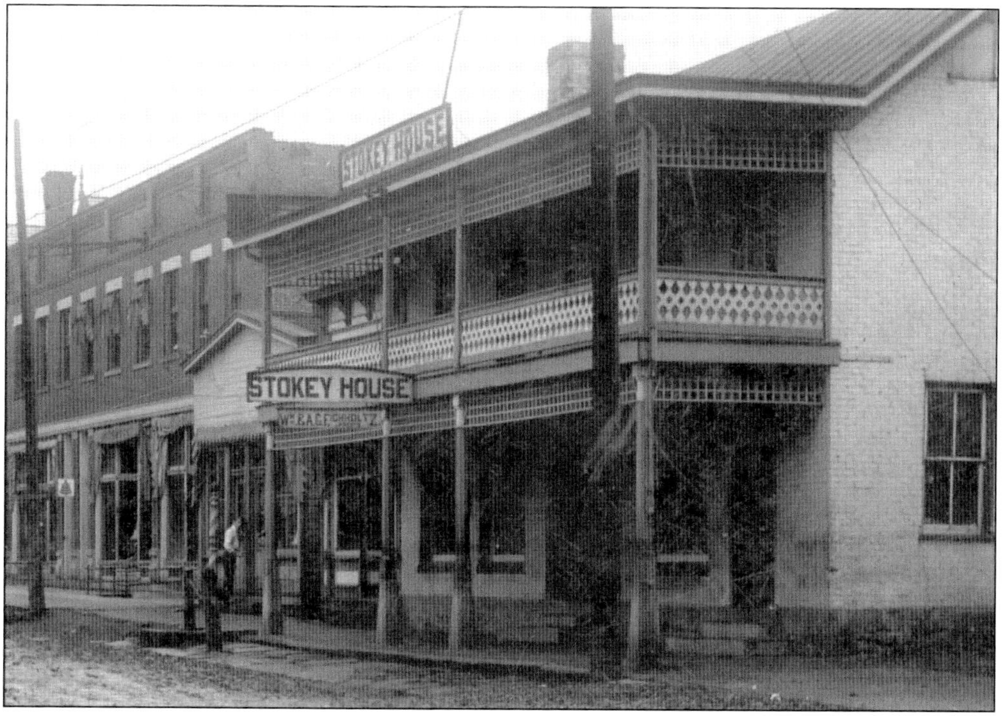

In the 1930 photograph above, the building on the far left is 106–114 South Main Street, where many merchants have been located over the years. The Jacob Schaffer Barbershop is between the buildings, and stairs are seen leading to the former basement bowling alley and poolroom. The 1886 photograph below is of the famous Stokey Hotel, with Charles Stokey leaning against the Gehring's Beer sign. This hotel at 118 South Main was built in 1825 by Rudolph Kelkers. It was known as the Golden Eagle Hotel, and then the Stokey Hotel when operated by Henry Stokey and son Charles. It later became the Miller Hotel, the Luek Hotel, and, lastly, the William Eichholtz Hotel. This old landmark hotel of stagecoach days was demolished in 1935. The Northwest Savings Bank is located here now. (Both, ZHS.)

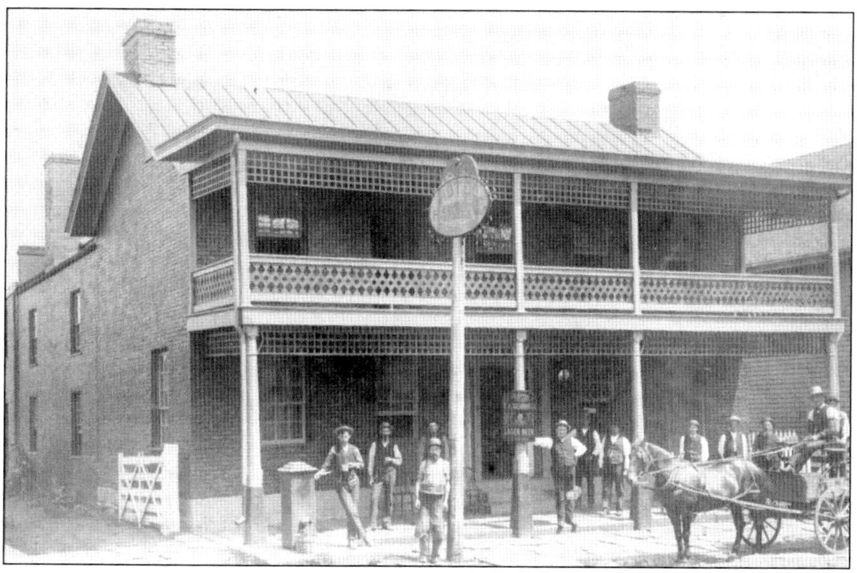

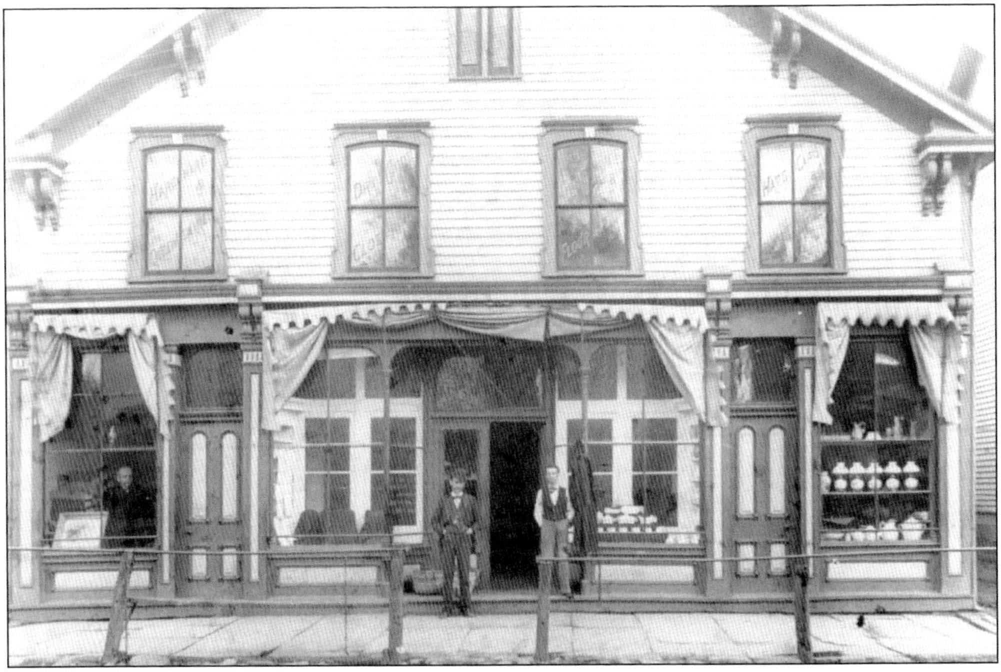

The photograph above of 128–132 South Main Street shows three stores with various dry goods, clothing, and hardware for sale. The building was later owned by Herbert Walters, who also had the Clover Farm grocery and a horse barn in the back. The 1950s photograph below shows Wright's Golden Dawn grocery and barbershop on the left. The K&K Hot Dog shop and several others were here later. The building now houses Kennedy-Meeder Insurance and Main Street's longest-running business on the left. This barbershop, spanning over 100 continuous years, was owned by William Kloffenstein in 1911, Carl Hartman in 1941, William Eppinger in 1968, and is now owned by Daniel Fritch, who joined in 2000. In the 1970s, the roof of the old wooden building was raised and a new concrete block building was built under it. (Both, BZC.)

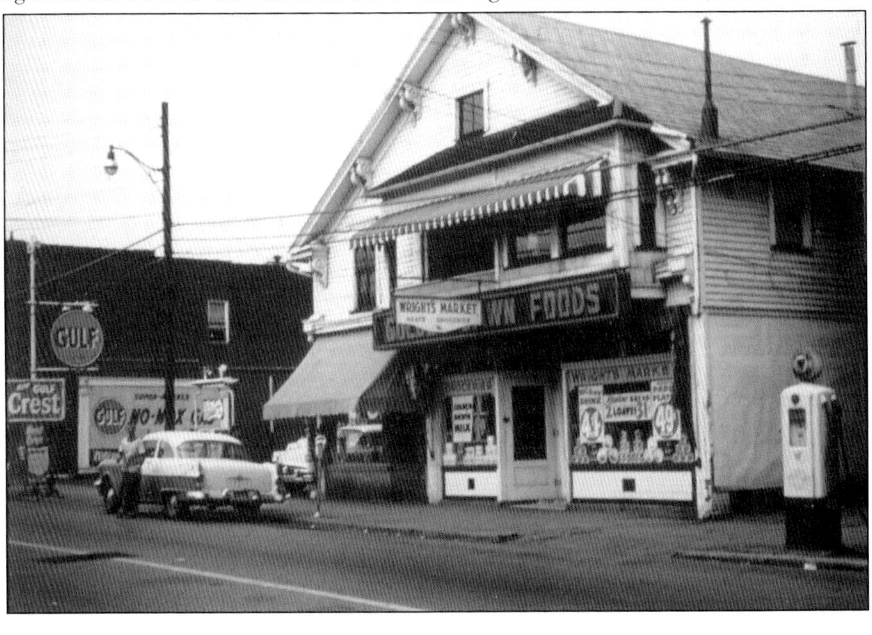

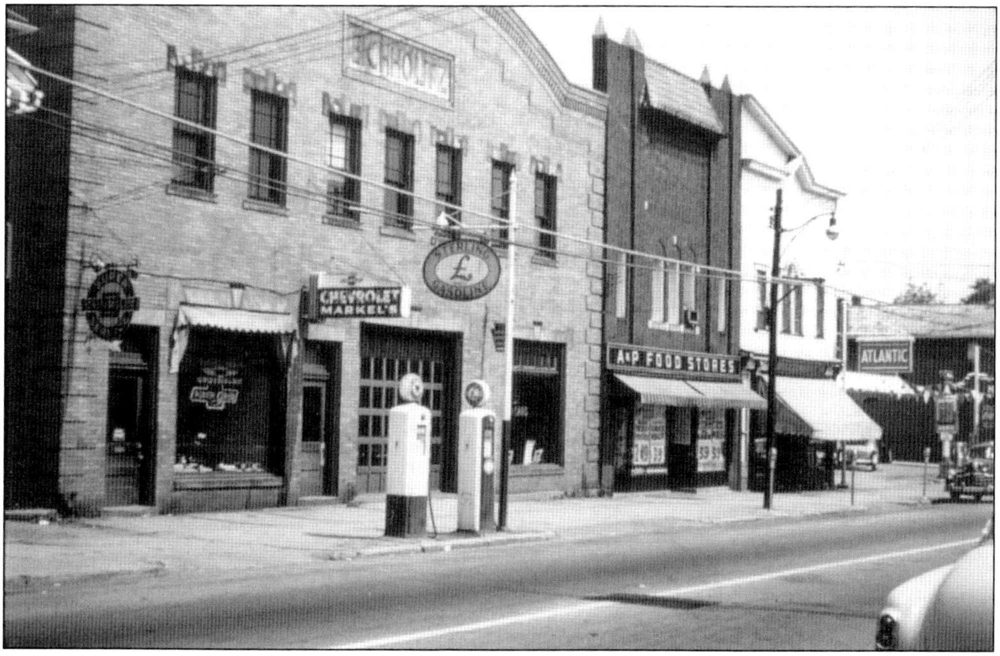

William Eichholtz built his Ford dealership at 134 South Main Street. The second floor was a basketball court and dance hall for teens in the 1920s. In the 1955 photograph above, it is Markel's Chevrolet, and later became the Golden Dawn Grocery. The building at 142 South Main Street was James Wilson Livery until it went out of business in 1928. Wilson erected a new brick building for the A&P food store and son Brandt's dental office. Since 1974, it has been Carol's Bakery. The building at 146 South Main Street was Kramer Wagons; it was later a duckpin bowling alley and the first nickelodeon in town. The 1916 photograph below shows Wilson in the middle, flanked by his two sons, Brandt and Warren, who would later become a dentist and doctor respectively, providing health care in the town for 50 years. (Above, BZC; below, Sharon Shanks.)

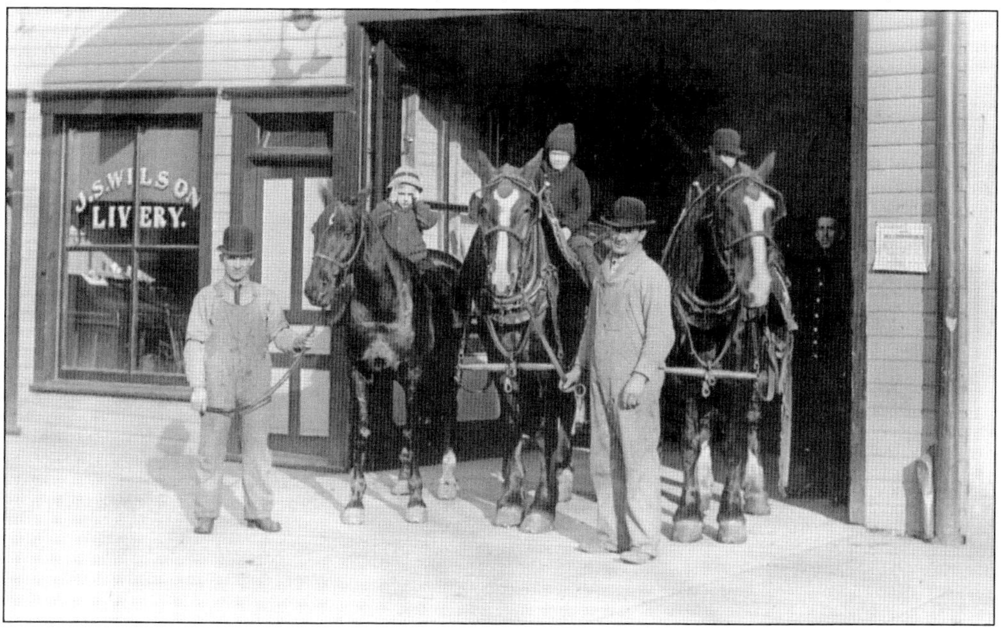

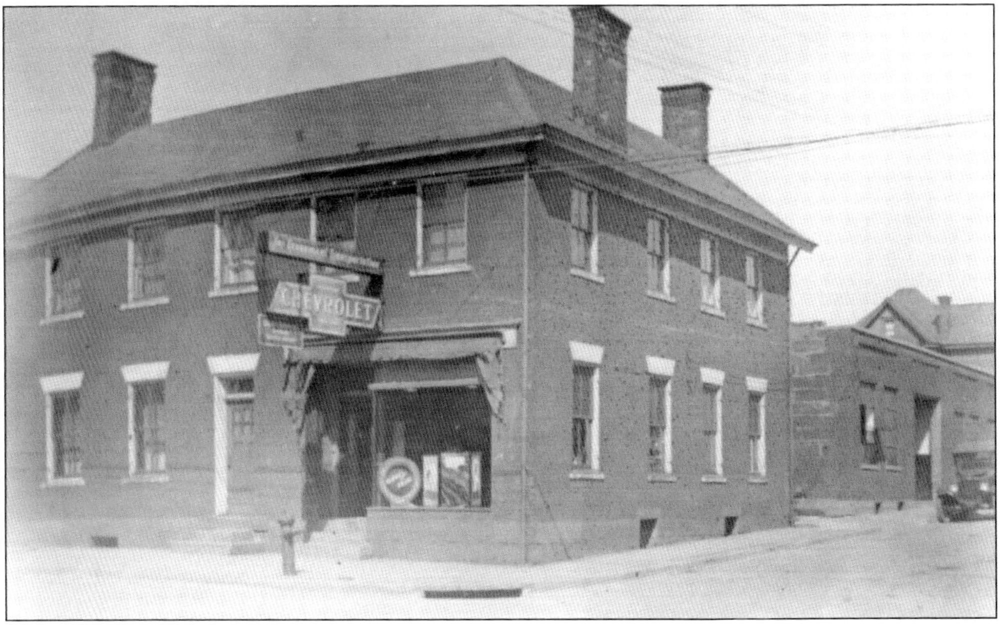

The 1921 photograph above depicts the brick residence of Eckert Bentle, later the home of Edward Mellon. In 1920, Harvey Harper Sr. bought this house at 154 South Main Street from tailor Herman Gross and built the automobile garage in the rear. He also bought the small lot and store to the left. Later, Harper built a new showroom building and connected it to the rear garage, as shown in the 1930 photograph below. During the years of the Pontiac dealership, Harvey Harper Jr. sold a Pontiac to cowboy movie star Gene Autry and to ballplayer Ralph Kiner, who played for the Pittsburgh Pirates from 1946 to 1953. William Harper now conducts his Outdoor Power Equipment business here, making him the third generation of Harpers to do business at this location. (Both, William Harper.)

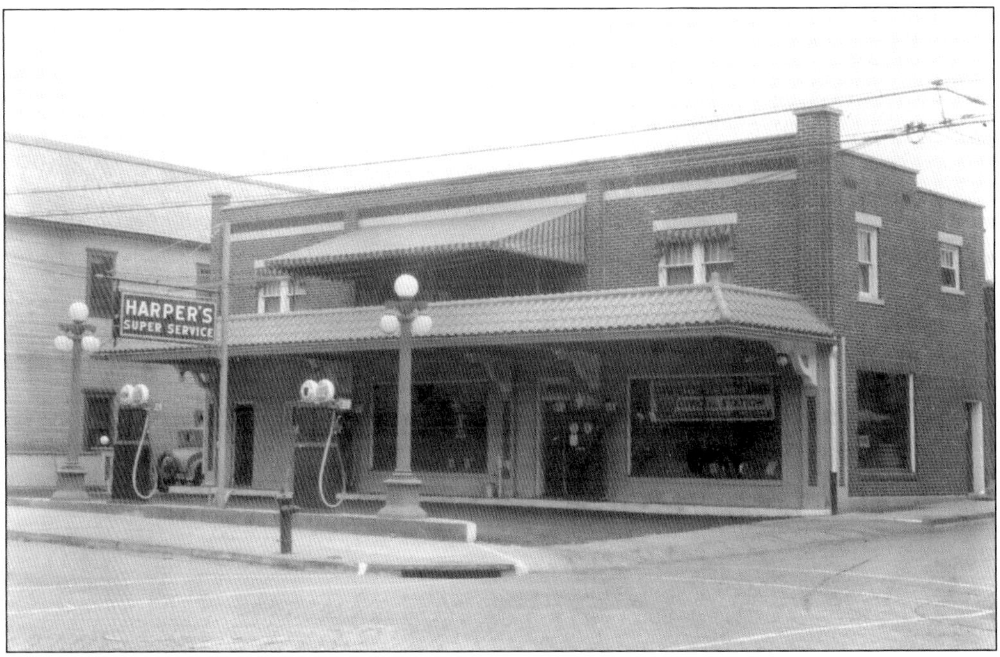

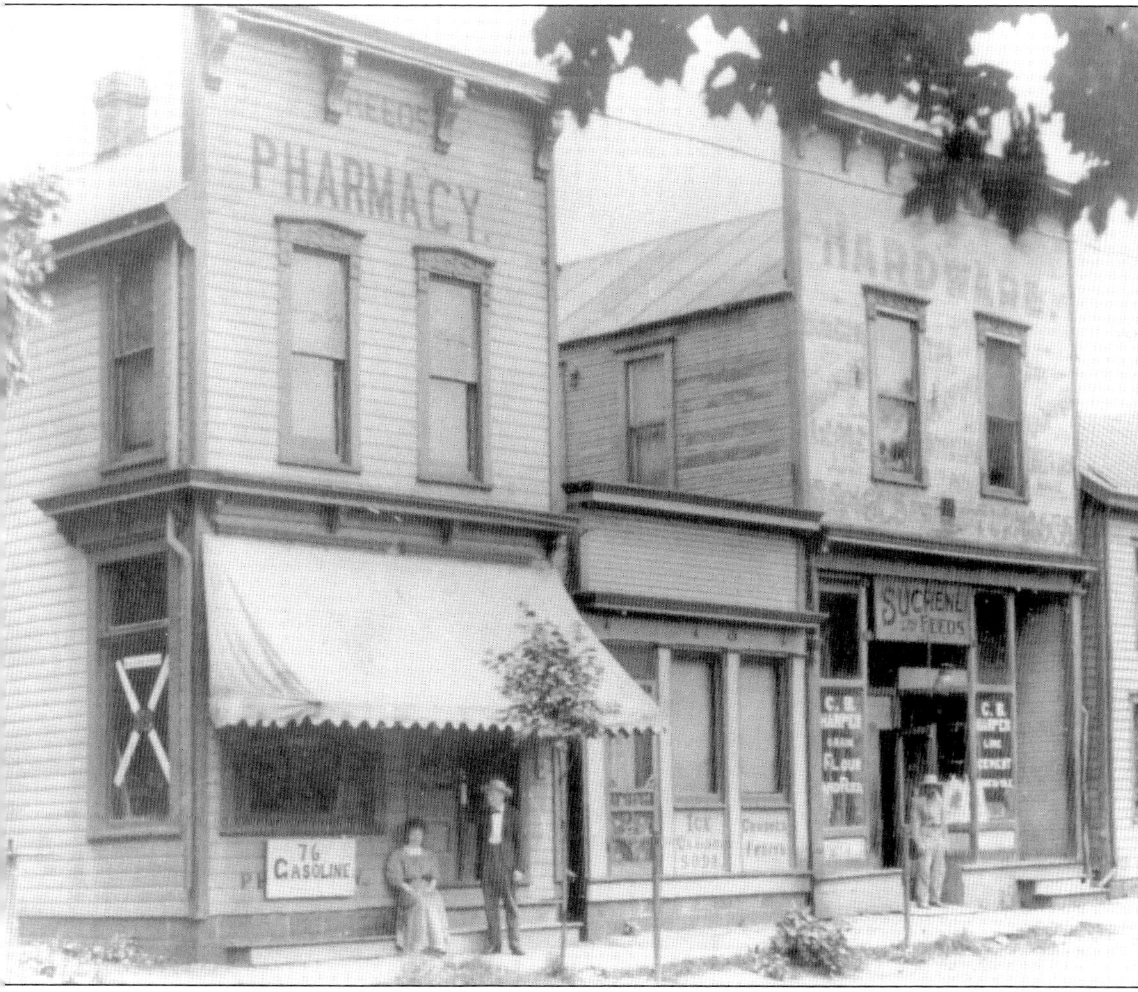

This 1902 photograph shows Charles and Jeanette Reed in front of Reed's Pharmacy at 200 South Main Street. The pharmacy sold gasoline and the water pump on the far left was a source of community well water back then. The small ice-cream parlor was at 202 South Main. The pharmacy was later bought by Alfred Sitler, then Alfred Campbell, and in 1940 by George Fishburn, who was in business there for 30 years. The structure then became Robert Steffler's Bicycle Shop, later an AAA Automobile office, and finally a travel agency. A devastating fire started here on May 10, 2008, and the entire block was in danger. A police officer was patrolling the area just after 3:00 a.m. when he noticed smoke coming from the building. Ten volunteer fire departments responded to the crisis and managed to contain the blaze. No one was injured, but three firefighters were temporarily trapped on the second floor when part of the ceiling fell on them. Unfortunately, all three of these buildings were lost. The one on the right at 204 South Main Street was Cyrus B. Harper's Hardware; the image shows him standing in front. He also owned a grain and feed mill along the Connoquenessing Creek. This building later was occupied by Penney's Hardware, C.T. McCormick's Hardware, Olde Attic Antiques, and Beecher's Coffee Shop. This structure was also destroyed in the fire and had been recently renovated to include Wi-Fi and live music, along with gourmet coffee. The building on the extreme right was also heavily damaged by the fire, but attorney Wesley Hamilton was able to salvage and restore the early 1800s structure, now currently serving as his office. Since 2014, Roach and Ziegler Interiors has occupied these three spaces in a new brick building. (ZHS.)

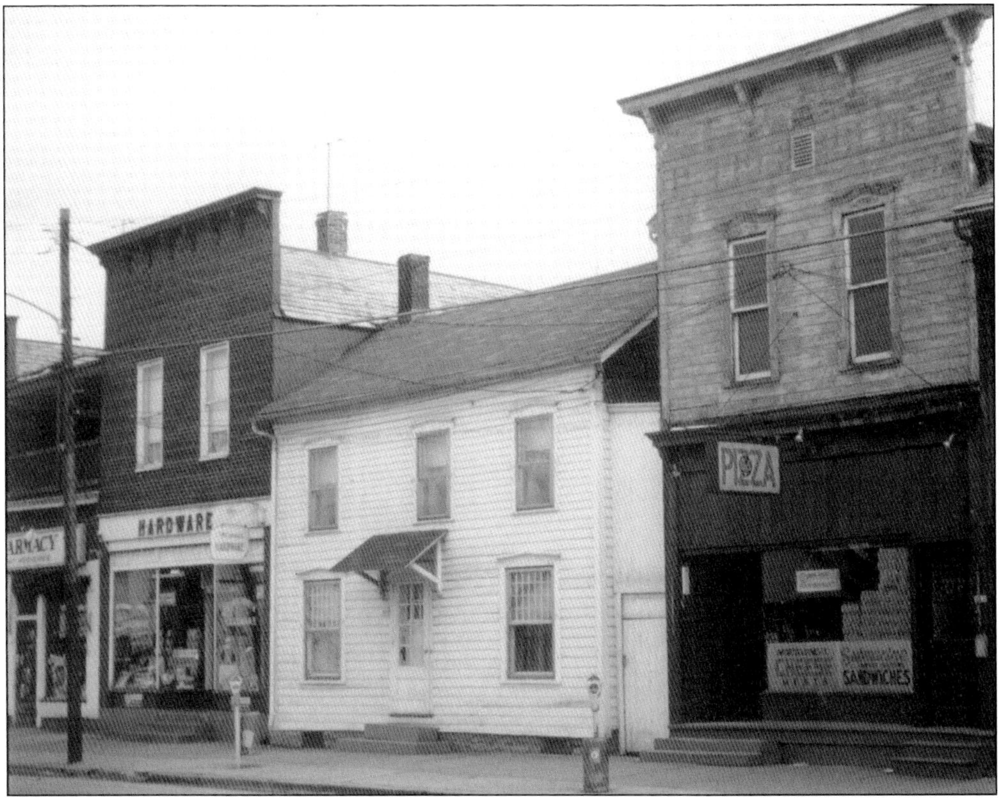

The 1970 photograph above shows Fishburn's Pharmacy, McCormick's Hardware, Attorney Hamilton's building, and Chef's Pizza. Attorney Wesley Hamilton's building at 208 South Main Street may be the last log structure on Main Street. The left half of this building is log, and the logs are exposed and finished on one of the interior walls. This was originally the home of Henry Householder, and on the right at 210 South Main Street was his bakery and bookbindery. The photograph below shows young Householder anxious to start the day's work in this vintage delivery van. The bakery later became the home of Chef's Pizza, which in 1960 was the first place in town to serve "pizza pies," as they were called then. (Both, BZC.)

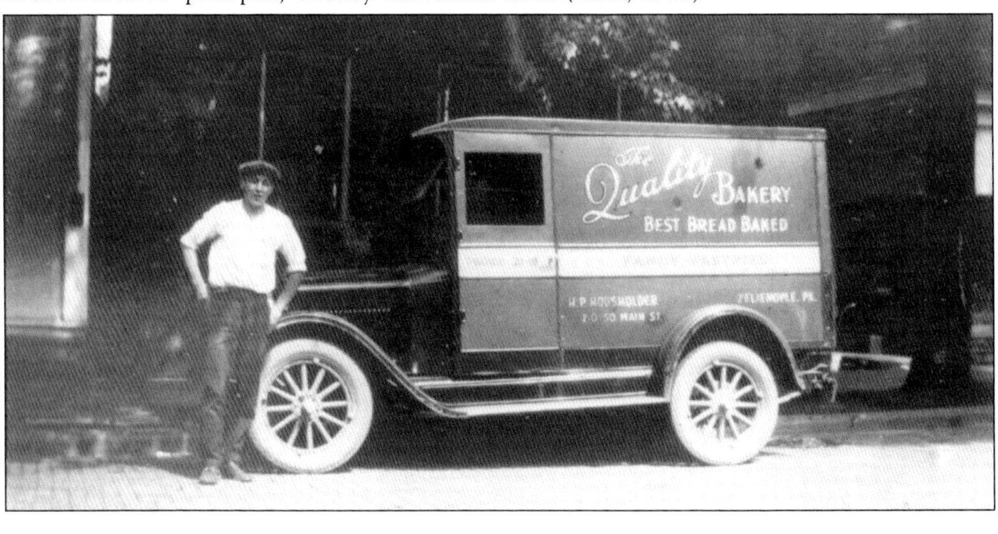

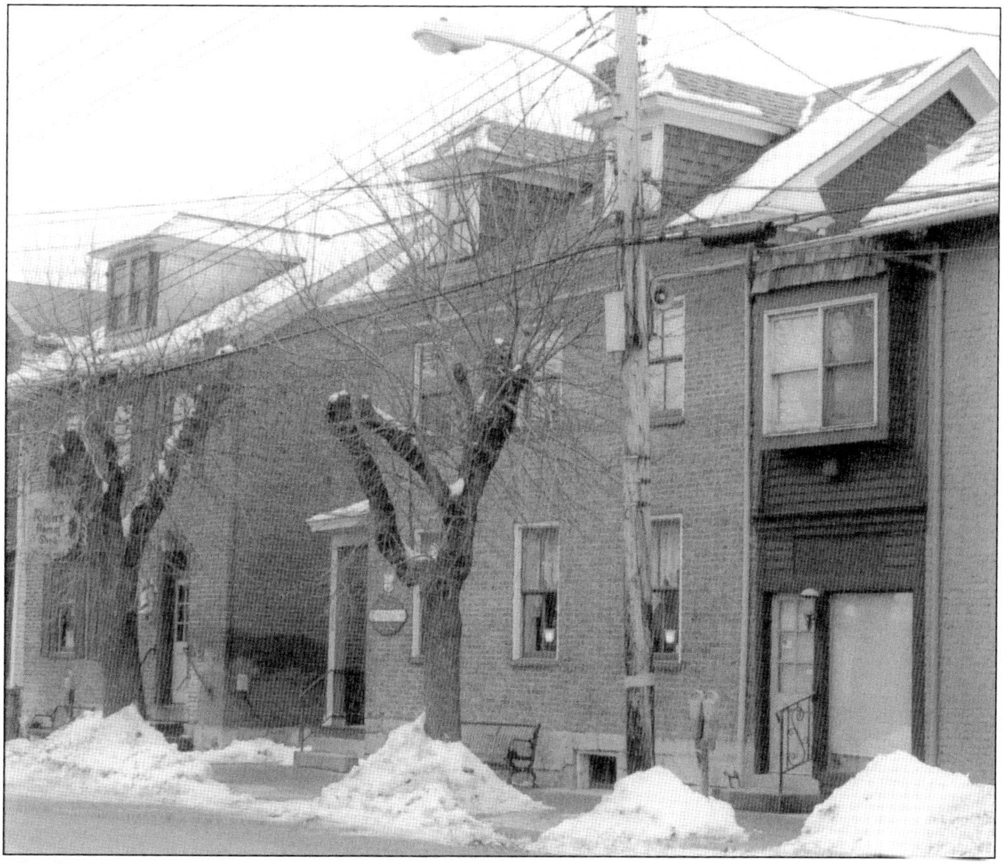

The four brick buildings at 214–226 South Main Street were all built in the late 1800s by pioneer residents of the town. They lived here and had various trade shops at these locations. There was Leonard Hallstein, who was a cabinetmaker and the first village undertaker, at 214 South Main Street. Art Frishkorn had a barbershop here, which is now owned by Rich Eppinger. William Allen Sr. and Jr. had homes at 220 and 226 South Main Street. James Greer, founder of the popular Newstand, lived at 226 South Main Street, as did Leo Hart of Hart's Newstand. All four houses have been converted into shops and offices. Citizens Bank, now NexTier, saved 226 South Main Street from the wrecking ball and now uses it for office space. (Both, ZHS.)

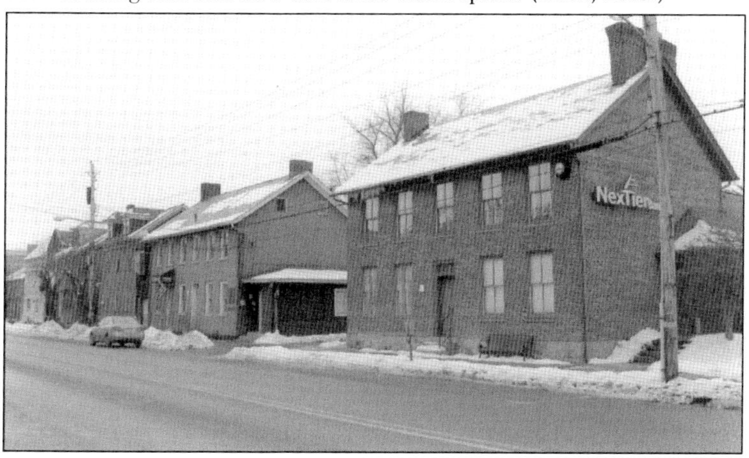

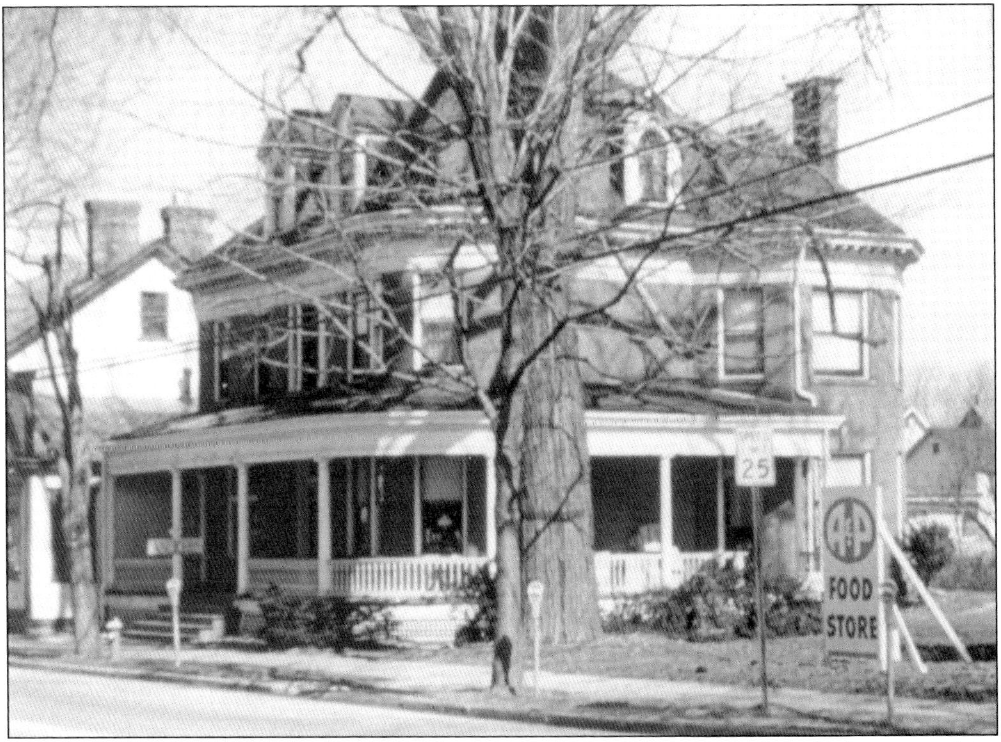

The parking lot at Walgreens drugstore at 230 South Main Street was once the location of the biggest and best house in town. The 1960 photograph above shows a fine Victorian mansion with an unusual wraparound porch. This Charles Passavant Jr. home was on a very large lot with a rose garden in the rear and a bridge over a small stream running through the property. This valuable home was lost when Charles Passavant III sold it to the A&P food store. The photograph below shows the A&P store after completion in 1961. The store later went out of business. The rear portion of this lot now serves as the location of the town's library on High Street. (Both, BZC.)

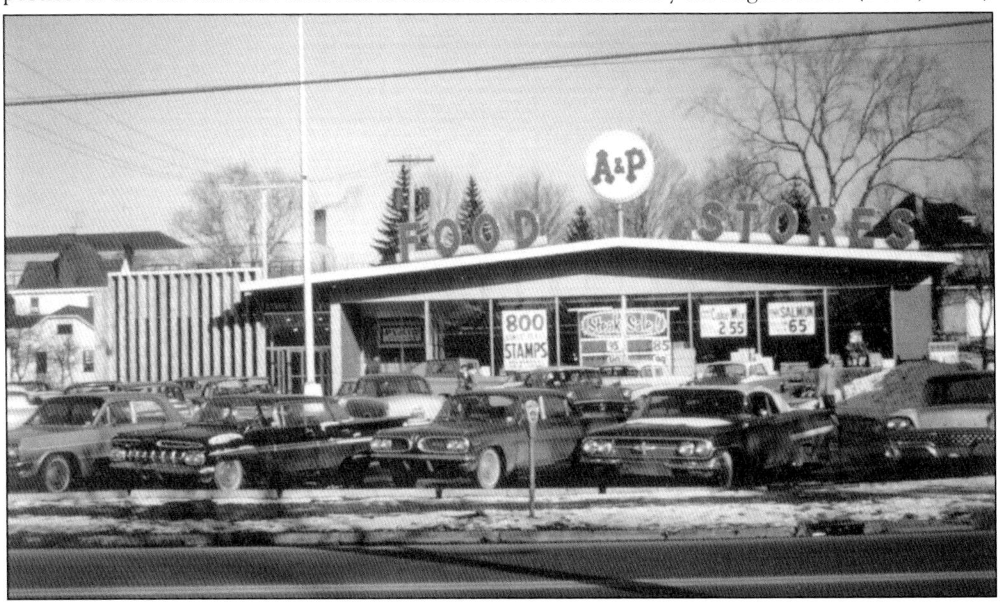

The house at 240 South Main was built in 1821 by pioneer John Reed. His son Charles Reed lived in this house and was the town druggist for 50 years. It was later owned by Col. George Gage, who was the supervisor of public schools, and by insurance agent William Uhl. Later, the Mel-Den TV and appliance store was in business here for 20 years. Now, the structure is the home of Hovis Auto Supply. (ZHS.)

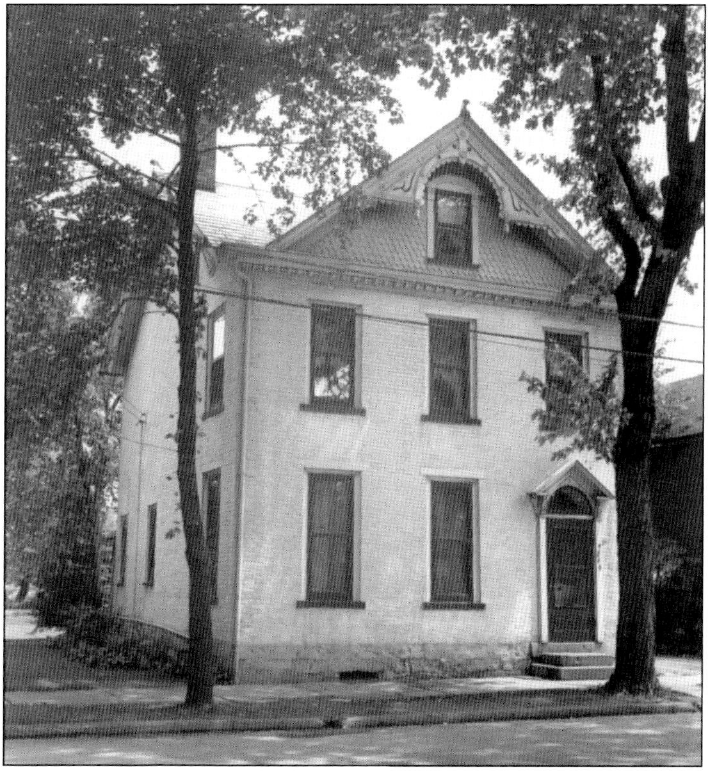

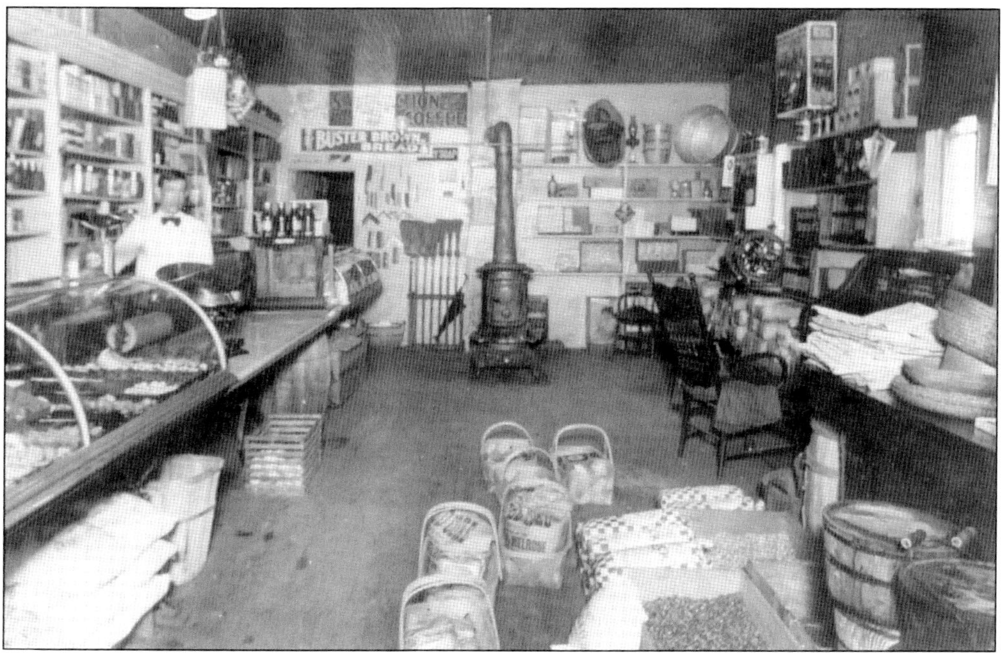

This 1916 photograph shows the interior of the grocery store located at 242 South Main Street, first operated by Ike Weiz (Wise), then by Walter Rogner. This wooden building was torn down and a brick home was built here. Other businesses have been located here over the years; the site is now a parking area for Hovis Auto Supply. (ZHS.)

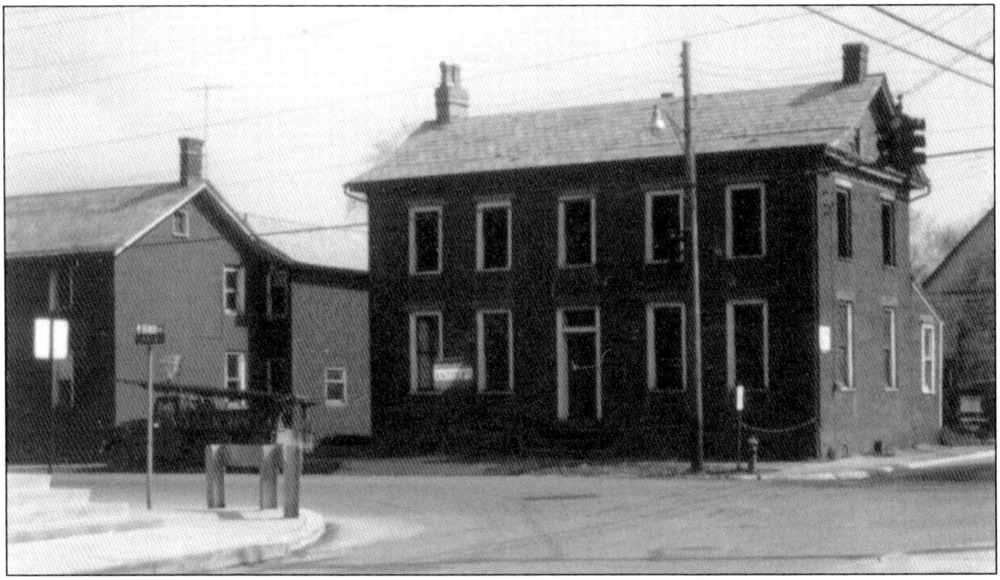

The photograph above shows two similar brick houses that were located at 242 and 246 South Main Street. On the right was the home of Lewis Reed, son of John Reed, who operated a tannery at this location. Later, there were other residents and businesses here until the buildings were demolished in the 1960s for the first of many gasoline stations that have been located at the site. At the extreme right of the photograph, a white wooden building can be seen in the rear. The photograph below shows that same old workshop and carriage house being moved from Beaver Street to High Street. Today, it sits in the backyard at the home of former high school art teacher Robert Bruker. (Both, BZC.)

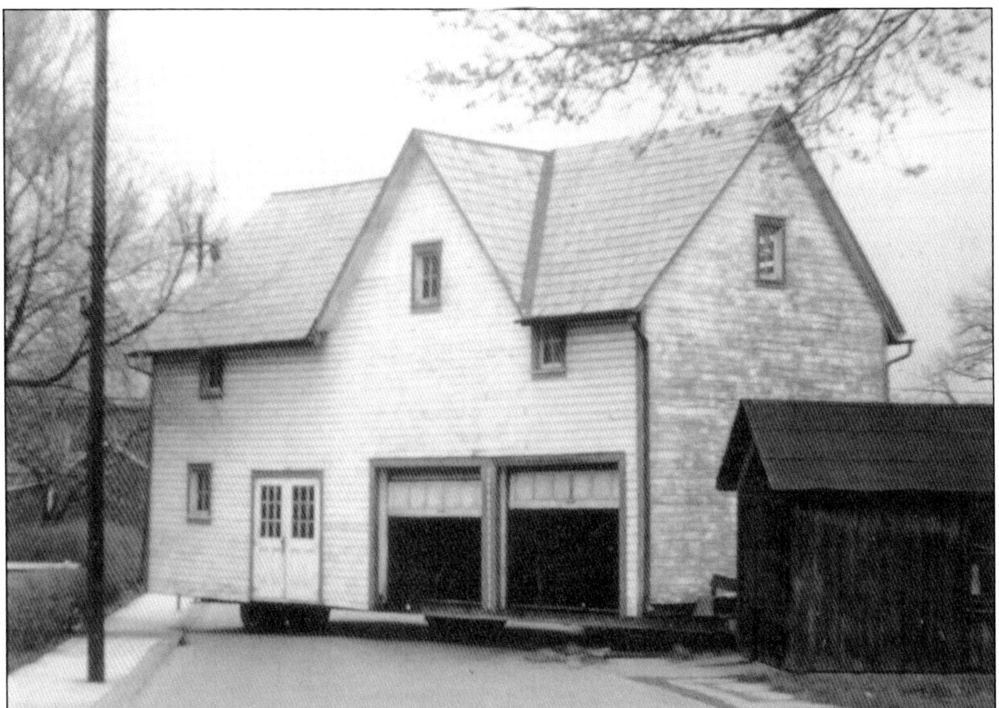

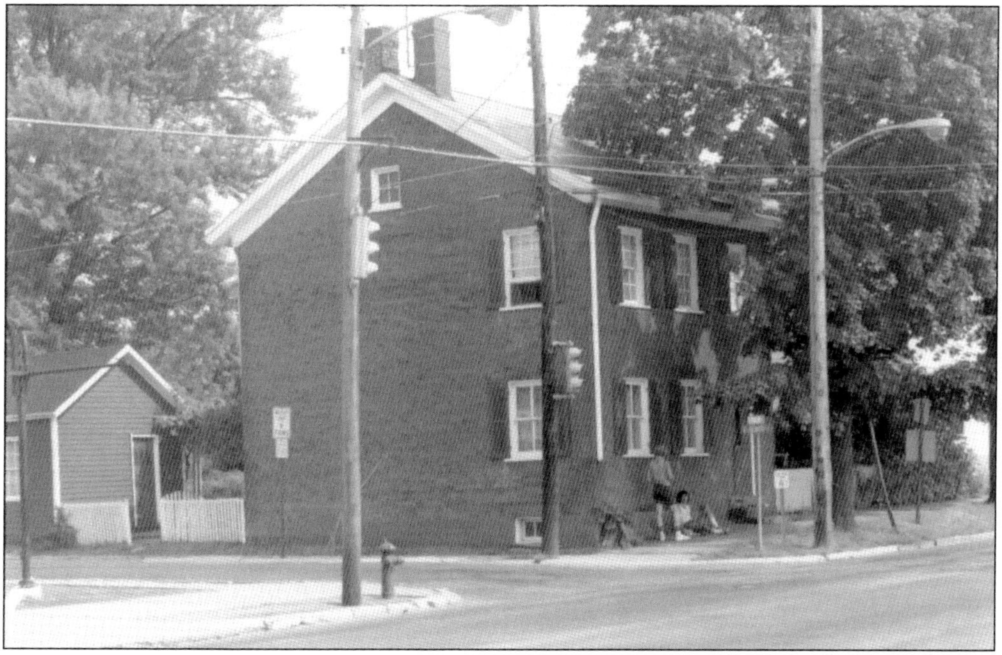

The 300 block of South Main Street contains homes that have been converted into offices. At 300 South Main Street is the 1847 home of Daniel Stauffer that was reportedly used as a stop on the Underground Railroad. The William Allen Jr. home at 304 South Main Street now serves as offices. At 310 South Main Street was the home of huckster Jacob Gudeholder, later the home and barbershop of William Eppinger and now Falk Investments. In 1871, the house at 314 South Main Street was the first English Lutheran Parsonage, later the home of C.W. Ohl of Ohl Hardware, and still later the offices of Foreman Architects. The home at 320 South Main Street is now Avada Hearing Center. The residence at 322 South Main Street was built by Jacob Kaufman, a carpenter who constructed many homes here. It was later owned by George Fishburn of Fishburn's Pharmacy, and now serves as medical offices. (Both, ZHS.)

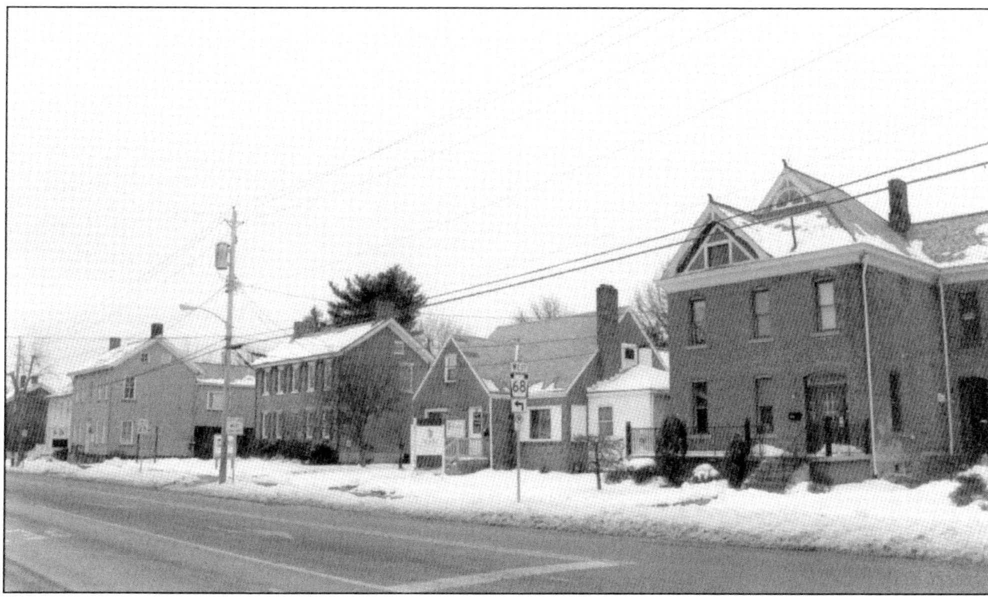

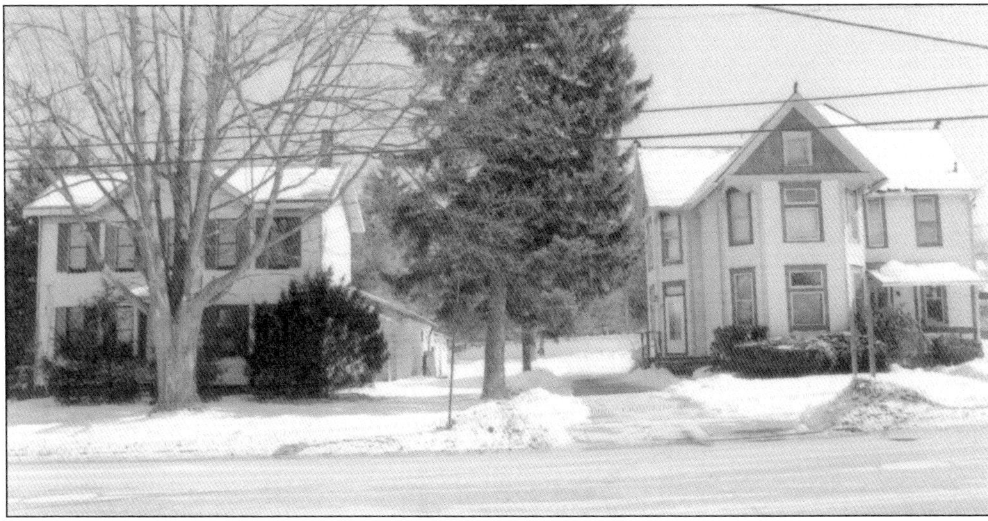

The 400 block of South Main Street contains homes that have been converted into businesses. In the photograph above, 402 South Main Street was the home of Ray Bauder, the butcher, and had a small store in the rear. Walter Zehner lived at 408 South Main Street, which is now a day care center. Walter Rogner lived at a house at 416 South Main Street; it later became Nesbitt's Cleaners, then Basilone's Cleaners. The T-Shirt Loft has been at 420 South Main Street for 30 years at the former Peffer house. The photograph below shows former mayor Jack Hockenberger at 424 South Main Street in his Mercury and AMC (American Motors Corporation) showroom, getting ready for the 1964 model year. His son currently owns a service business there. Ronald Clouse, high school principal, lived at 434 South Main Street. The houses at 438 and 442 South Main Street were owned by the Henderson and Robinson families, owners of Robinson Ventilating in Harmony. (Above, ZHS; below, Hockenberger Motors.)

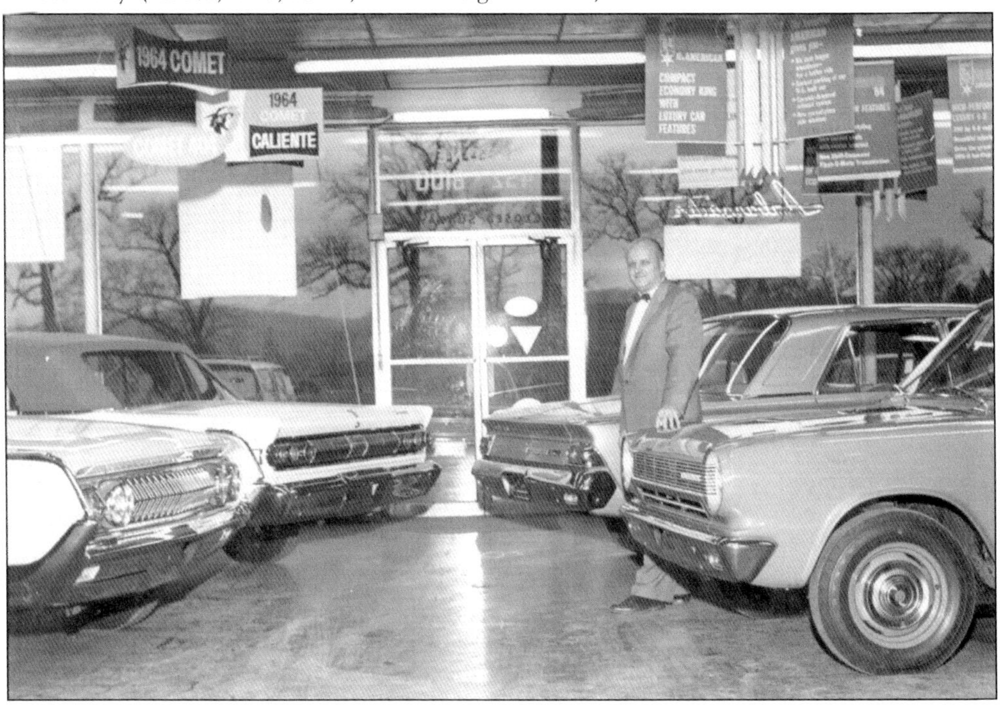

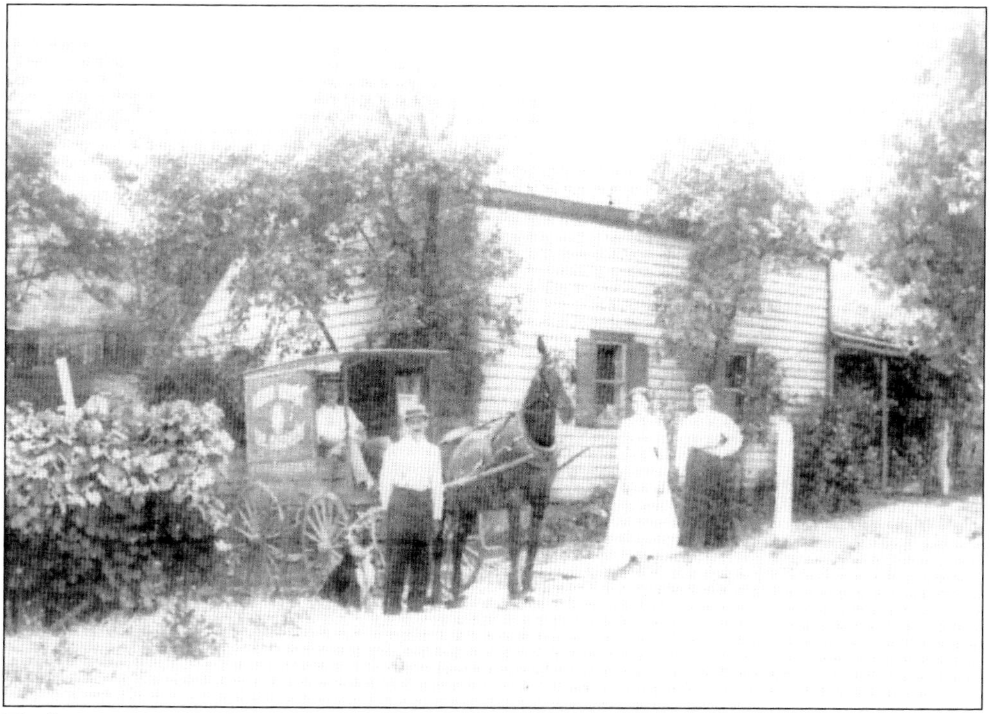

The house at 450 South Main Street was built by Francis Burkhart, a charter member of Zelienople Council in 1840. The log portion of the house is still intact and has an Underground Railroad trap door. Since 1892, this home has been owned by Annie Schomberg Birch and her descendants. This 1910 photograph shows, from left to right, an A&P tea company driver, A&P tea company agent Henry Birch, his daughter Ivie, and his wife, Annie. (Janice Black.)

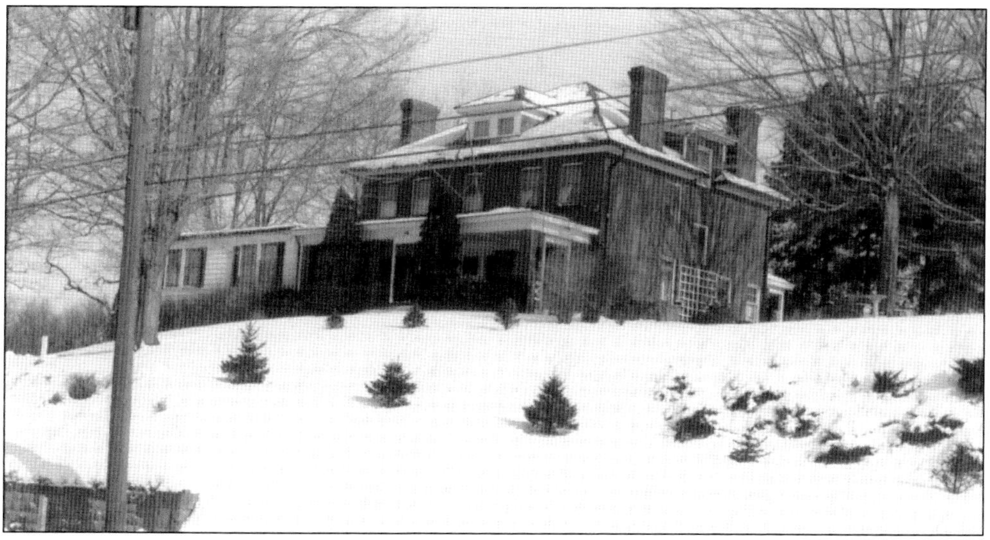

The home at 500 South Main Street was built about 1900 by a Mr. Poher of Pittsburgh and later purchased by attorney Thomas Chalmers Duff, who operated a tearoom and bed-and-breakfast here, calling it Duffmont. Around 1935, it was the home of Thomas C. North, president of Universal Manufacturing, and his wife, Grace, who was a church organist. The home is now Penberthy Photography Studio. (BZC.)

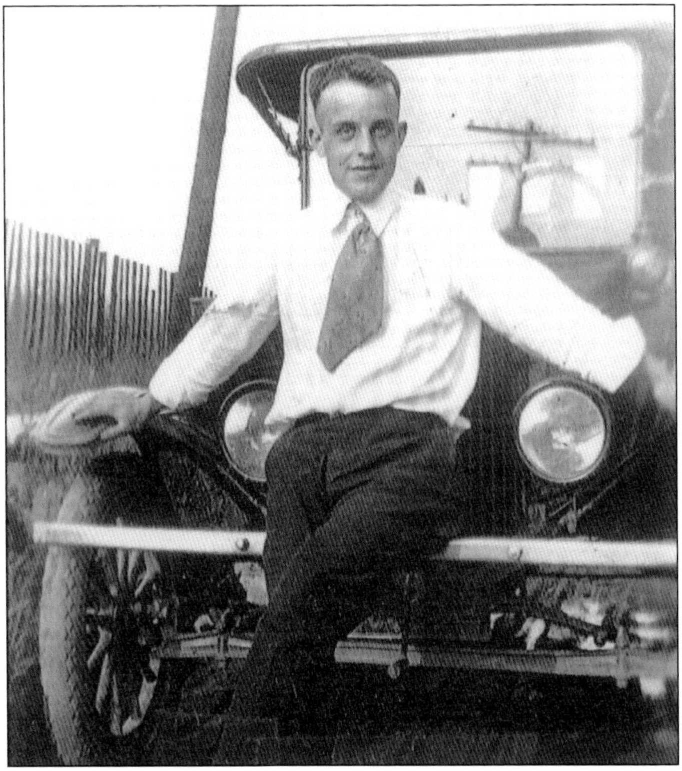

The Willys-Knight was an automobile produced between 1914 and 1933 by the Willys-Overland Company of Toledo, Ohio. It became the Willys-Knight Company and produced higher priced automobiles, and later the World War II Willys Jeep. This 1920 photograph shows Richard Allen displaying his latest model at the Householder-Allen dealership of Zelienople. The business may have been located in a building at the rear of the Householder home and bakery on Main Street. (ZHS.)

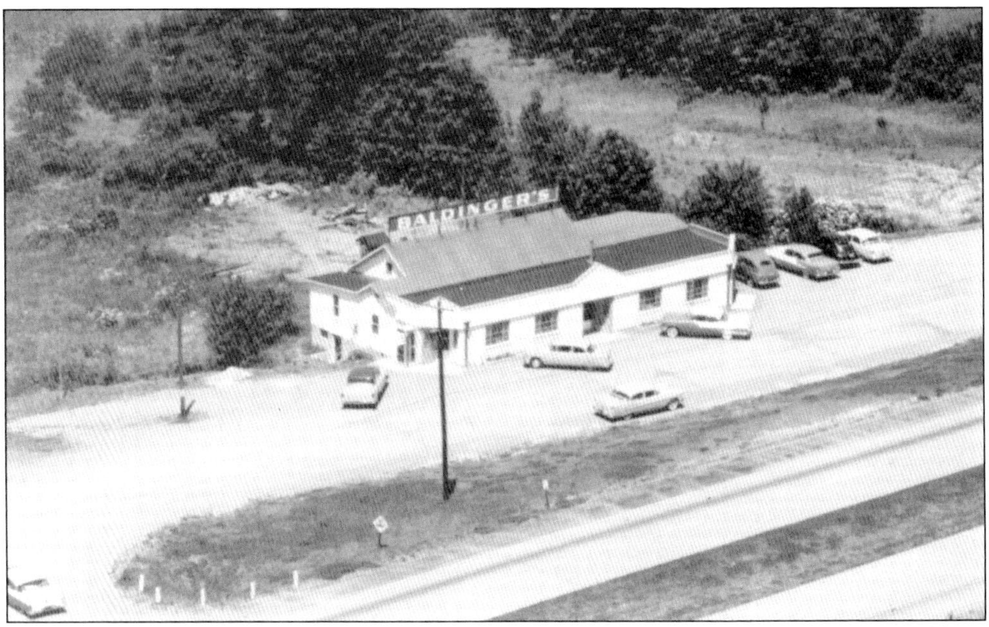

Baldinger's was built south of Zelienople along the old Perry Highway in 1933. The "Food from all Nations" store has been visited by people from all over the United States. In 2008, the store celebrated its 75th anniversary and relocated closer to town, bringing along its old mechanical cash register, which only records purchases up to $9.99. The parking area shown is the old two-lane Route 19 highway in 1955. (Larry Parisi.)

Five

MANUFACTURING IN ZELIENOPLE

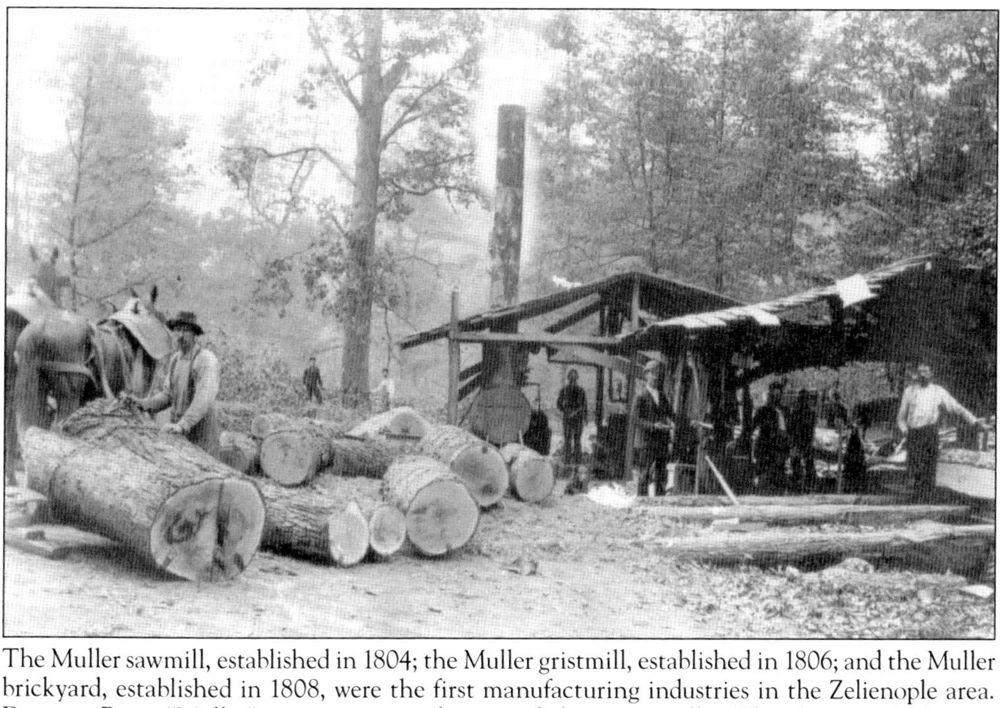

The Muller sawmill, established in 1804; the Muller gristmill, established in 1806; and the Muller brickyard, established in 1808, were the first manufacturing industries in the Zelienople area. Dettmar Basse "Muller" was a name used to signify he was a miller. The photograph shows a local "in the field" sawmill operated by a steam-powered saw and real horsepower hauling the logs. (ZHS.)

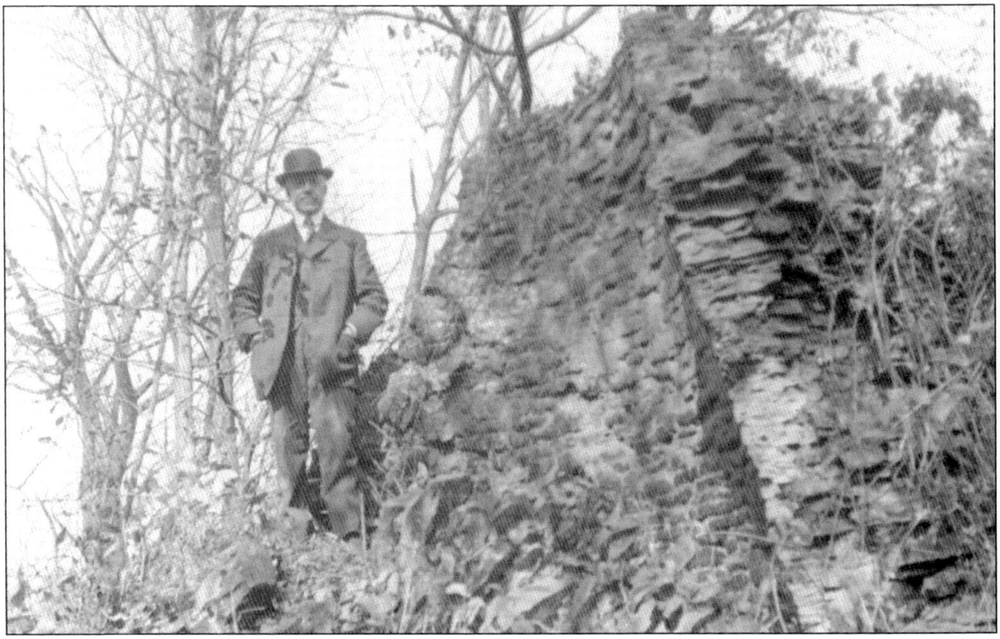

Manufacturing history is seen in the 1910 photograph above. Rev. Dettmar L. Passavant (1859–1932), son of Rev. William A. Passavant, is standing next to the remains of his great-grandfather's famous 1813 Bassenheim Furnace. This furnace was one of the first iron-manufacturing operations in western Pennsylvania, and it used iron ore found on Dettmar Basse's land. Production was for large kettles, stoves, and fire irons, but what was left over was cast into pigs or shot. The furnace was in operation for 10 years before the local ore ran out. The photograph below shows a great example of an 1816 cast-iron fireplace made at this furnace. It is now in the living room of the Passavant House at 243 South Main Street. The "Bassenheim Furnace" name can be seen along the top. (Both, ZHS.)

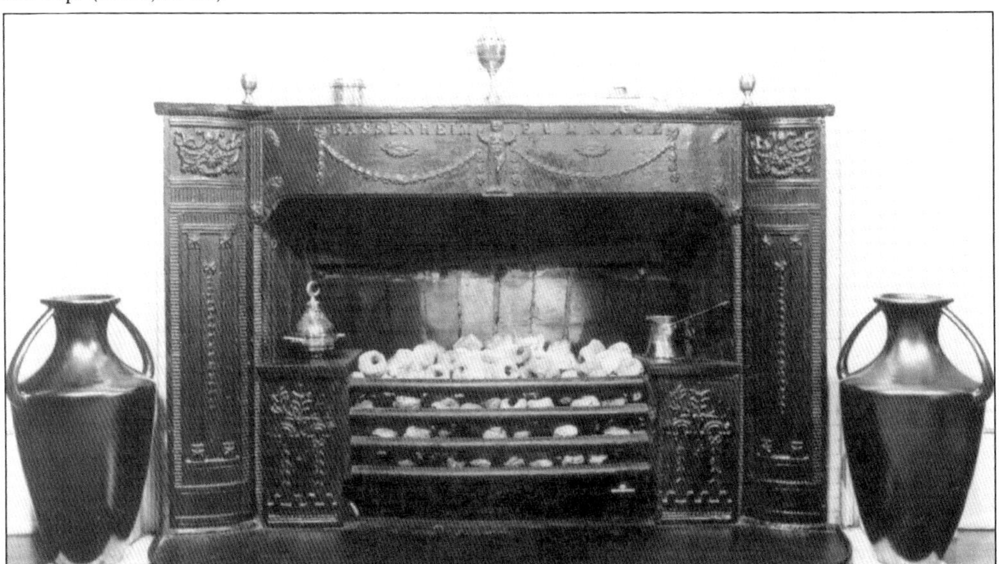

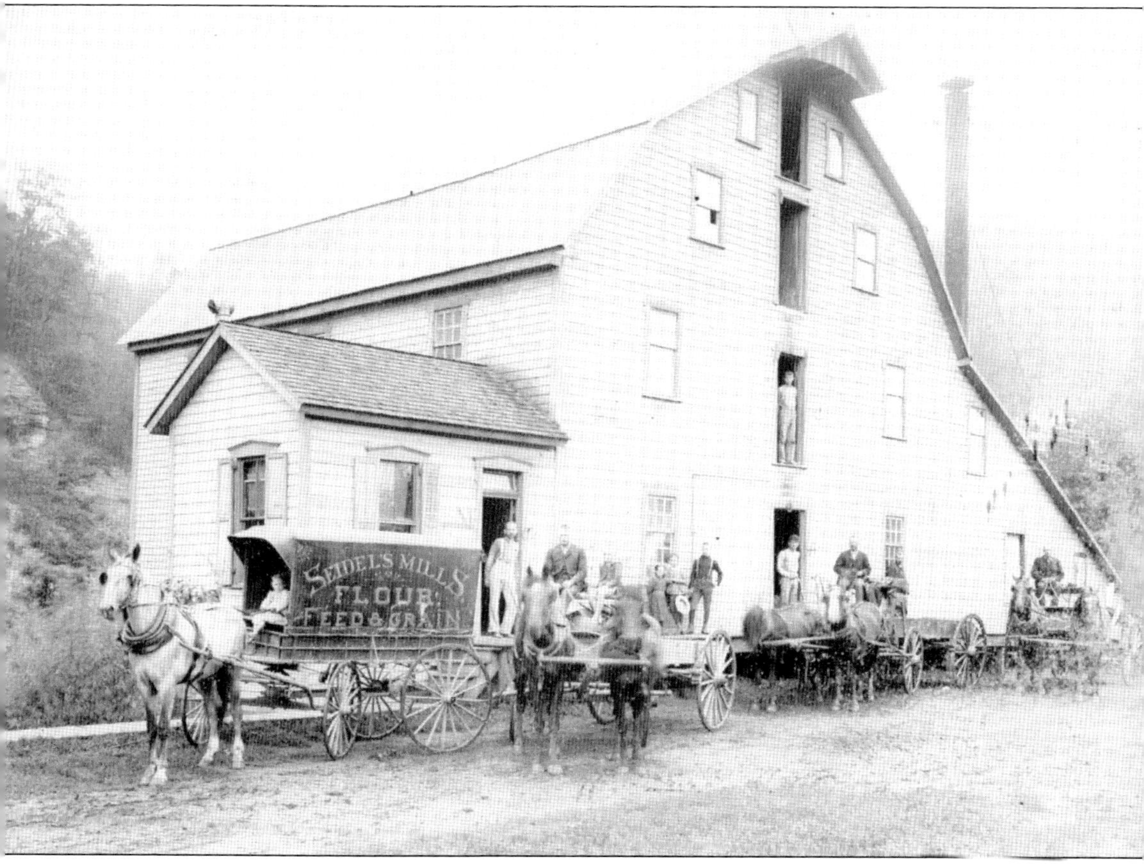

In 1806, Dettmar Basse constructed the first gristmill along the Connoquenessing Creek, just west and downstream of Zelienople. In 1857, John Herr's mill, in a similar location, became the property of Albert Seidel, and after 1880 it was operated by his sons. In 1892, Cyrus B. Harper became the sole owner and operated the mill until it met with disaster in 1911. "Harper Mill is in Ashes" is the headline of the April 27, 1911, edition of the *Connoquenessing Valley News*. The article states that "Mr. Harper was alone in the mill at night, filling a special order when the fire occurred. He thought he smelled smoke and going upstairs to the third floor, discovered flames near the cleaner. He fought the fire as best he could, but when he discovered the flames were in the dust room, he knew all hope was lost. He quickly descended to the first floor just in time to prevent his escape from being cut off by the flames. It was a total loss of $20,000 including milling equipment, wheat, flour, middlings, bran, buckwheat, and seed." Harper rebuilt the mill, but it burned again the following year and it was never rebuilt. In the 1898 photograph, the boy in the first wagon is Harvey Harper Sr., the man in the left doorway is owner Cyrus Harper, the man in the right doorway is Albert Harper, and the man above him on the second floor is Charles Harper. Waterpower to run the milling equipment was provided by a large wooden dam across the creek. Later, it was replaced by a smaller concrete dam, but flooding eventually caused it to fail also. Small sections of the concrete dam can still be seen near the canoe launch on Halstead Boulevard. (William Harper.)

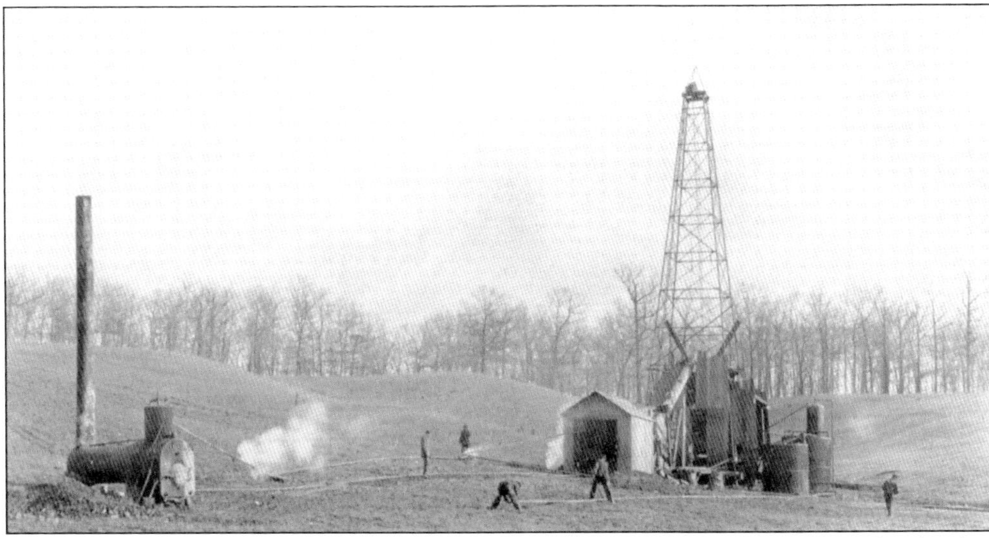

The world's first successful oil well was drilled at Titusville, Pennsylvania, in 1859 with a depth of 70 feet, starting the oil boom in America. Locally, over 100 wells were drilled in Evans City and several in Harmony. This early 1900s photograph shows several men operating a steam-operated oil-drilling rig on the Rader farm, just outside Zelienople. (ZHS.)

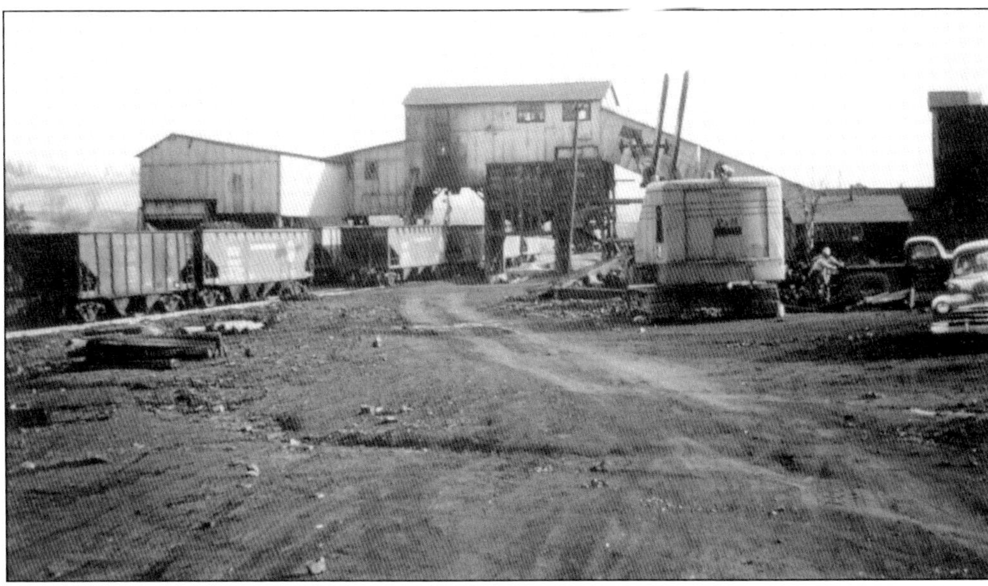

In past decades, coal was a major industry in the area, with strip mines in every direction. Many homes still had coal furnaces, requiring the owner to keep a fire going all day. Most homes had a coal cellar under a porch. The well-known local coal companies included Cunningham, Old Furnace, Shirley, and Tasa. This photograph shows the Shirley Coal Tipple loading railroad cars in 1952. It was located behind Universal Manufacturing. (BZC.)

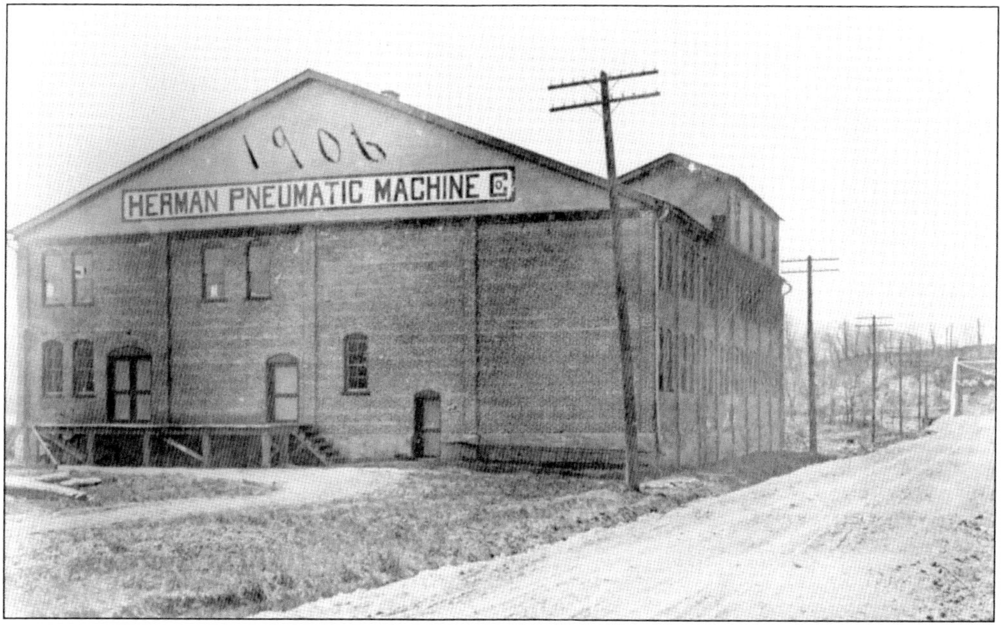

Charles Herman, a native of Germany, came to Zelienople in 1904 and founded the Herman Pneumatic Machine Company. He invented the pneumatic jarring machine used in the foundry industry and other machine operation patents. The 1906 photograph above shows the company's first building along a dirt New Castle Street. Notice all road traffic had to make a sharp left turn after crossing the bridge and go around Allen's Hill. In 1908, the Harmony Short Line Railroad would make a narrow cut through the hill for its electric trolley line. This was also the location of Dettmar Basse's Bassenheim Castle from 1802 to 1841. He personally had this road cut through the woods from the mansion into the village, and he petitioned the state to build a bridge across the Connoquenessing Creek. The photograph below shows a gathering of Herman employees at Thanksgiving in 1953. This plant is now ATI Precision Finishing. (Both, ZHS.)

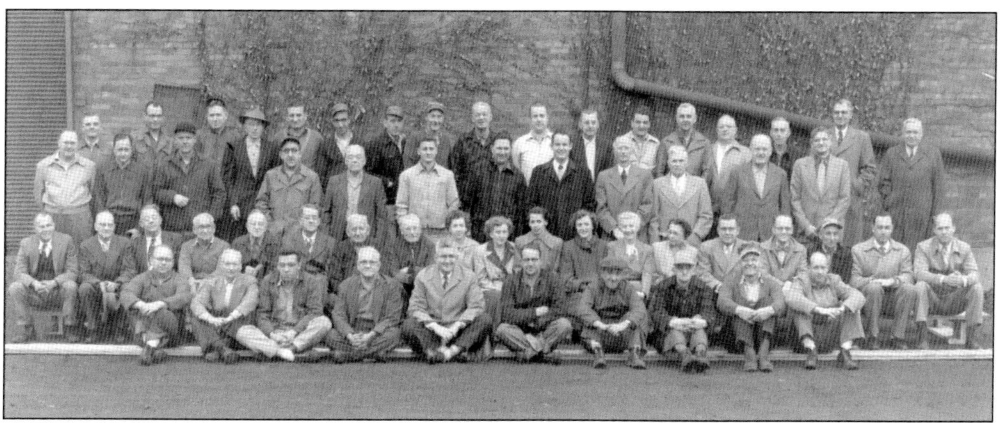

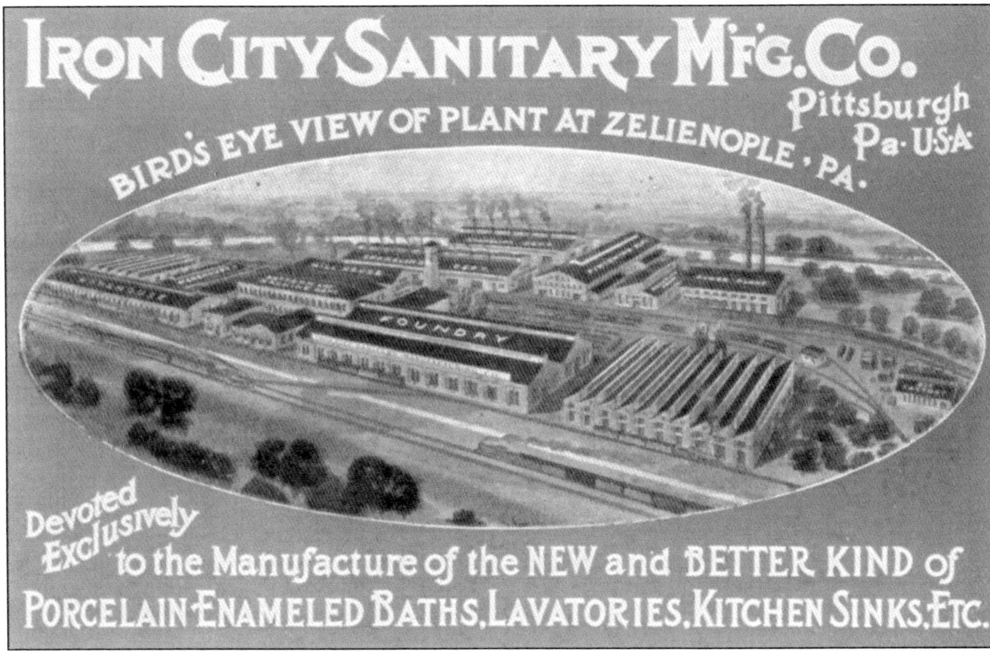

This photograph is a rare postcard of the Iron City Sanitation Company. In 1905, the company added a new 158-foot, two-story building to its plant and announced plans to add 6,000 square feet of space to its foundry. The firm made cast-iron bathroom fixtures, usually with a white porcelain enameled finish. The plant was closed in 1930. (Gregory Cowell.)

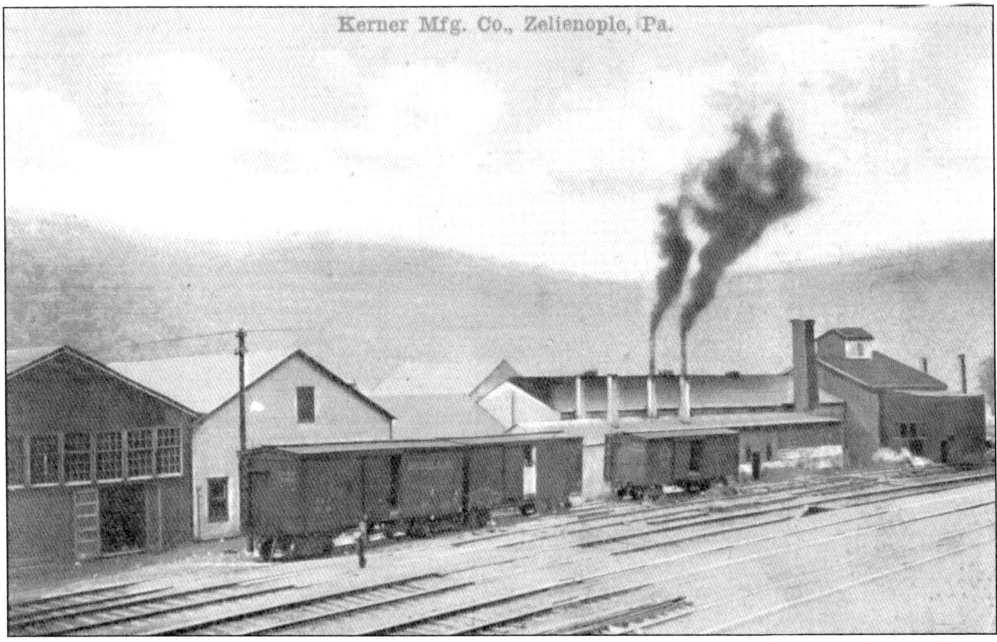

The Kerner Manufacturing Company was very similar to Iron City, as its also manufactured cast-iron bathroom fixtures. In 1910, the company announced a melting of 2,400 tons of iron for use in its business. It also shared an office building with Herman Pneumatic. This postcard shows the plant in operation along the railroad tracks, near the Herman plant. (Larry Parisi.)

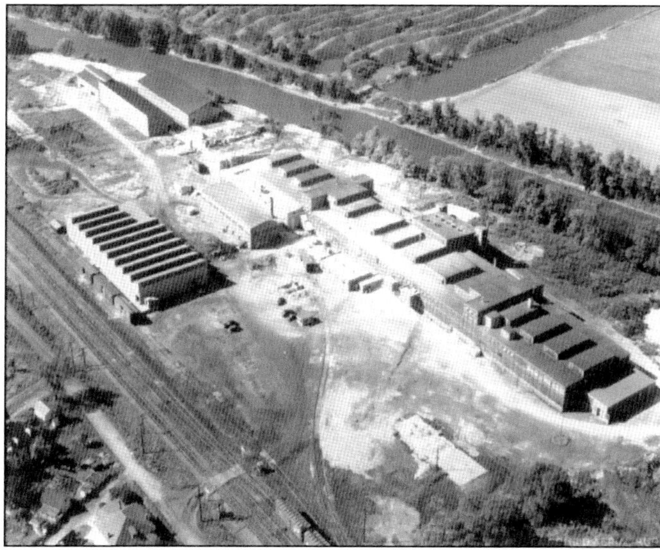

In 1940, the Johns Manville Corporation announced it had purchased the old Iron City Sanitation plant in Zelienople that had stood vacant for 10 years. The plant manufactured asbestos brick, tile, and insulation materials. Due to the number of lawsuits for asbestos-related illnesses, Manville voluntarily filed for bankruptcy reorganization in 1982, and the Zelienople plant closed. This 1940s photograph is an aerial view of the plant. (ZHS.)

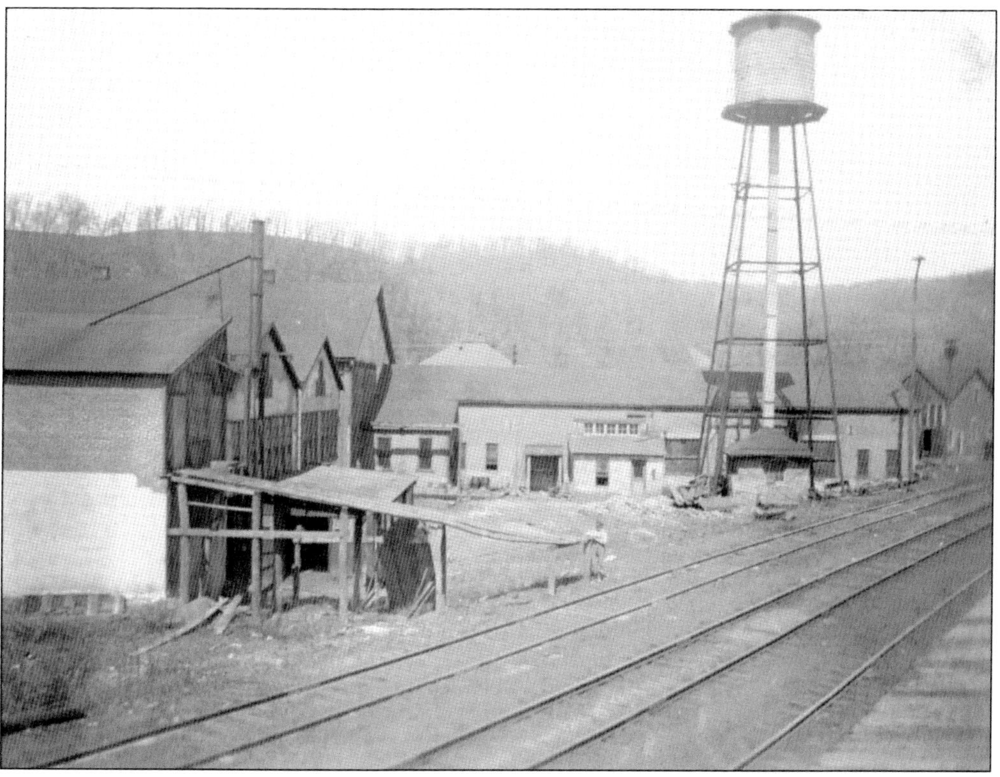

The American Flexible Bolt Company was in operation in Zelienople from 1910 to 1921. It made specialized bolts for bolting large boiler plates together, used in ships, trains, and industry. Normal bolts continually failed until they were made of a special charcoal malleable iron. Holes were drilled through the length of the bolt so that a steam leak would show if it started to fail. The closed plant was later bought by Universal Manufacturing. (ZHS.)

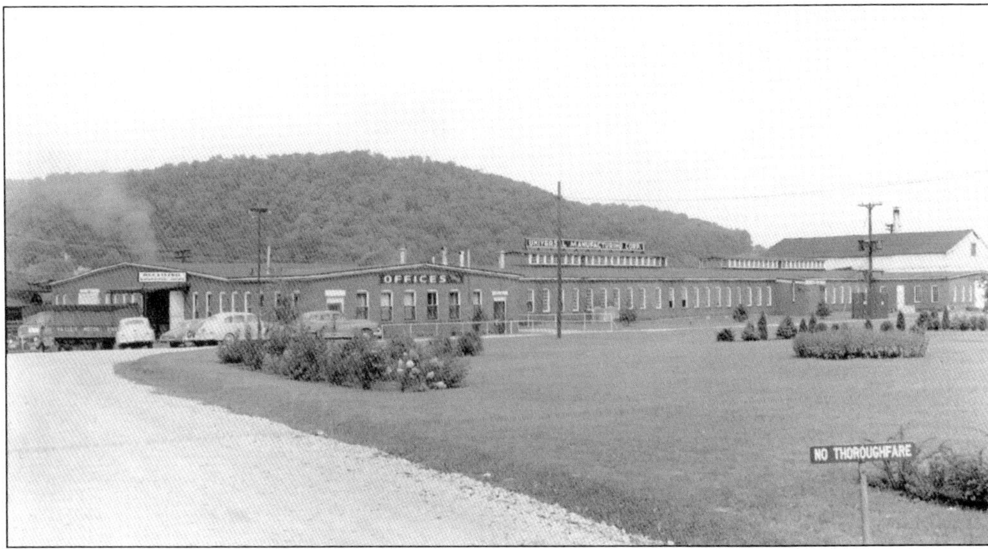

In 1934, Zelienople was chosen as the site for the operations of the Universal Fittings and Scaffolding Company. The old Flexible Bolt Factory was purchased by Universal Fittings' first president, Thomas C. North of Blairsville. Seventeen workers moved to Zelienople and brought the machinery to produce various types of ladders, platforms, and steel scaffolding. North later sold the company to Robert Carbeau Sr., who changed the name to Universal Manufacturing. The company is now located on West New Castle Street, with Robert Carbeau Jr. serving as president. It produces scaffolding and platforms for wide variety of uses in the construction industry. In the 1960s, its products were used at Cape Kennedy and at the US Capitol. The photograph above shows the plant in the late 1940s; the 1950 photograph below is of a company gathering of employees. (Both, ZHS.)

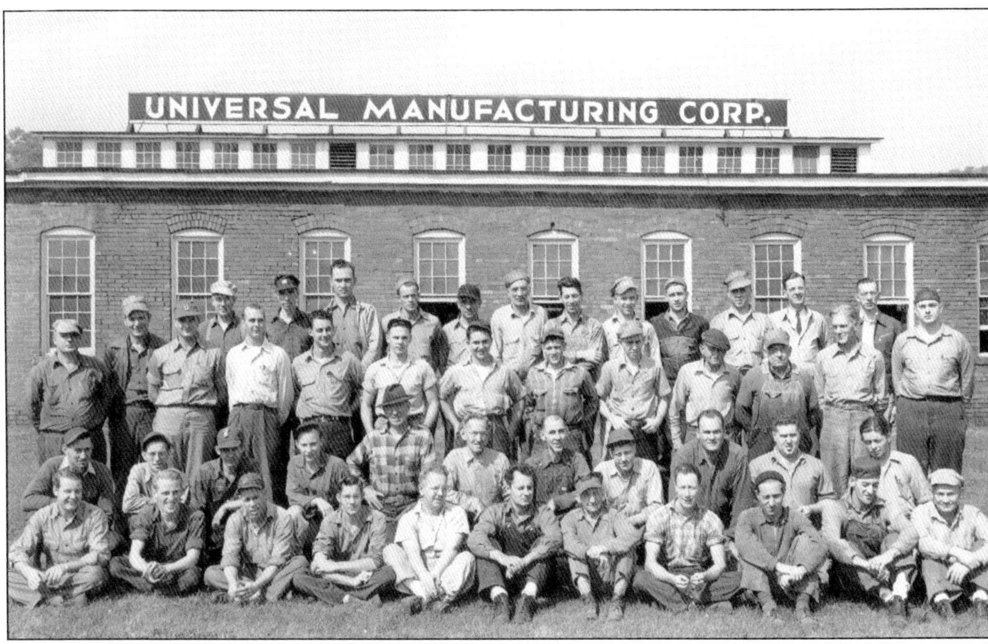

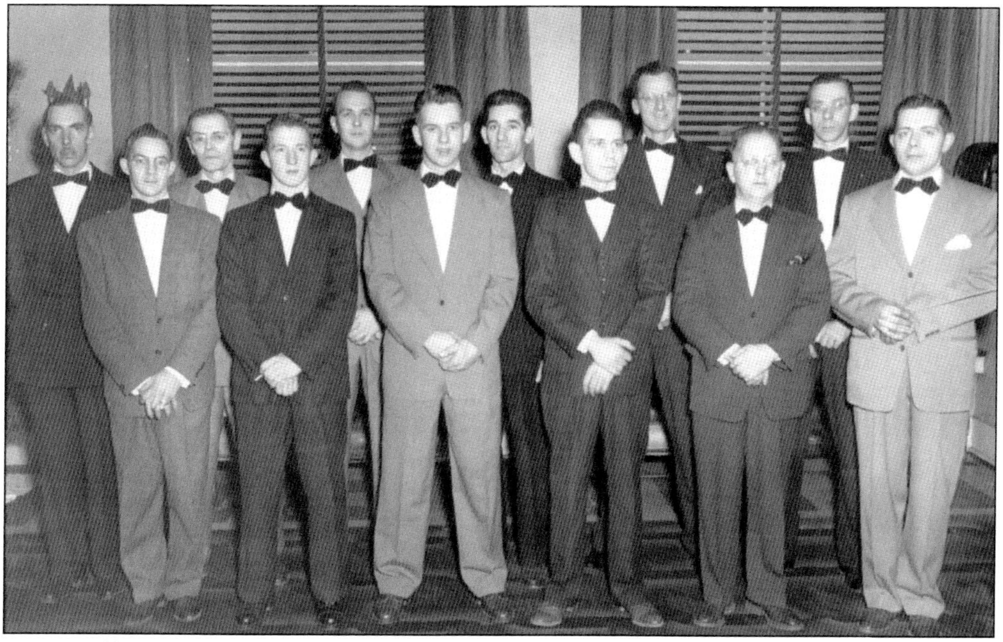

Historically, a glee club is a choir group of male voices specializing in the singing of short songs, or glees. In the late 19th century, it was very popular in most American high schools. Universal Manufacturing had its own glee club during the 1940s under the direction of Thomas W. North (first row, far right), son of company founder Thomas C. North. (ZHS.)

When all the local factories were in full operation, times were good for the companies and the employees, and they held intramural sporting events between the companies. There were basketball games, softball games, bowling, and others. There was an open area in front of Universal's plant that was used as a ball field. This 1949 photograph shows the Universal basketball team. (ZHS.)

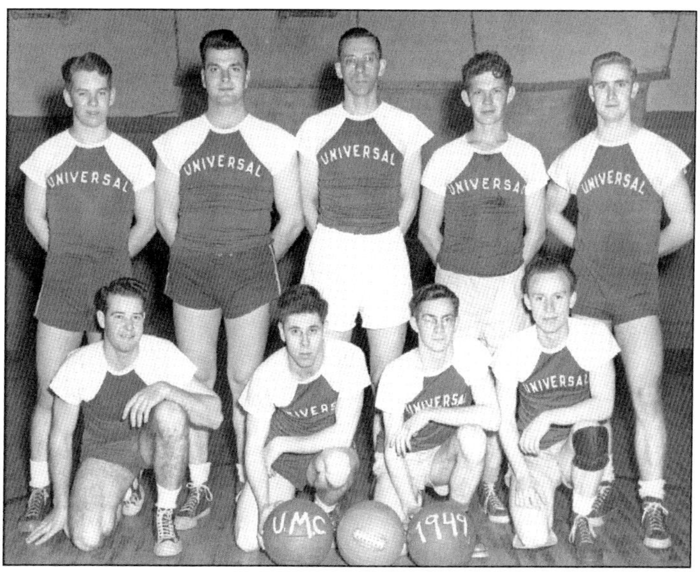

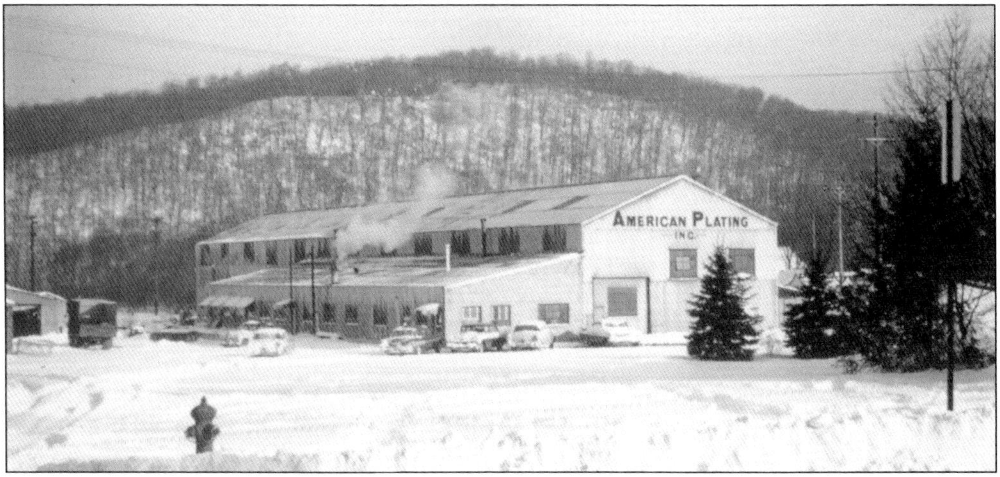

The American Plating Company was founded in 1951 and is still in operation in Zelienople. It is located on West New Castle Street beside Universal Manufacturing and handles all the plating needs required for Universal's products. This photograph was taken on a snowy day in 1956. (BZC.)

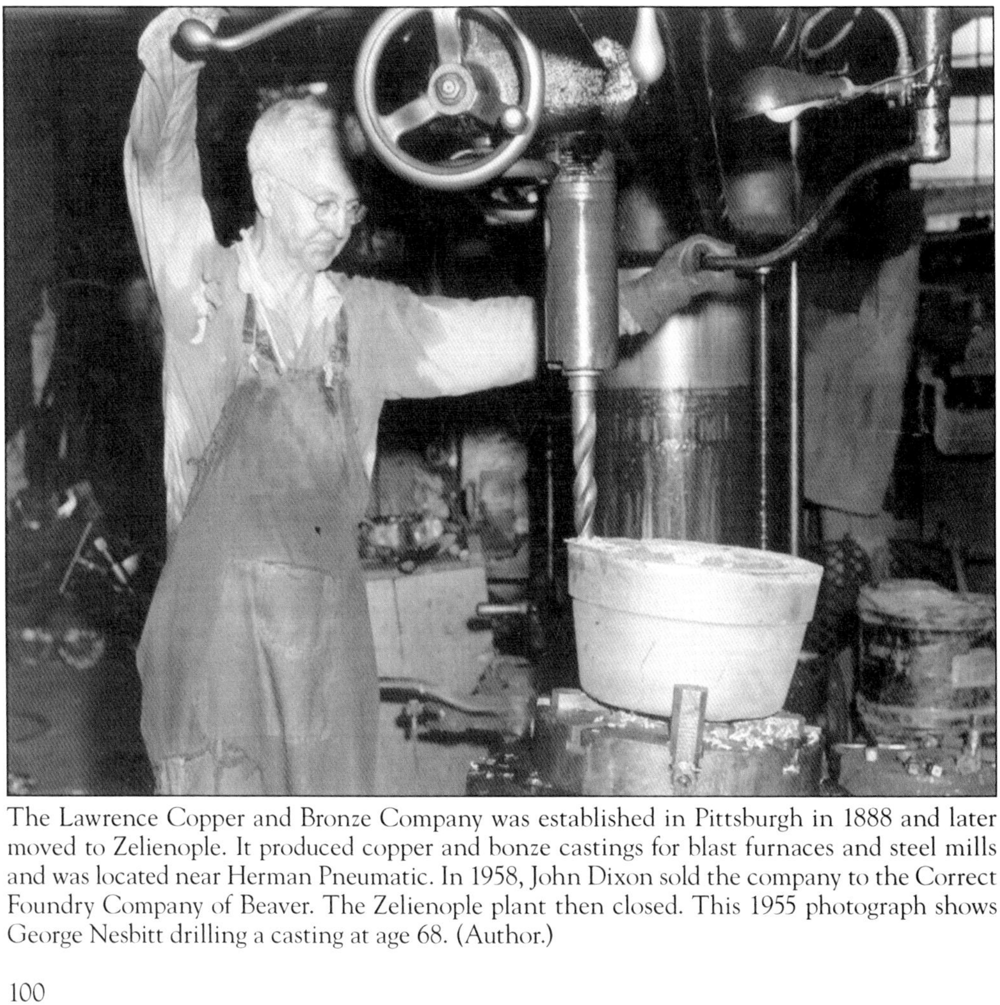

The Lawrence Copper and Bronze Company was established in Pittsburgh in 1888 and later moved to Zelienople. It produced copper and bonze castings for blast furnaces and steel mills and was located near Herman Pneumatic. In 1958, John Dixon sold the company to the Correct Foundry Company of Beaver. The Zelienople plant then closed. This 1955 photograph shows George Nesbitt drilling a casting at age 68. (Author.)

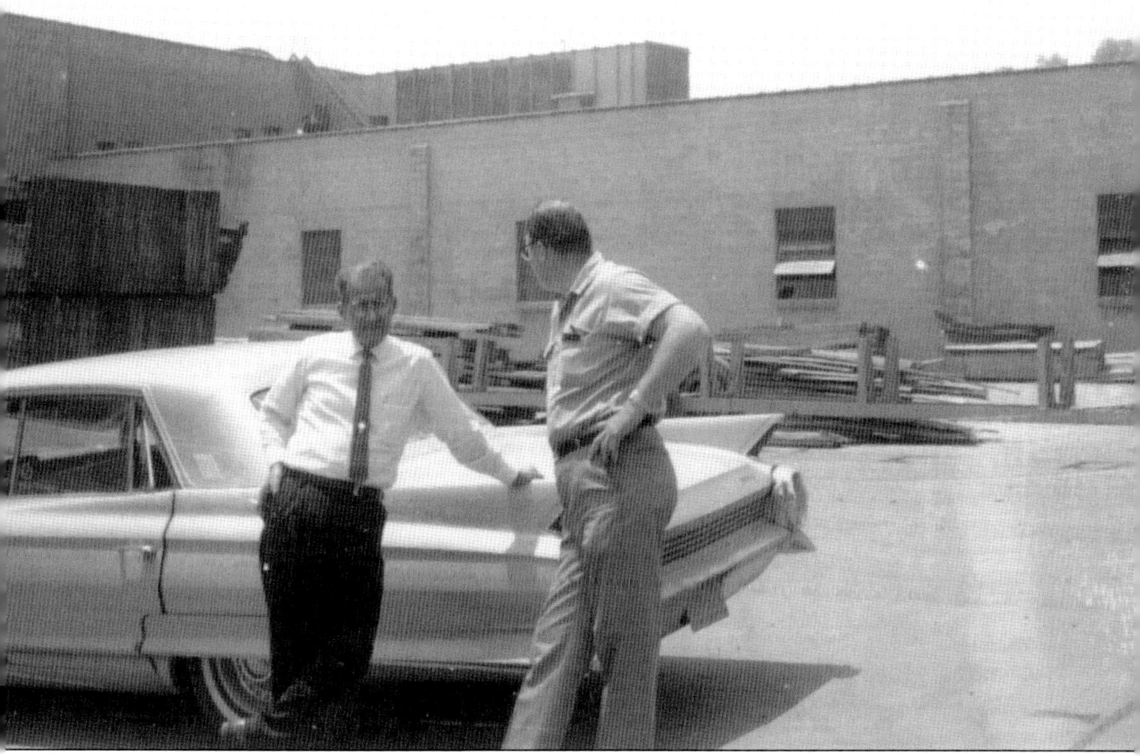

In 1935, Halstead Industries began in Pittsburgh, using an enlarged garage as its place of business. The company operated as a partnership between Byron Halstead and Caroline Mitchell. In 1947, the business moved to Zelienople, bringing along managers David Bonomo, Frank Buczkowski, and other employees. In 1948, a 10,000-square-foot plant was constructed on West New Castle Street. The plant was expanded many times until it occupied 500,000 square feet on 23 acres. It produced industrial air handlers, cooling towers, coils, and condensers. Halstead Metal Products was formed to produce copper tubing, first for Halstead, then for other manufacturers. In 1973, the Halstead and Mitchell Division was moved to Scottsboro, Alabama. Halstead Metal Products remained in Zelienople and continued to produce copper tubing until August 31, 1990, when it closed its doors forever. During the 1960s, there were 500 Halstead employees in Zelienople, making it the largest employer to ever reside in the area. This 1965 photograph shows managers Robert Hartmann (left) and David Bonomo at the rear of the plant. (Robert Hartmann Jr.)

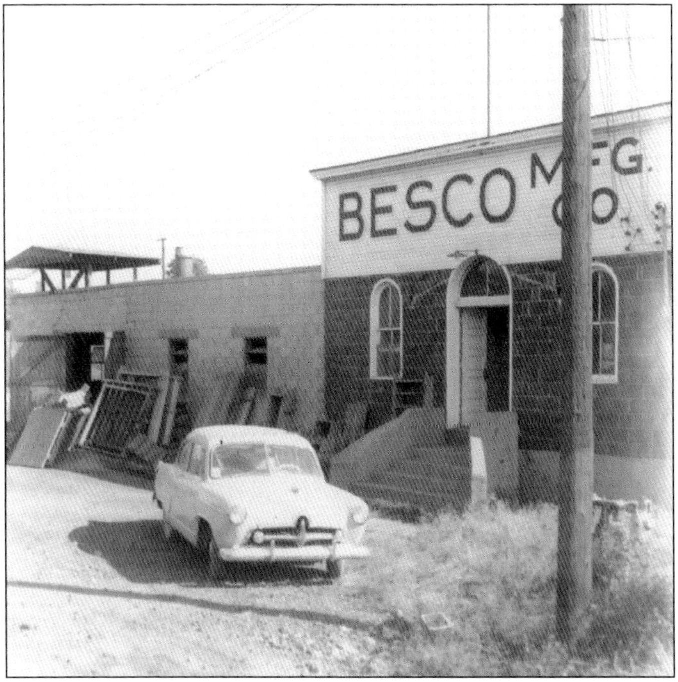

The Besco Company was founded in 1952 by father-and-son team George and William Bessor, with William becoming president in 1966, and grandson Bryan assuming that role in the 1990s. It produced aluminum sand castings for industry and federal contracts for the military, including the B-1 bomber. Due to increased use of other high-tech materials, the company ceased operations in 2005. This 1950s photograph shows its location at the former Romanian Hall on Ziegler Street. (ZHS.)

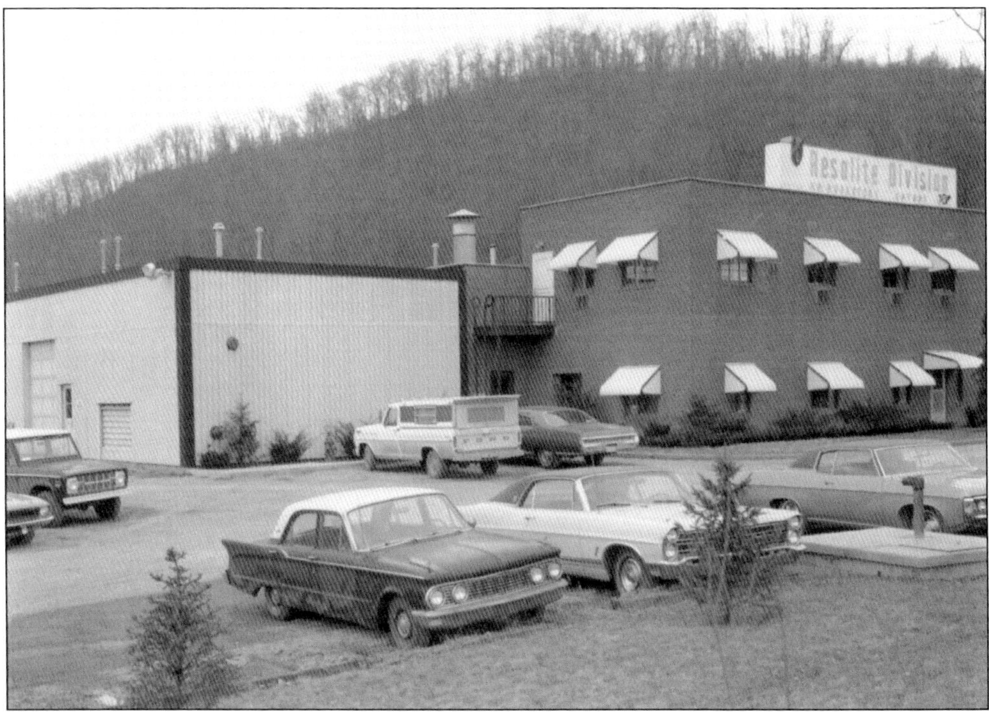

The Resolite Company started in Zelienople in 1951 and was located just north of town. It manufactured lightweight fiberglass panels for use by building architects and contractors when corrosion resistance was the principal consideration. This photograph from 1970 shows its location; in 1990, the company moved to Tennessee. The Creekside shopping plaza is located at this site now. (ZHS.)

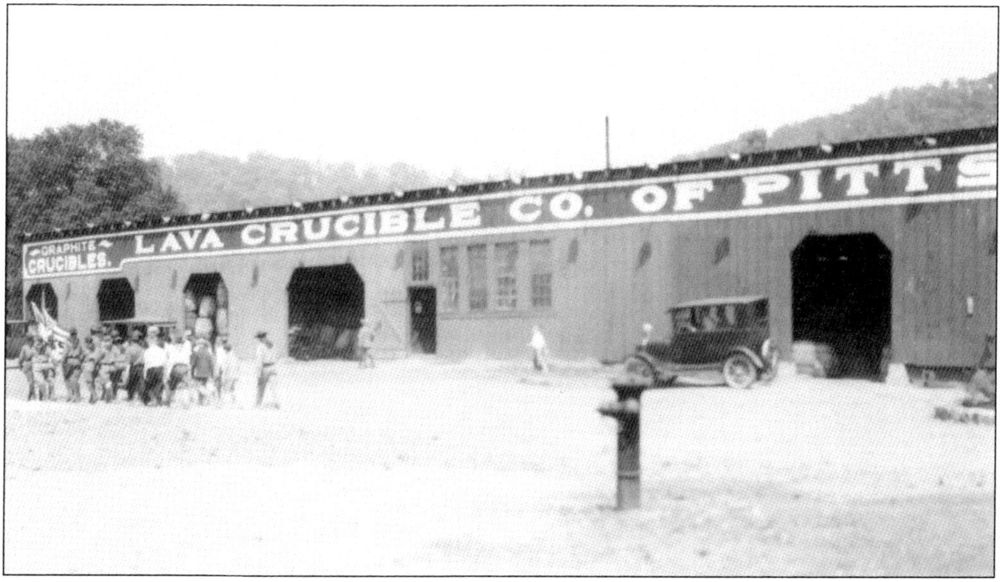

During World War I, Belgian chemist Jean Hubert Luis Debates came to Zelienople and developed a way to make crucibles and exotic alloys for melting steel. Debates set up his laboratory in a former buggy-and-wagon works on the west side of Main Street. Later, the Lava Crucible plant opened, covered 100,000 square feet, and was situated on 25 acres along the Connoquenessing Creek. Its crucibles were in high demand in the United States during wartime, as war manufacturing was at its peak. The name was later changed to Vesuvius Lava Company. The photograph above shows a group of Boy Scouts visiting the Lava plant in the 1920s. The photograph below is a more modern aerial view, from 1965. The plant is now closed. (Both, ZHS.)

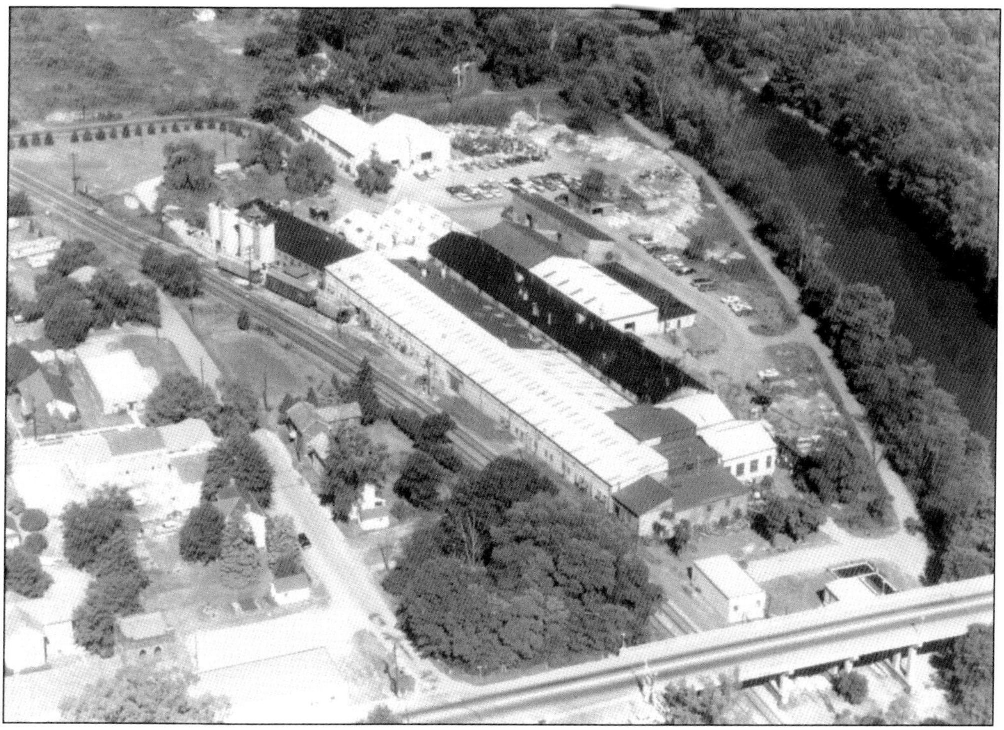

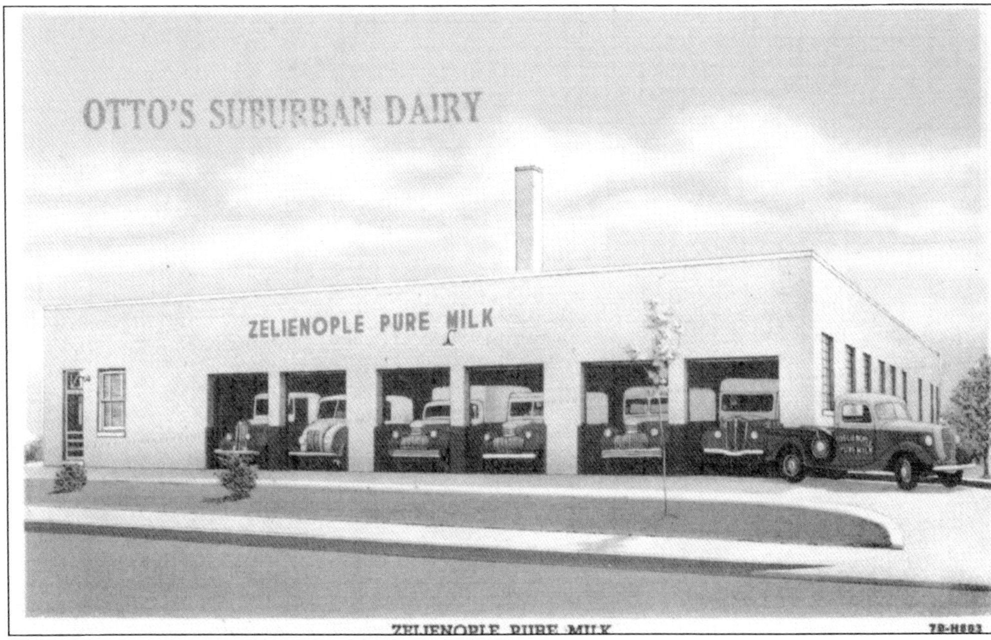

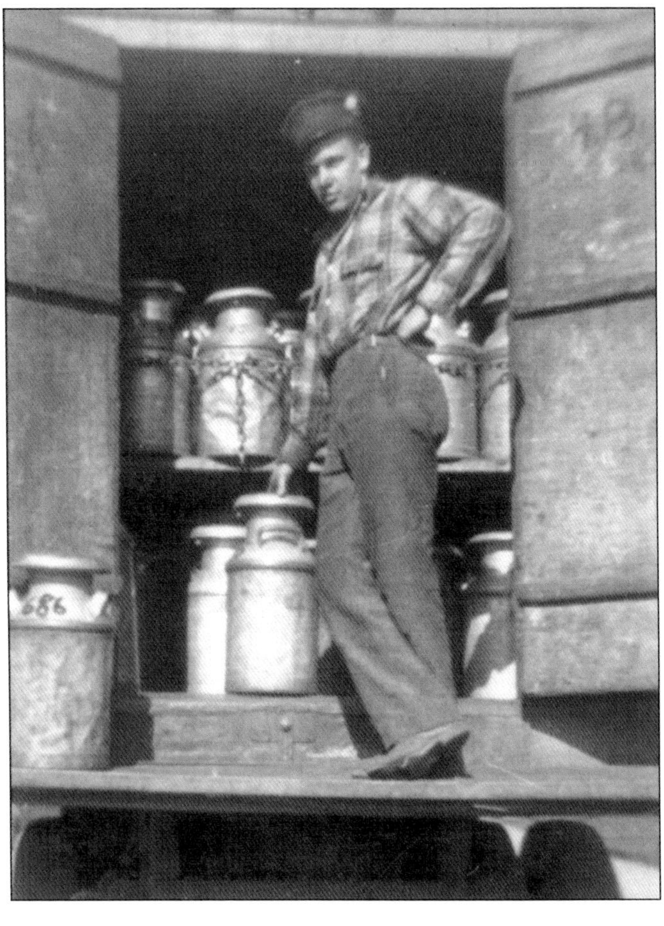

Located at Beaver and Division Streets near the community park, the Zelienople Pure Milk Company was founded in 1922 by Peter Dambaugh. The 1940s postcard above shows it was later bought by the Otto Milk Company. Otto and other area co-op drivers had to manually load the five-gallon cans, which weight 40 pounds when full, at nearby farms and drive to the Otto Pasteurizing Plant at Twenty-Fifth and Smallman Streets in the Strip District of Pittsburgh. The photograph on the left shows co-op driver John Burkett of Zelienople getting ready for work in 1947. Later, the Zelienople Milk Dairy building became Leopold, a water treatment specialist. After 30 years, it was bought by the Xylem Company, which maintains offices there today. (Above, ZHS; left, Mary Lou Burkett.)

Six

Civil, Military, and Social Organizations

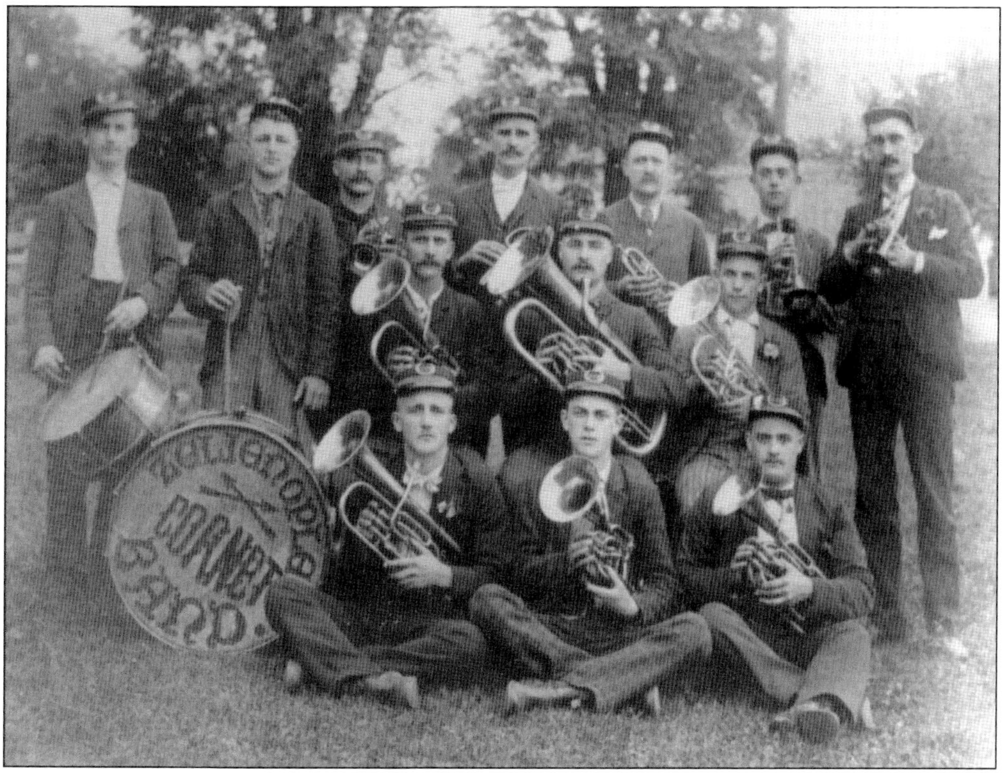

This rare undated photograph shows the Zelienople Cornet Band. A cornet band was a common designation for bands organized during the Gilded Age (1870–1900). This 13-piece band was brass and percussion only, and it used cornets, which produce a mellower sound that trumpets, along with the various baritone instruments shown. (ZHS.)

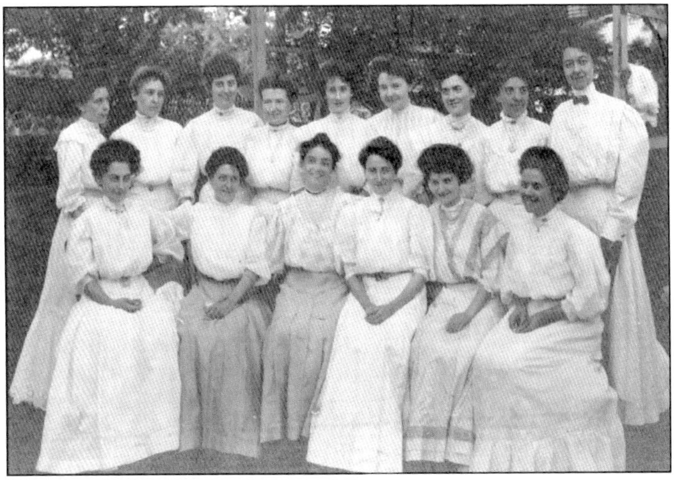

The Fortnightly Club of Zelienople was active in the early 1900s. This women's group was formed as a social gathering and goodwill group and met every two weeks (fortnightly). Members included Emma Passavant, Stella Dindinger, Altha Endres, Alva Fogel, Mary Goehring, Fanny Kildoo, Joanne and Edith Gelbach, Bess Reed, Margaret McClure, Carrie Stokey, and Anna Wild. (ZHS.)

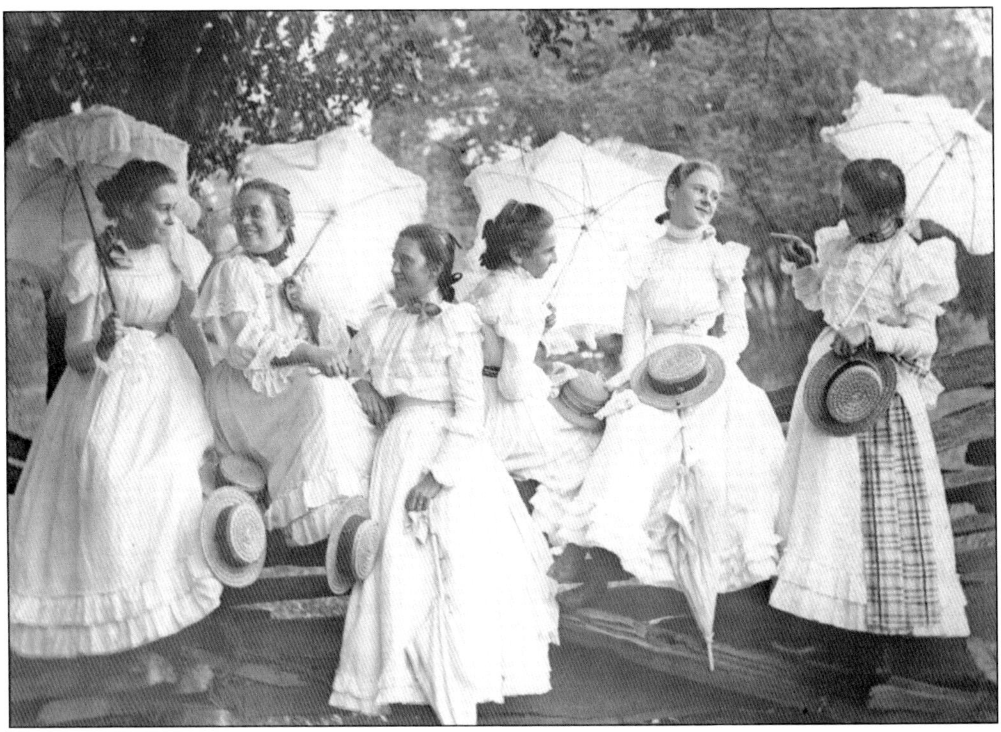

This photograph shows a carefree life on a spring day during the late 1890s. From left to right are Mabel Fiedler Wallace, Sweet Knox Householder, Fanny Kildoo Rogner, Virginia Ziegler Kelly, Edna Heller, and local historian Nell Wilson Campbell. This photograph appears in the Lester R. Mohr's 1940 book, *Centennial History of Zelienople.* (ZHS.)

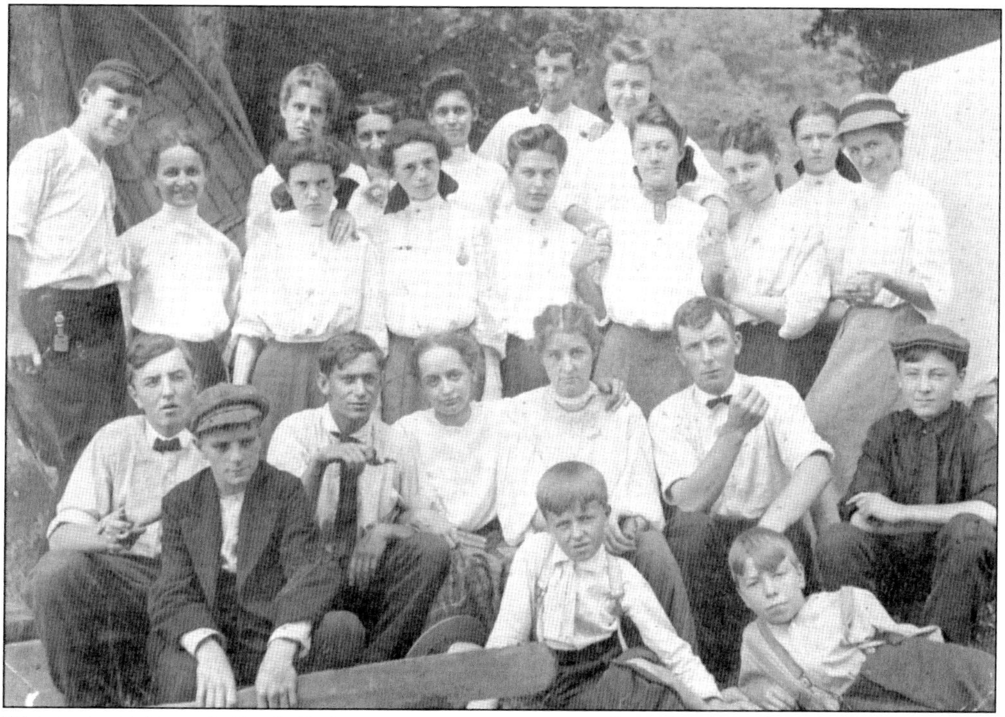

This is the Zelienople Book Club on a camping trip in 1905, complete with canoes, paddles, and tents. It appears that the club members are a little weary after a day's outing on Connoquenessing Creek in those long pants and dresses. (ZHS.)

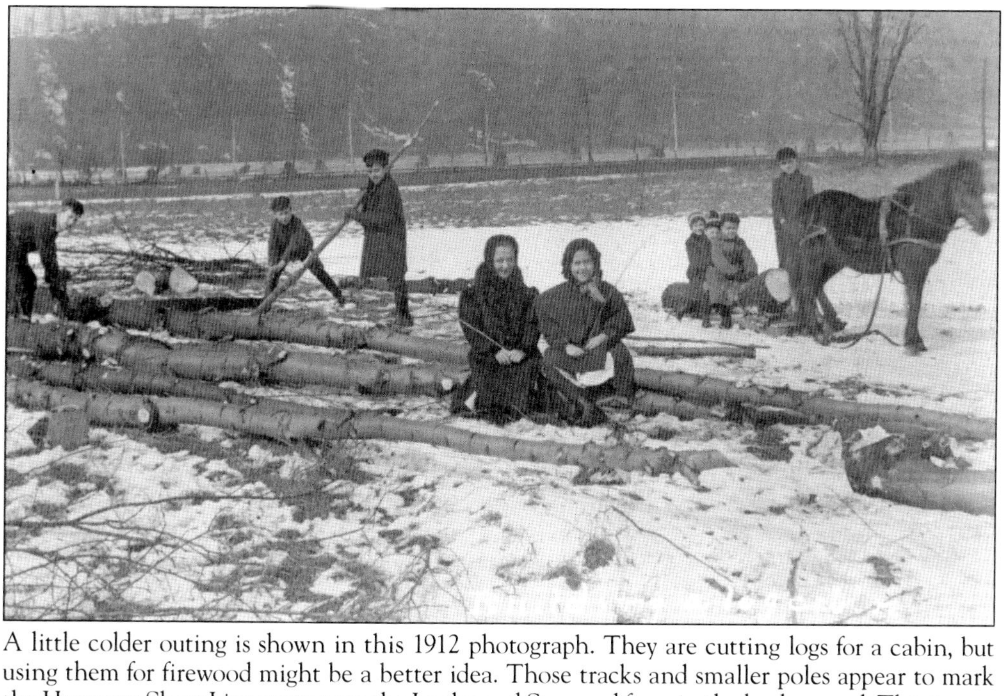

A little colder outing is shown in this 1912 photograph. They are cutting logs for a cabin, but using them for firewood might be a better idea. Those tracks and smaller poles appear to mark the Harmony Short Line route near the Lockwood Stop and farm in the background. This is now the industrial area along Halstead Boulevard. (ZHS.)

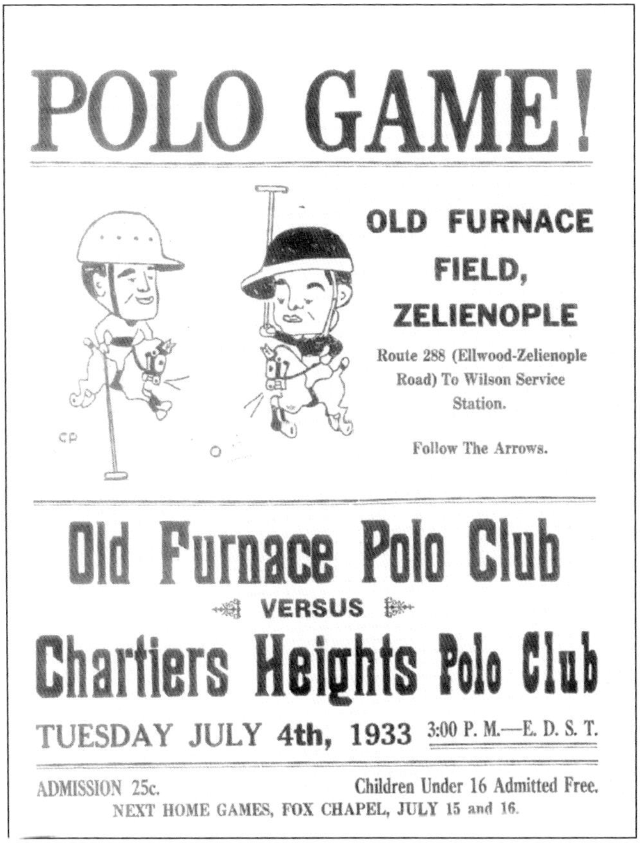

In the early 1930s, local farmers and other residents began to use their horses for pleasure rather than transportation or farmwork. They started playing informal pickup polo games at the Wilson Farm on Route 288, west of town. Harlan, Thomas, and Warren Wilson, Charles and Louis Passavant, Hiram Ball, John Troutmann, George McCormick, and Harold White were among the early players. The poster on the left is from 1933 and shows the formation of the Old Furnace Polo Club, named for the old Bassenheim Furnace. The photograph below shows the men in action, with Dr. Warren Wilson on the far right. Notice Allen's Hill in the background that, as part of Wilson's farm, was a pasture. This was originally owned by Dettmar Basse, then later by Joseph Allen. (Both, Sharon Shanks.)

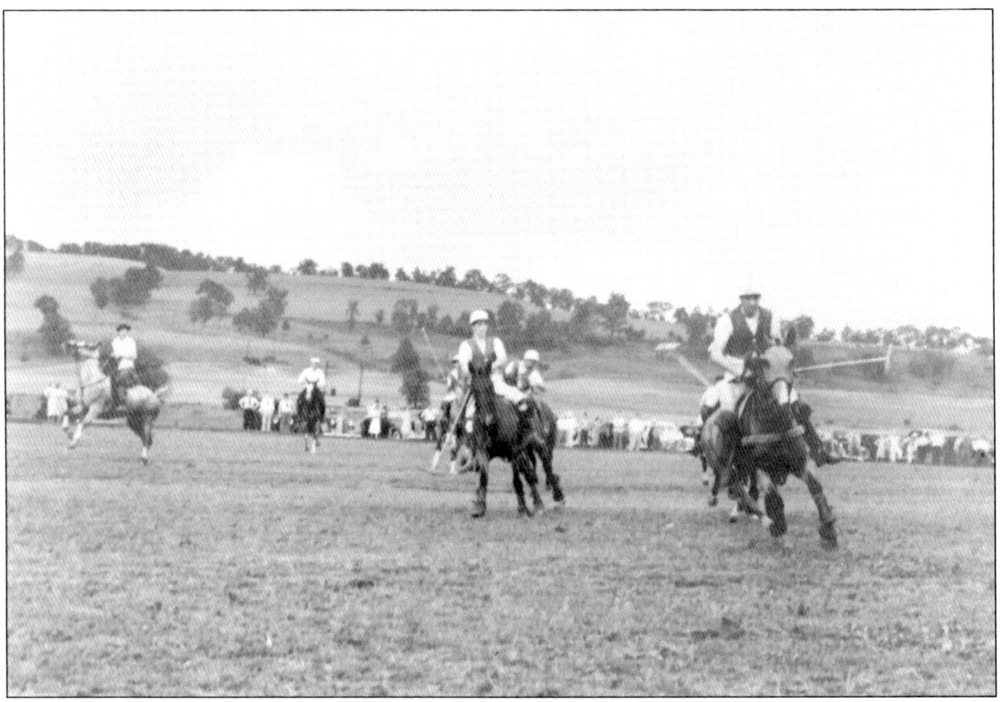

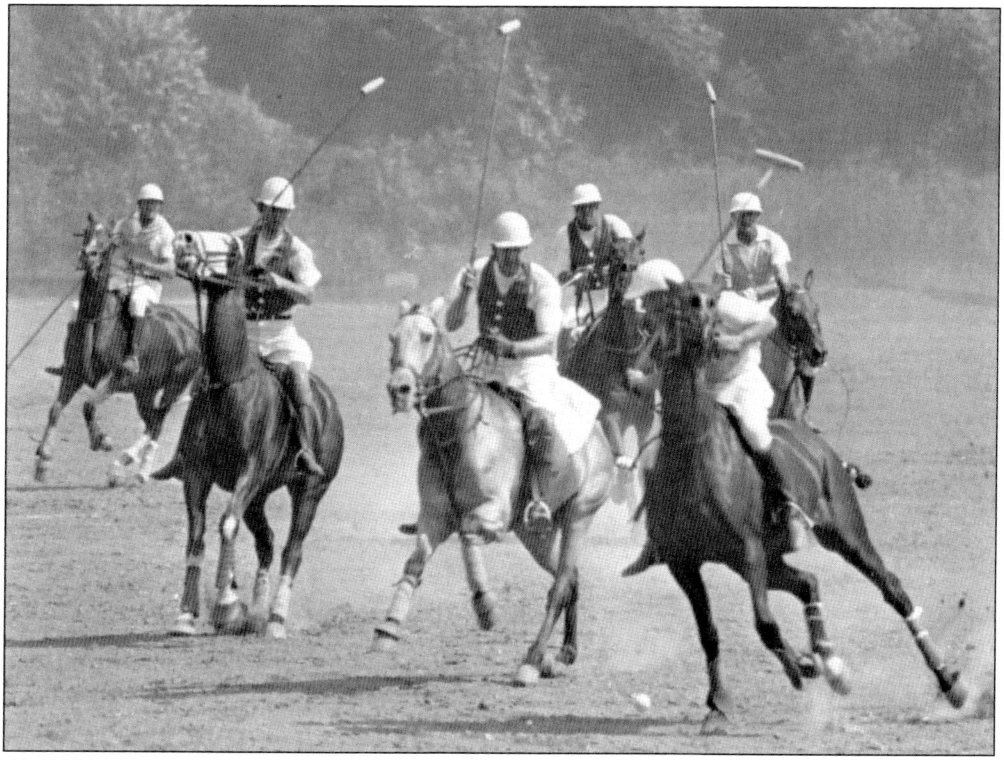

The Old Furnace Polo Club competed against local teams from Wexford, Monongahela City, South Park, and Library in Pennsylvania, and Akron, Poland, Salem, Alliance, Chagrin Falls, Columbus, and Buckeye Lake in Ohio. Enthusiastic spectators attended the polo games on Sunday afternoons throughout each summer until the late 1940s. During the winter, the team played games at indoor facilities in Pittsburgh, Cleveland, Akron, and Ithaca, New York. In Zelienople, practices and games were held inside the vacant Iron City Sanitary Manufacturing plant. When the team disbanded, the remaining players joined the Darlington Polo Club, which still competes today. The photograph above shows the team in action, and the photograph below shows team members, from left to right, Harlan Wilson, William McClaren, Dr. Warren Wilson, Lloyd Wilson, and Chester Shagetts. (Both, Sharon Shanks.)

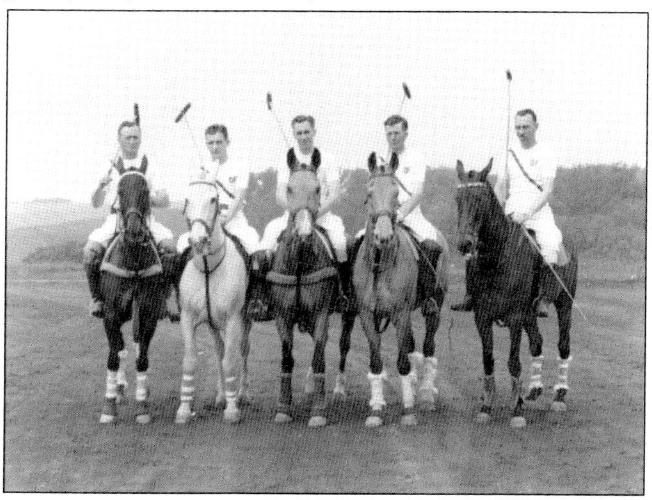

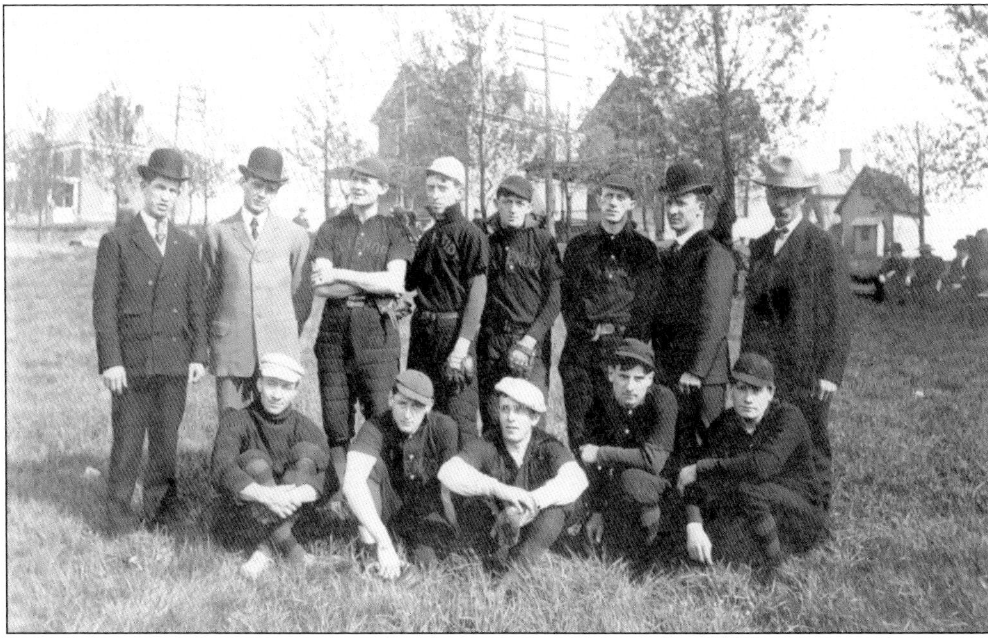

Zelienople's first organized baseball team, the Zelienople Reds, won the championship in 1905 that included Beaver, Butler, and Lawrence Counties. In the photograph above, from left to right, are (first row) right fielder Rev. Hugh Leith (also pastor of the Presbyterian church), second baseman George Lusk, third baseman Michael Carr, left fielder Harry Young, and catcher and shortstop Charles Garman; (second row) catcher Walter Rogner, manager William Meeder, pitcher Joseph Cavanaugh, center fielder Joseph Rebley, pitcher Ralph Cunningham, first baseman Frederick Jackson, left fielder Edward Young, and constable and mascot Edward Knauff. The team practiced in a vacant field on West New Castle Street near Universal Manufacturing. In the background are the homes of local historians Gertrude Ziegler (far left) and Blair Zeigler (center). The photograph below shows another of the Reds teams. (Both, BZC.)

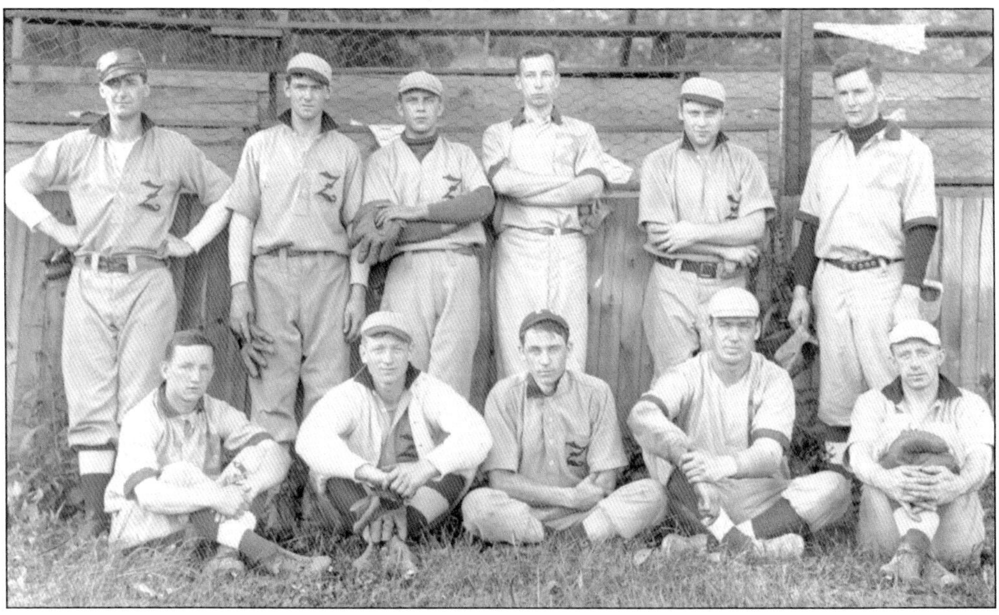

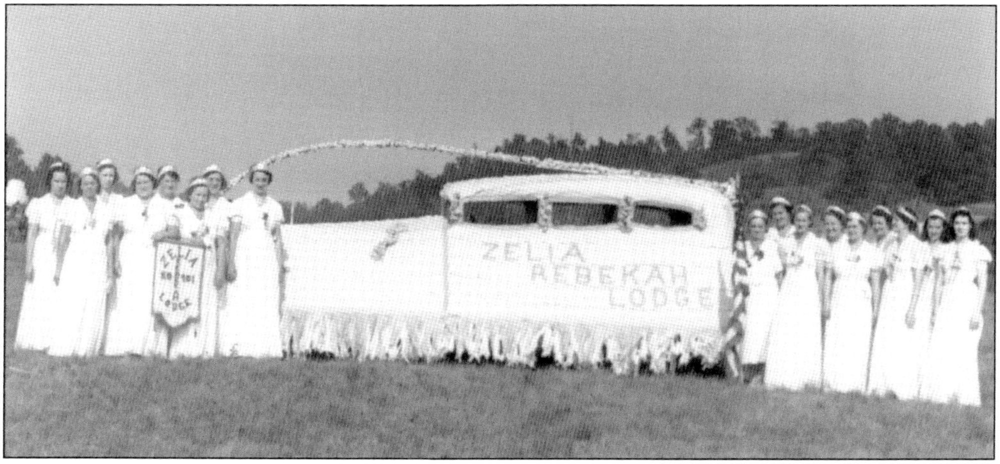

Initially designated as the female auxiliary of the Odd Fellows, the Zelia Rebekah Lodge 401 was founded in Zelienople in 1911. It celebrated its 50th anniversary in 1961 with a dinner at the elementary school; Saraellen Weyman was the dinner chairperson. The women met monthly above Hartmann's Drug Store and held various fundraising activities to help local residents. (ZHS.)

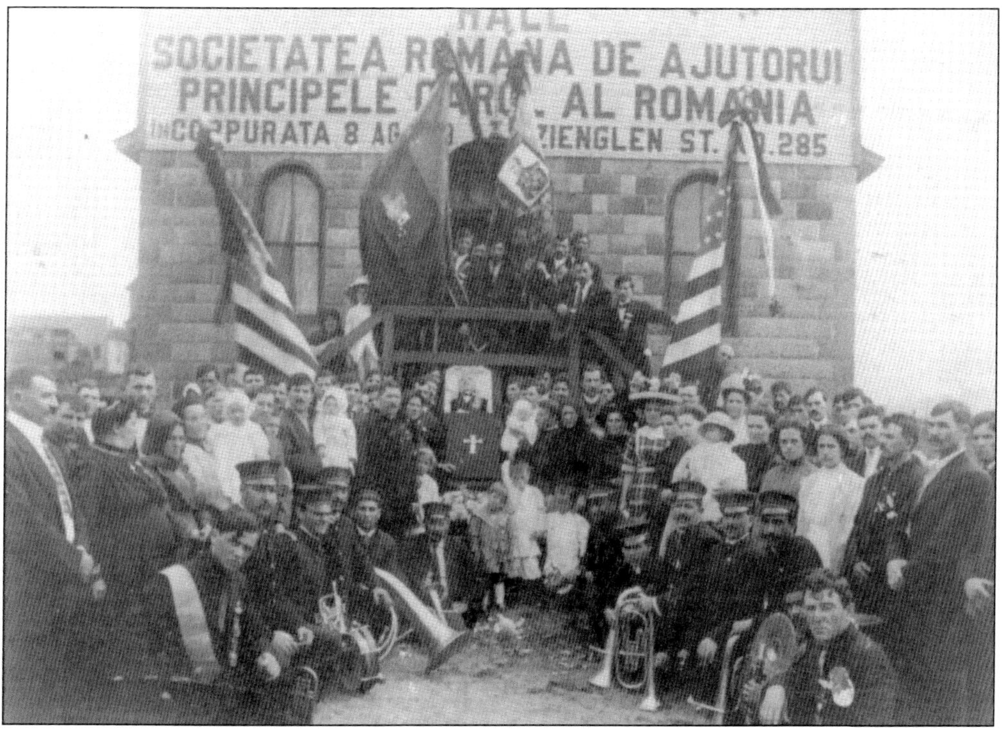

The Prince Carol Romanian Society was organized in Zelienople in 1909. It constructed the Romanian Hall on Ziegler Street, as seen in this 1921 photograph. Notice the coffin in the center of the image. After 1952, this building was home to the Besco Company. (BZC.)

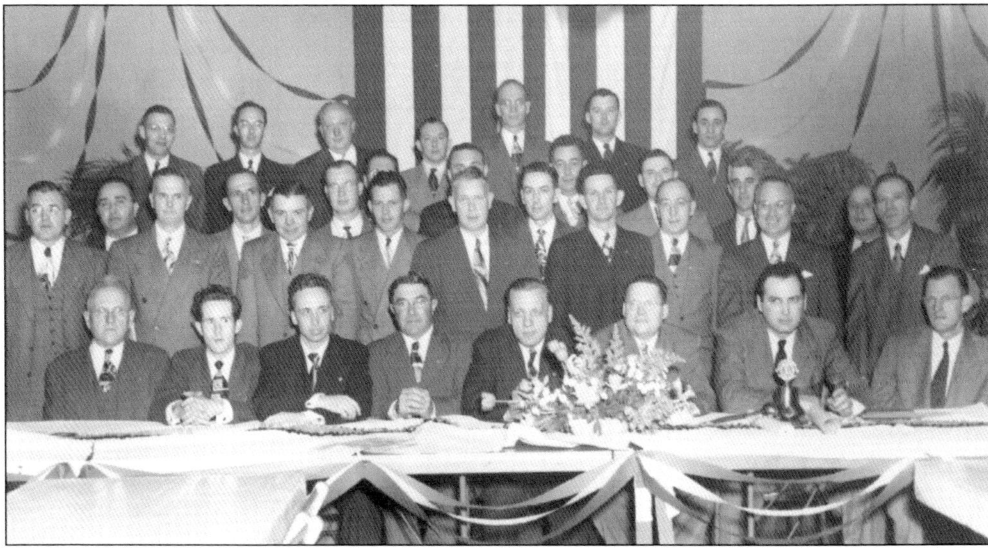

The Zelienople Lions Club was founded in February 1949 by men interested in community service and in promoting the ideals of the Lions Club International, which includes a spirit of understanding among the people of the world, good citizenship, and good government. (BZC.)

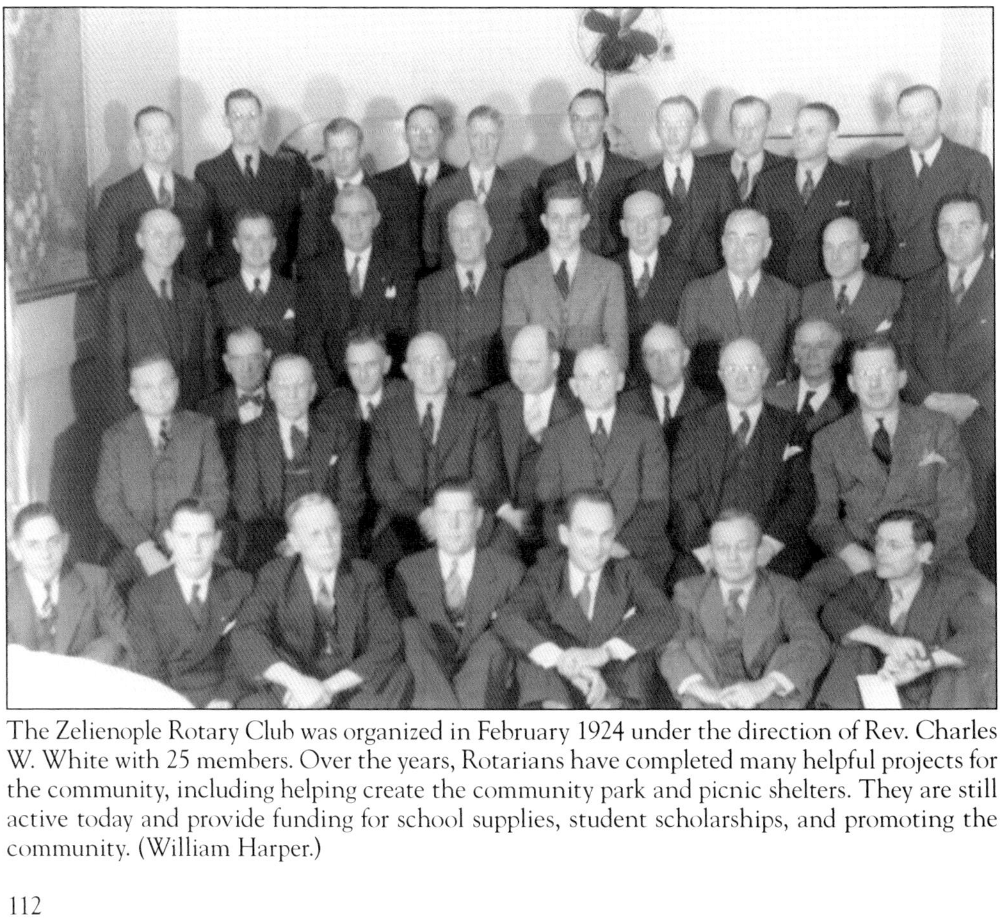

The Zelienople Rotary Club was organized in February 1924 under the direction of Rev. Charles W. White with 25 members. Over the years, Rotarians have completed many helpful projects for the community, including helping create the community park and picnic shelters. They are still active today and provide funding for school supplies, student scholarships, and promoting the community. (William Harper.)

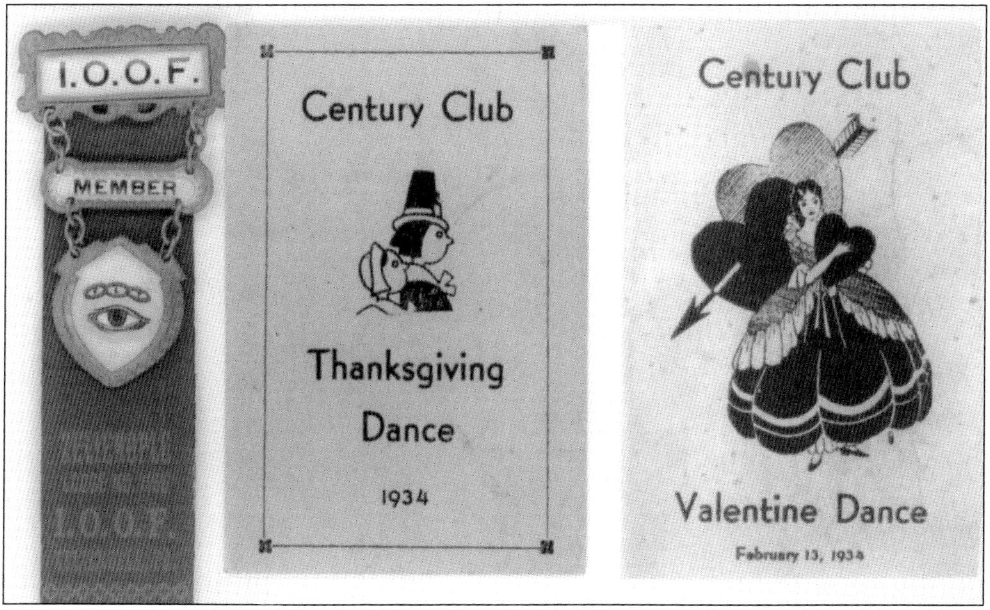

The Odd Fellows Lodge No. 1166 of the Independent Order of Odd Fellows was started in Zelienople in February 1910. This was a goodwill group of men who contributed to the community. The dance cards were for young ladies who attended dances at Zelienople's Century Club. The club was for single men over 21 who wanted a place of their own for socializing. They met during the 1930s above the First National Bank. (ZHS.)

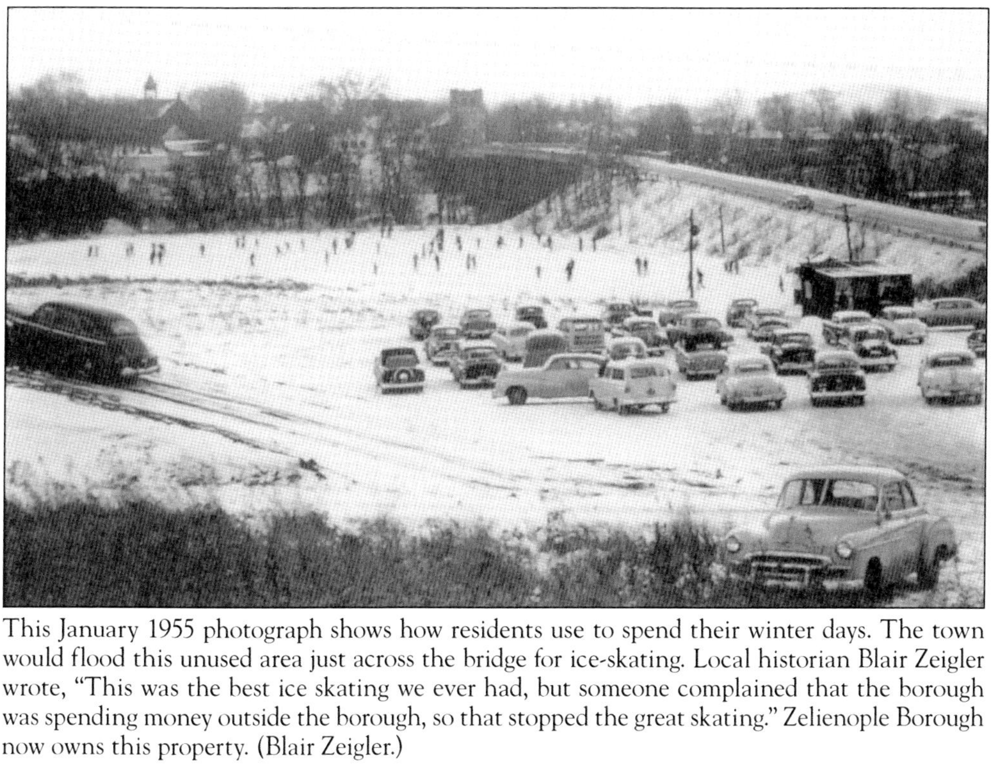

This January 1955 photograph shows how residents use to spend their winter days. The town would flood this unused area just across the bridge for ice-skating. Local historian Blair Zeigler wrote, "This was the best ice skating we ever had, but someone complained that the borough was spending money outside the borough, so that stopped the great skating." Zelienople Borough now owns this property. (Blair Zeigler.)

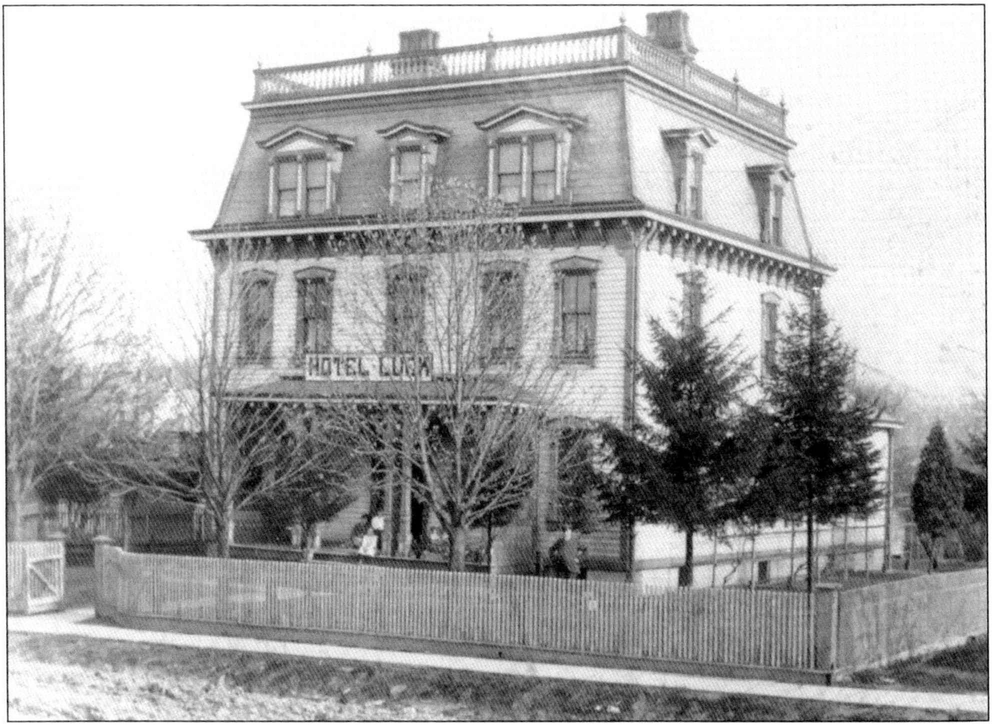

The photograph above is the Hotel Luek, a very handsome, three-story Victorian structure that was located at 308 West New Castle Street. In later years, it deteriorated and was owned by the Bales family as a private home. It was purchased by the Zelienople American Legion Post 474, which was founded on November 11, 1919, with James Britt was the first commander. The old structure was demolished and a temporary Quonset hut was built for the Legion, as shown below. That temporary Quonset hut lasted for 50 years, until a new, modern brick facility was built in 1989. Today, the Legion has a modern banquet room and facilities for dinners, weddings, and other occasions. This post has a Legion Auxiliary, organized in 1930 by Emma Evans, that helps veterans and their families. (Above, ZHS; below, BZC.)

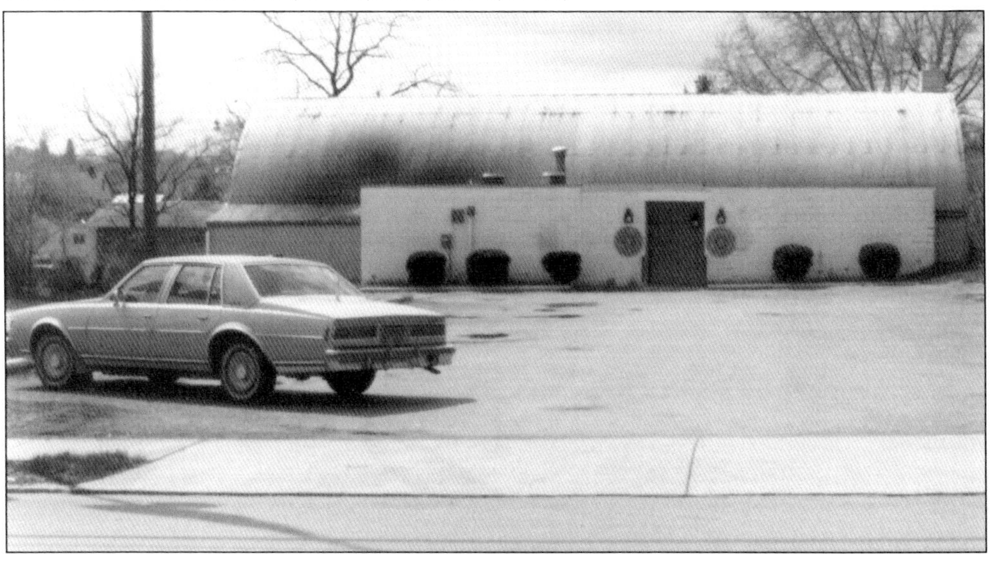

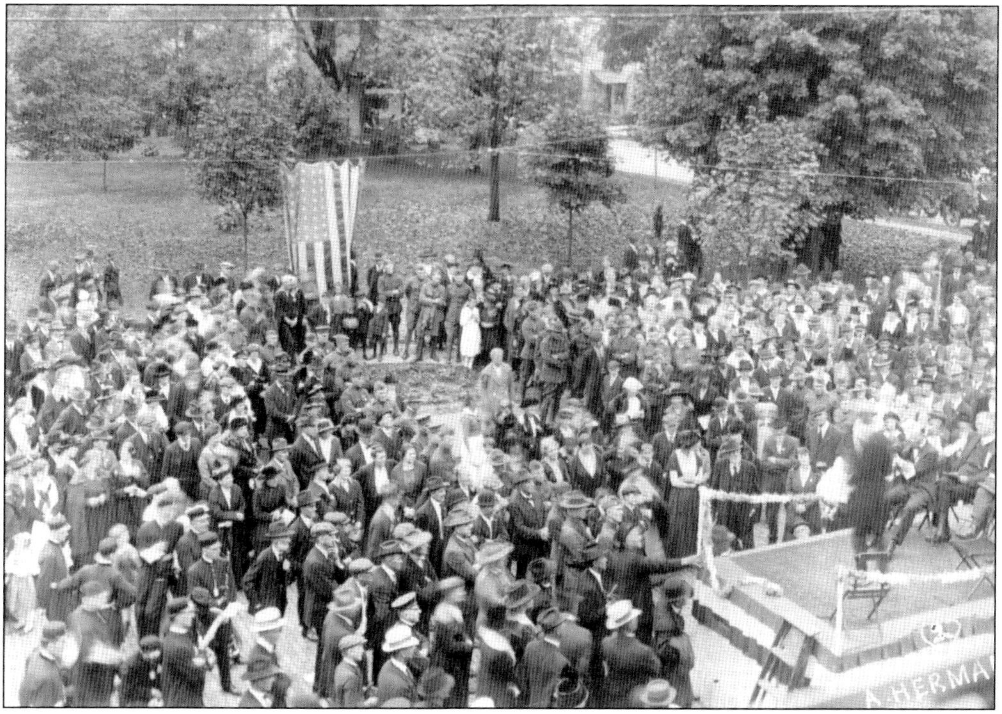

This unique photograph shows the World War I memorial marker being dedicated in the Main Street Park on October 15, 1919. This was the start of the small area along Main Street that contains memorials to those who served in all the important wars and conflicts of the United States. In this photograph, the new memorial is located behind the American flag. (ZHS.)

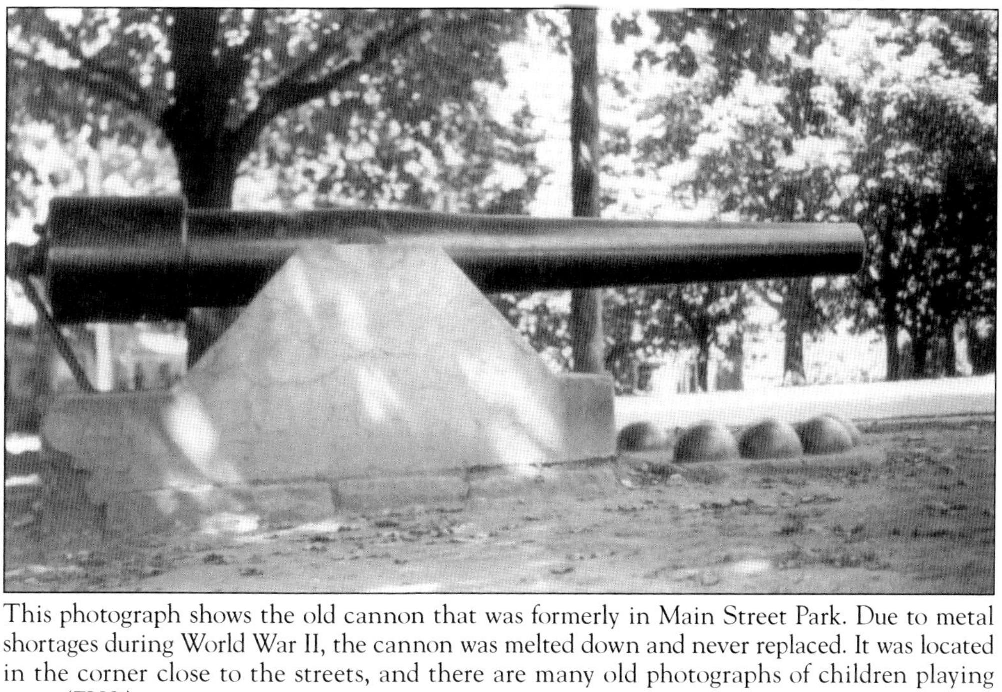

This photograph shows the old cannon that was formerly in Main Street Park. Due to metal shortages during World War II, the cannon was melted down and never replaced. It was located in the corner close to the streets, and there are many old photographs of children playing on it. (ZHS.)

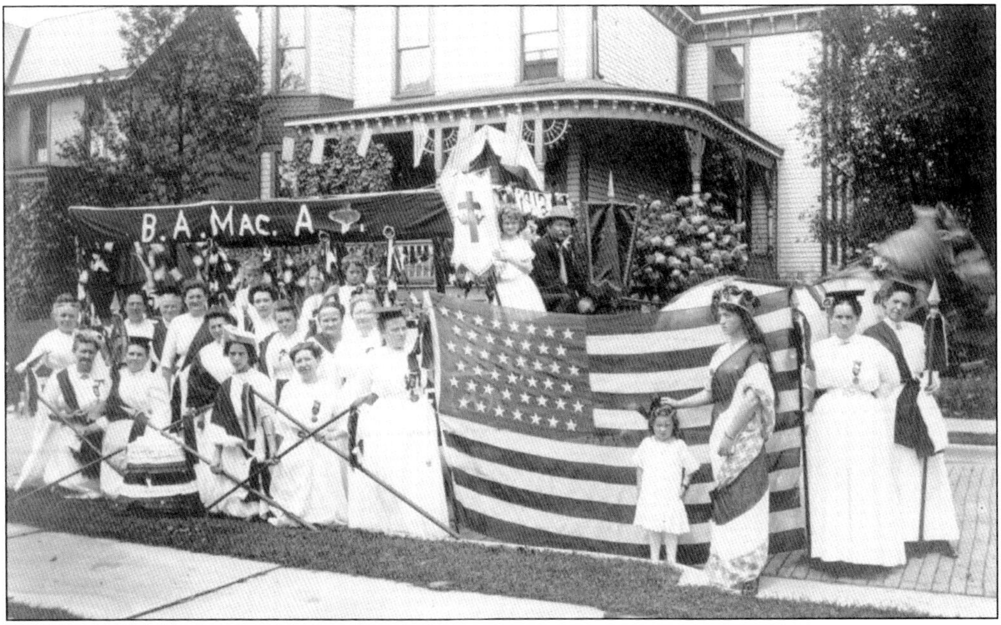

The Ladies of the Maccabees Lodge was a goodwill group organized in Zelienople in 1900 by Janet Rice. Bertha Winters was the first commander and Amelia Dindinger was the first the lieutenant commander. The group met monthly in the Dindinger Building on Main Street. This float, sitting on East New Castle Street, is getting ready for the 1912 Fourth of July Parade. The crowned queen is Alice Sisson. (ZHS.)

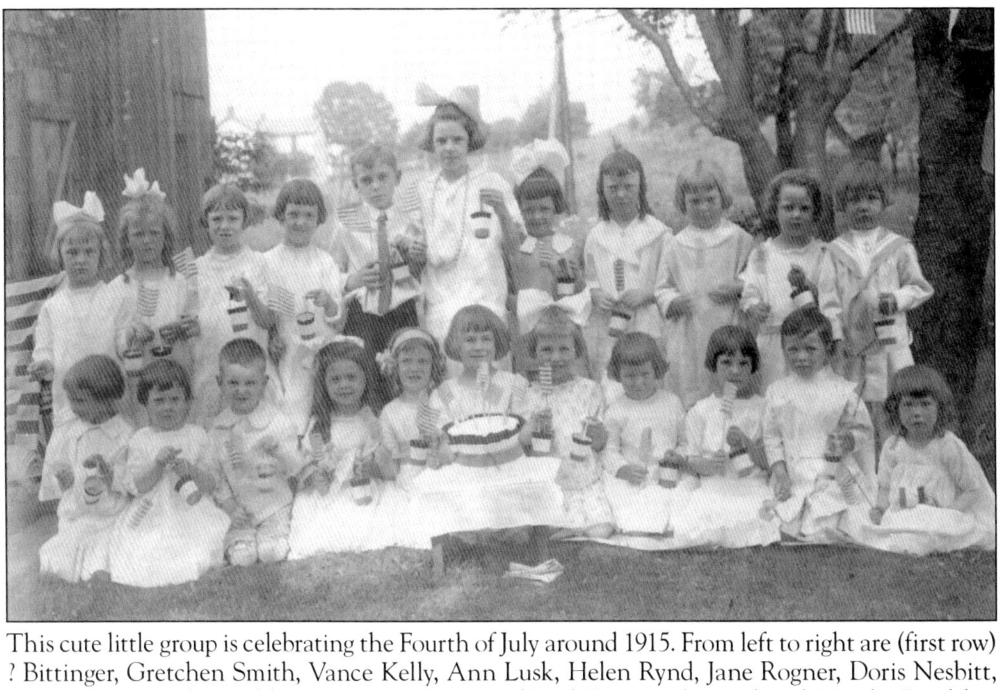

This cute little group is celebrating the Fourth of July around 1915. From left to right are (first row) ? Bittinger, Gretchen Smith, Vance Kelly, Ann Lusk, Helen Rynd, Jane Rogner, Doris Nesbitt, Jean Kocher, Gladys Frishkorn, Levon Meyers, and Ruth Rogner; (second row) Martha Beighley, Anna Kirker, Ethel Lutz, Marion Louden, Don Oesterling, Ethel Grey, Isabel Kaufman, Esther Danver, Margaret McWithey, Viola Nesbitt, and Robert Ringle. (ZHS.)

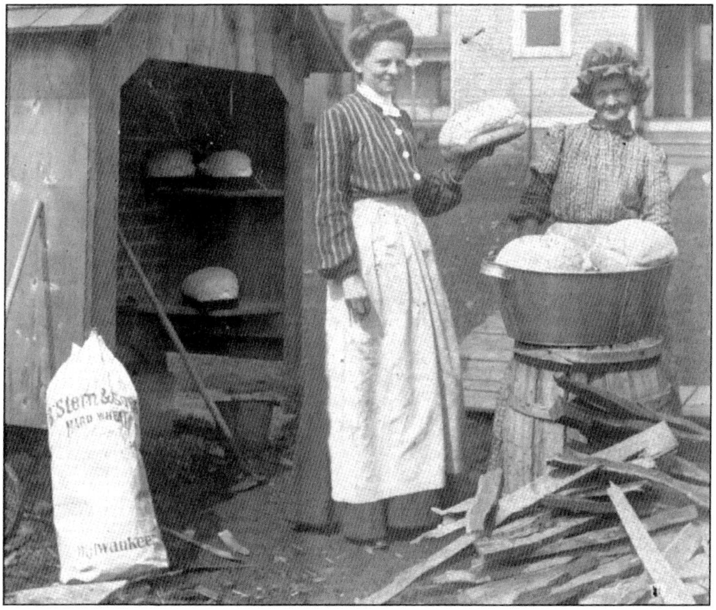

This 1910 photograph shows Julia Bassler on the left and neighbor Elizabeth Rape on the right at 306 East New Castle Street. They look like they are enjoying making bread from scratch. All it took was a backyard oven, a bag of wheat flour, yeast, and other secret ingredients. Julia was the wife and assistant of well-known photographer William Bassler, who took many early photographs of Zelienople. (Susan Pickford.)

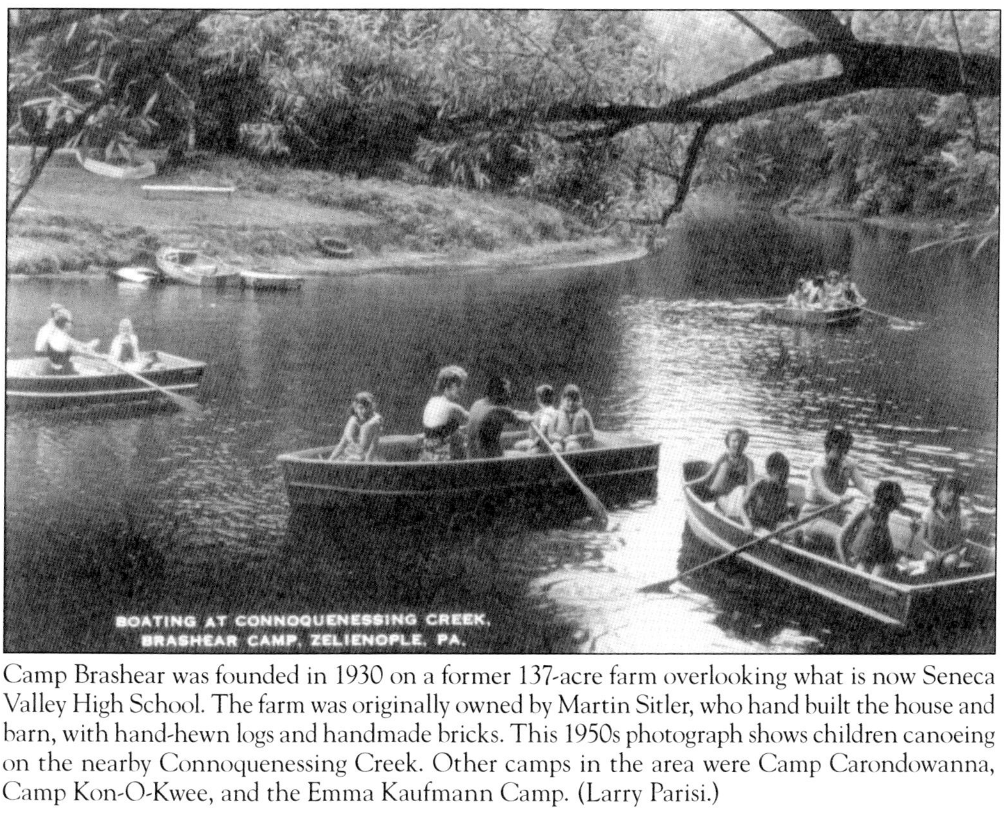

Camp Brashear was founded in 1930 on a former 137-acre farm overlooking what is now Seneca Valley High School. The farm was originally owned by Martin Sitler, who hand built the house and barn, with hand-hewn logs and handmade bricks. This 1950s photograph shows children canoeing on the nearby Connoquenessing Creek. Other camps in the area were Camp Carondowanna, Camp Kon-O-Kwee, and the Emma Kaufmann Camp. (Larry Parisi.)

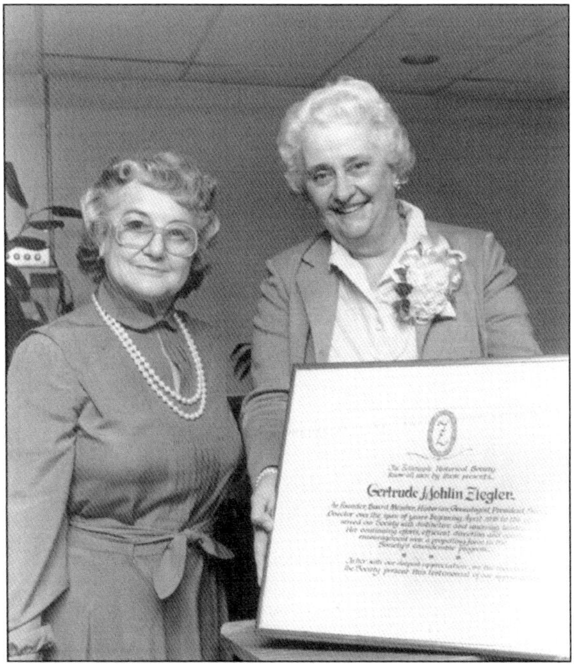

The Travelers Club was a women's club founded in 1906 by first president Martha Lockwood French, who held the first meeting at the Main Street school. Its purpose was to provide opportunities for travel, fine arts, and science. The photograph shows Yvonne Johnson (left) and Gertrude Ziegler, past presidents of the Travelers Club and the Historical Society. The club was active until the 1990s. (Shelby Ruch.)

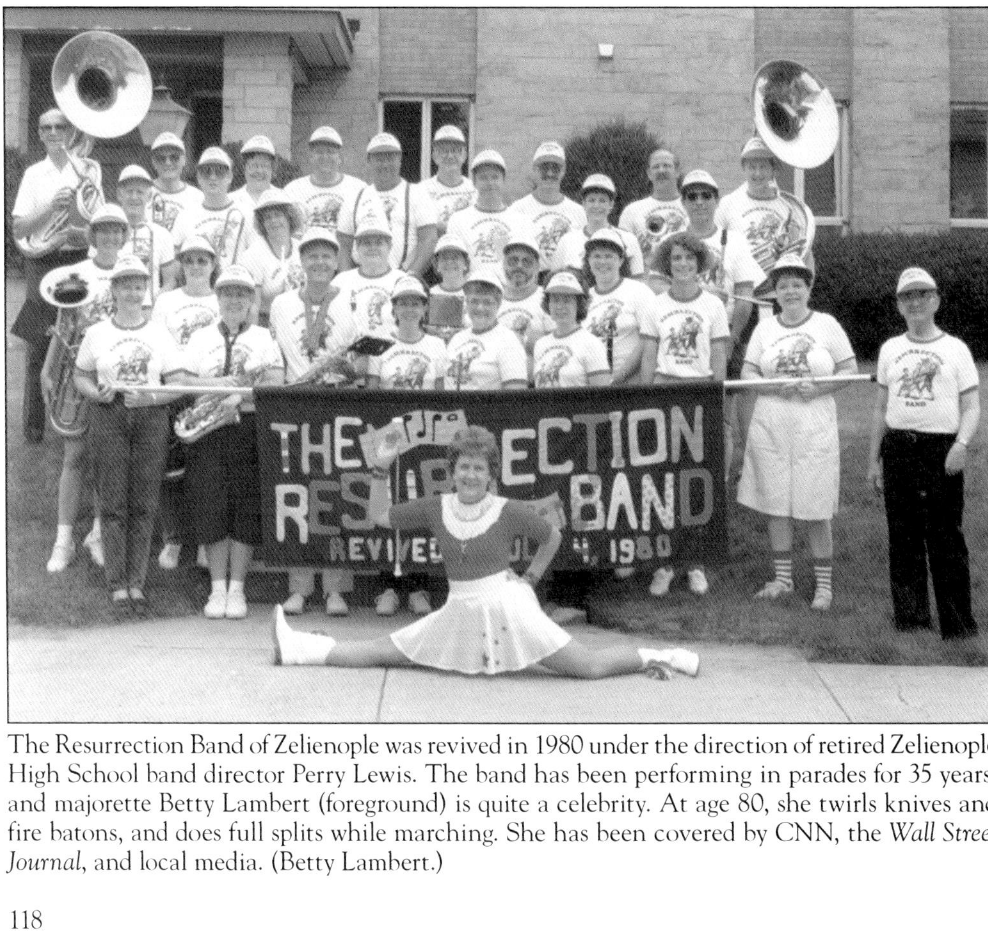

The Resurrection Band of Zelienople was revived in 1980 under the direction of retired Zelienople High School band director Perry Lewis. The band has been performing in parades for 35 years, and majorette Betty Lambert (foreground) is quite a celebrity. At age 80, she twirls knives and fire batons, and does full splits while marching. She has been covered by CNN, the *Wall Street Journal*, and local media. (Betty Lambert.)

Seven

Stately Homes and Farms

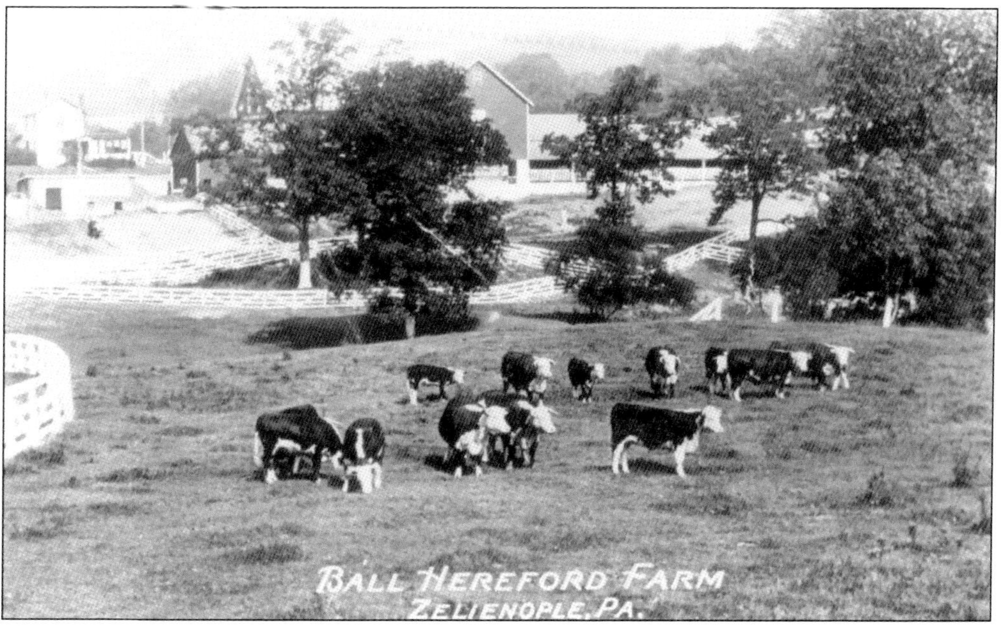

The beautiful George Ball Hereford Manor Farm was located just west of Zelienople on Route 288. In the 1950s, owner J.H. Cunningham had extensive strip mining done there. Afterwards, he built two earthen dams and created fishing lakes for which he charged a fee to use. They were enjoyed by local residents for 50 years. Due to recent legislation prohibiting earthen dams, the state permanently drained the lakes in 2012. (ZHS.)

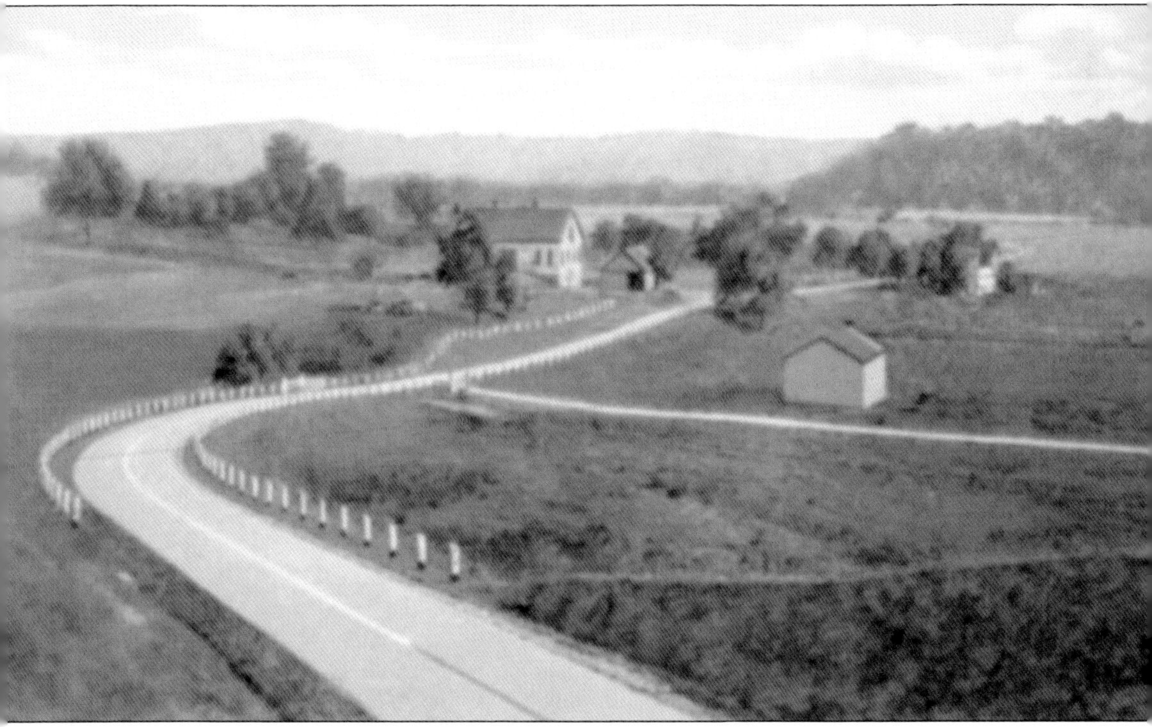

In 1803, Thomas Wilson Jr. and his brother William came from eastern Pennsylvania and purchased two tracts of land in the Camp Run area just west of Zelienople. In 1837, Thomas purchased two more tracts—the Zelienople Airport site and the Hereford Manor Lake site. Several sons and daughters built homes and farmed the 1,000 contiguous acres. Thomas's son Joseph (1820–1862) had a law degree, served as district attorney, and also served in the state legislature. In 1861, Joseph was elected colonel of the newly formed Keystone Regiment, and served as its commander at Yorktown and Williamsburg during the Civil War. He died of typhoid fever in Virginia in 1862, but his remains were interred in the Zelienople Cemetery. This 1930s postcard view of the Creek Meadows farm was taken from the Hereford Manor Lake location, showing the barn, house, and land that would later become the airport site. The cornerstone of the old farmhouse was laid in 1837. The farm passed down to descendant Francis Wilson, then to William T. Wilson, who had the land strip-mined by the Tasa Coal Company. After mining was finished, the grass airport strip was built by Halstead-Mitchell. William's sons—Harlan, Kenneth, and Thomas—inherited portions of the farm that finally passed out of the Wilson family in 1992. (Beth Wilson and Sharon Shanks.)

The Bastian House at 401 West New Castle Street was built in 1858 by William Bastian (1813–1887). In 1859, he built the Bastian House hotel on the present site of the Kaufman House. He traveled to California by covered wagon on the Overland Trail and kept a diary of his adventure. His son David lived here as a taxidermist and showed his prized animal collection to many schoolchildren. (ZHS.)

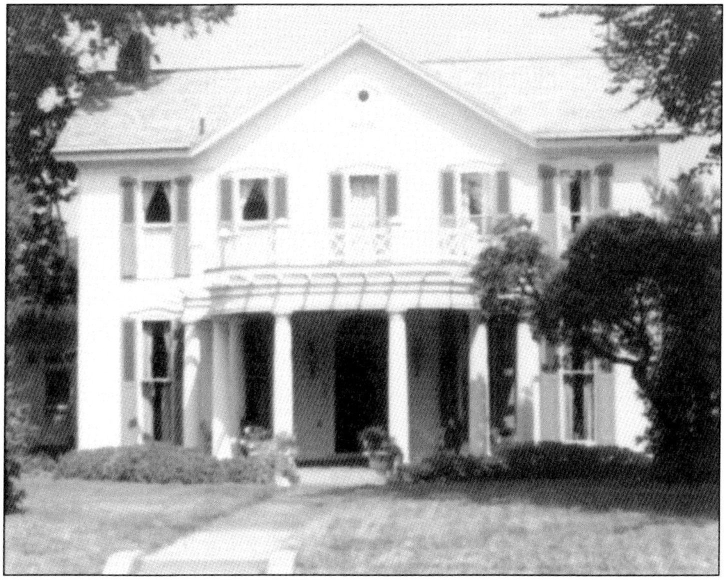

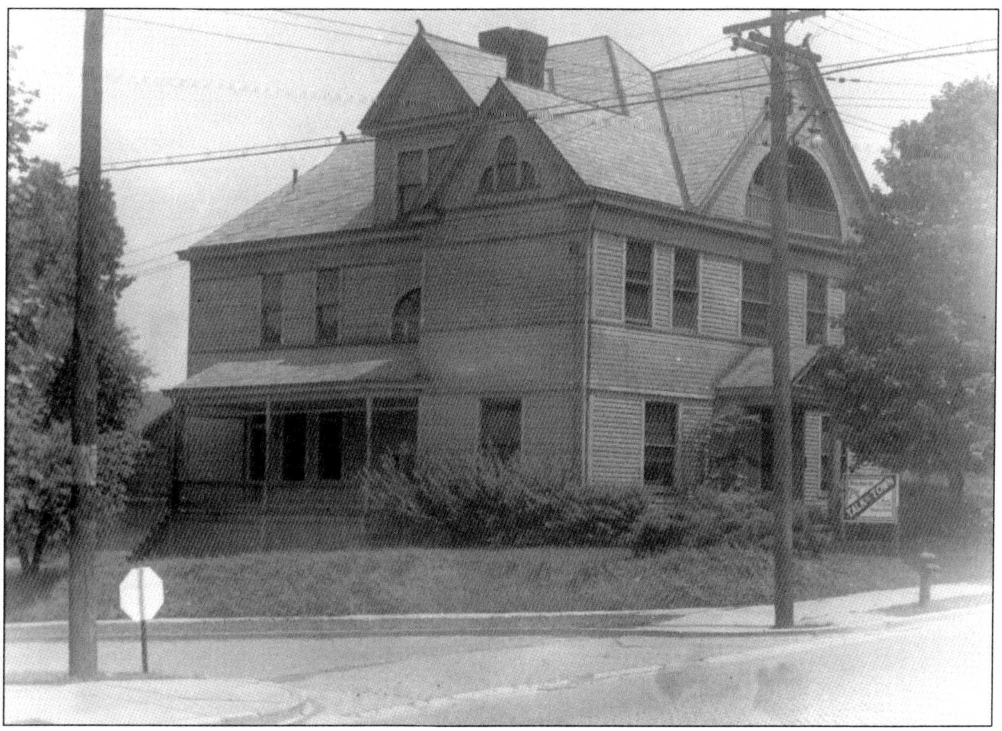

This massive house at 419 West New Castle Street was one of the largest homes in town. It was owned by George W. Bessor and was later divided into apartments, which is typical of these older Victorian homes. It was a total loss in 1952 when the wooden structure burned to the ground. It is believed that an electrical overload caused the fire. (BZC.)

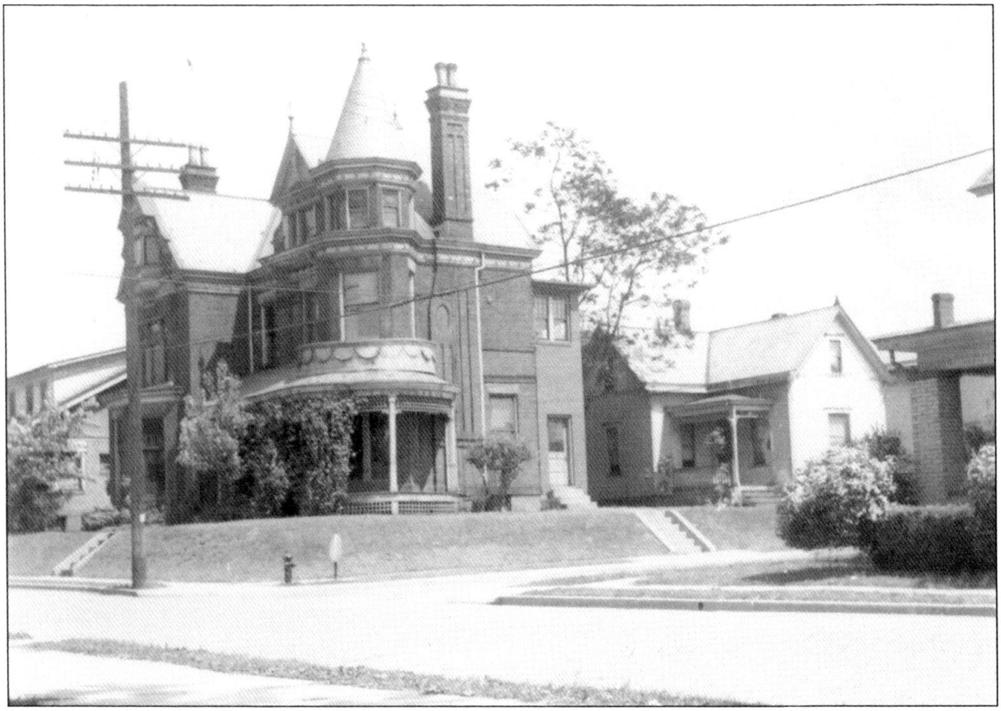

The large Victorian home at 120 West New Castle Street was built by William Goehring (1859–1945). It was later the residence of his daughter Nell Goehring (1886–1987), who lived to be over 100 years old. She was the valedictorian of her Zelienople High School class and later taught there. The Zelienople Historical Society had an honorary tea for her in 1980. This home may soon be demolished for parking. (BZC.)

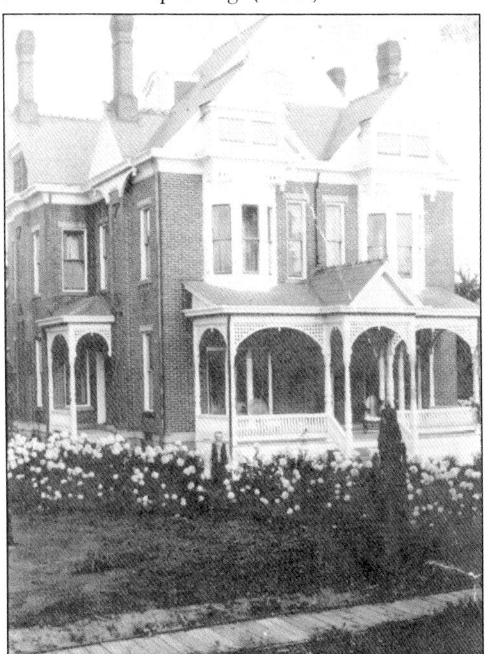

This impressive home at 120 South High Street was built in 1890 by John Ifft. This fortress was built with two layers of brick, four inches of air, and two more layers of brick. The photograph shows John Ifft in the front yard with his prized hydrangeas. He owned a lumber mill on North Clay Street that burned down around 1910. The house survives and is currently divided into apartments. (ZHS.)

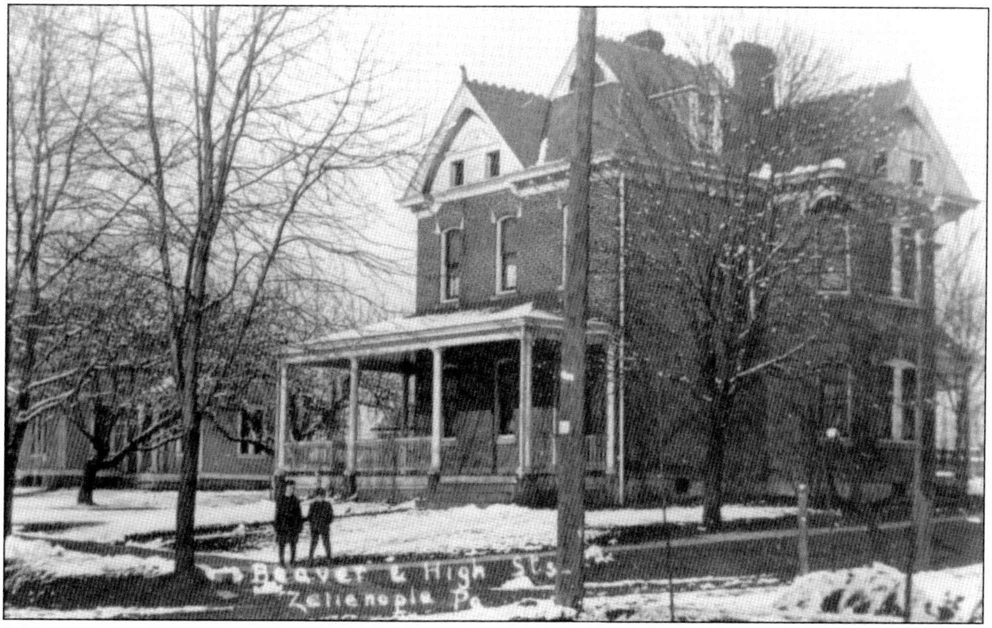

This 1910 Bassler photograph shows the large brick home at 240 South High Street that was built before 1900. For many years, it was the residence of Lawrence Markel, owner of Markel's Chevrolet at 134 South Main Street. When it was built, it had a narrow carriage house instead of a wider automobile garage. It has since been divided into apartments and updated. (BZC.)

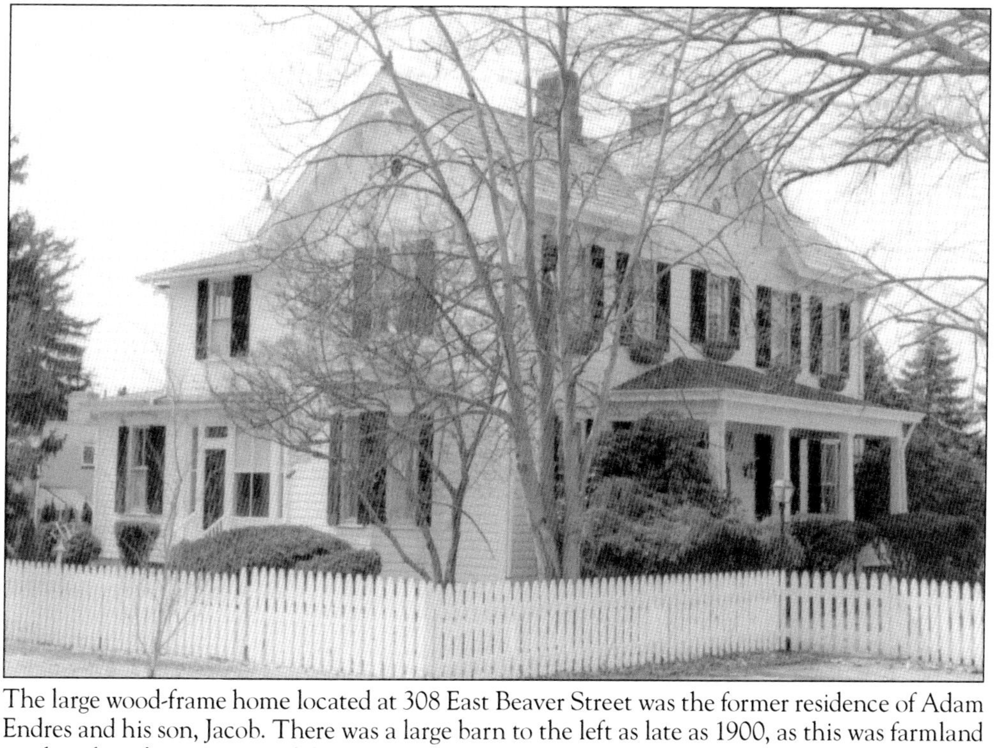

The large wood-frame home located at 308 East Beaver Street was the former residence of Adam Endres and his son, Jacob. There was a large barn to the left as late as 1900, as this was farmland on the edge of town. Most of the community park was once part of this Endres farm. This home was later owned by the Dodds and Gutzwiller families. (ZHS.)

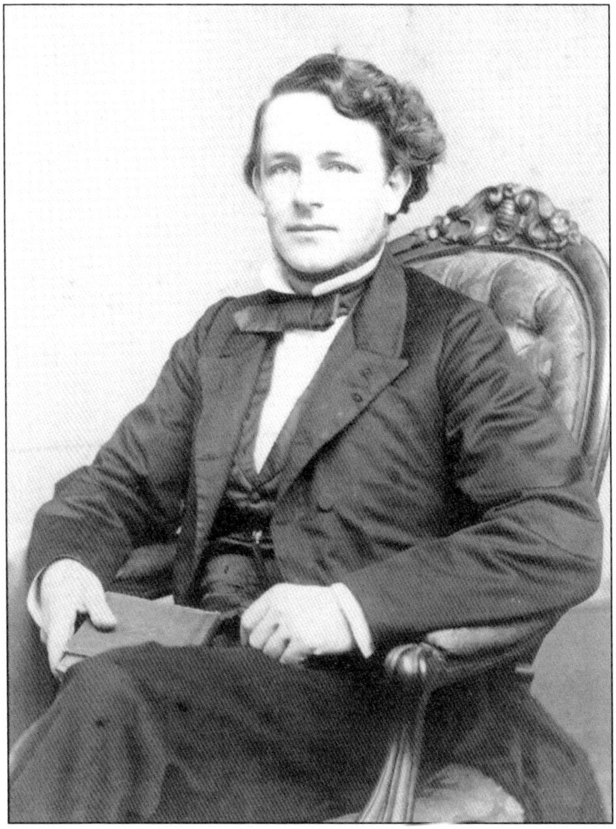

William Alfred Passavant (1821–1894) was born in Zelienople as the youngest son of Philipp and Zelie Passavant. He attended Jefferson College and later Gettysburg Seminary in preparation for a career in the ministry. William's life was devoted principally to the founding of benevolent institutions like the Pittsburgh Infirmary, now the Passavant Hospital. He also founded missions, hospitals, orphanages, colleges, and seminaries throughout the country. He is considered by many to be the greatest institutional leader the Lutheran Church has ever produced in America. (ZHS.)

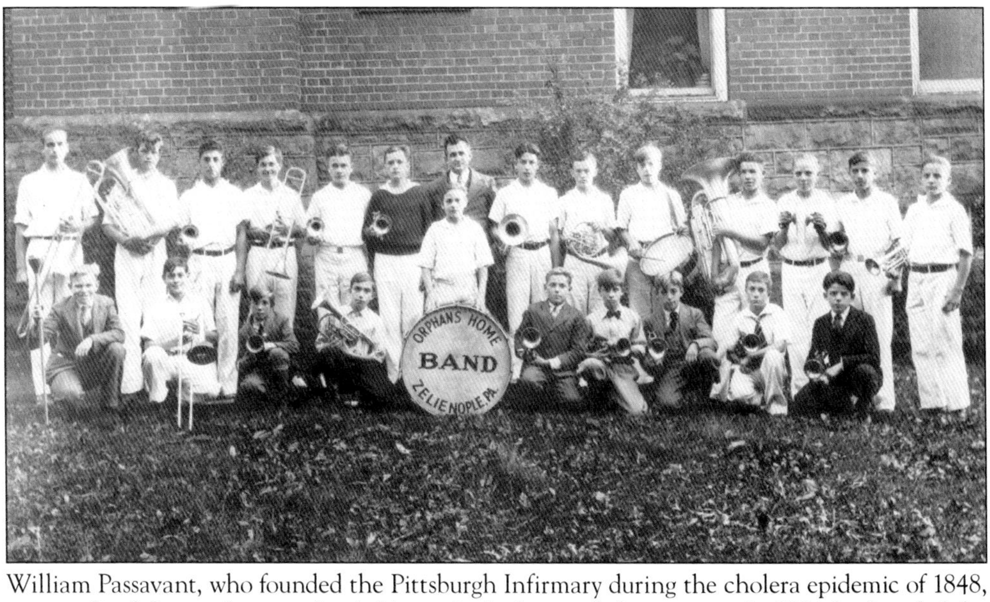

William Passavant, who founded the Pittsburgh Infirmary during the cholera epidemic of 1848, soon realized the need to care for children who had recently lost parents. In 1854, he founded the Zelienople Orphans Home and Farm School on 400 acres and called on Rev. Gottlieb Bassler to be the first director. This photograph confirms the children made their own entertainment there. (ZHS.)

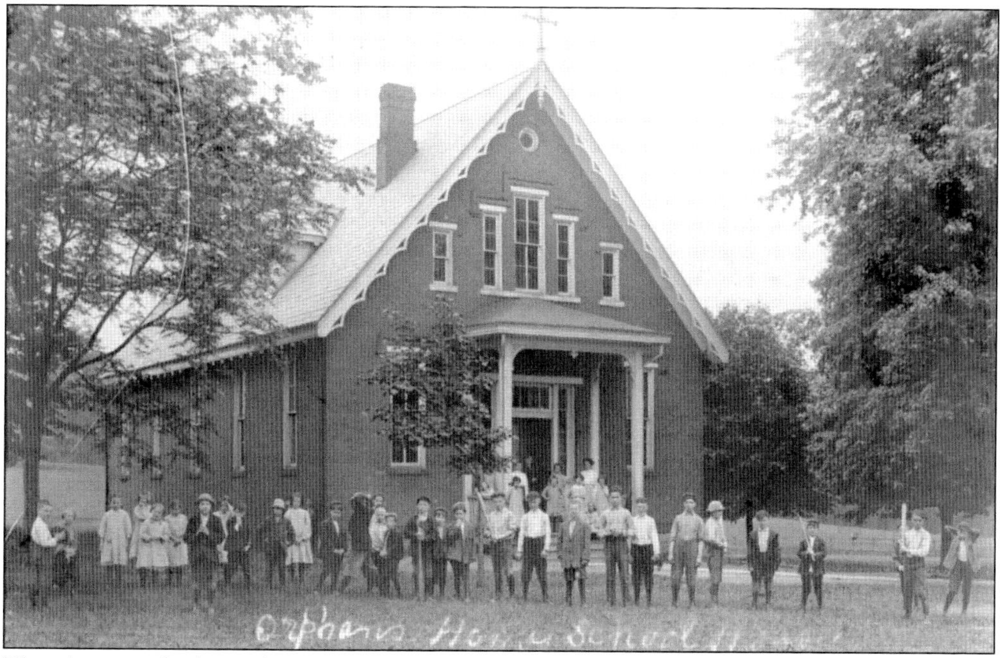

The photograph above shows a small schoolhouse located on the Orphans Home campus in the 1800s. The photograph below shows young girls learning to sew and holding up what they have created. All the basics were taught on campus, and later the children could attend the Connoquenessing Academy on Main Street in Zelienople. Professors there included George Holls and Rev. Gottlieb Bassler. The academy was operated by Asa H. Waters under the direction of Rev. William Passavant. There was no high school until 1896. (Both, ZHS.)

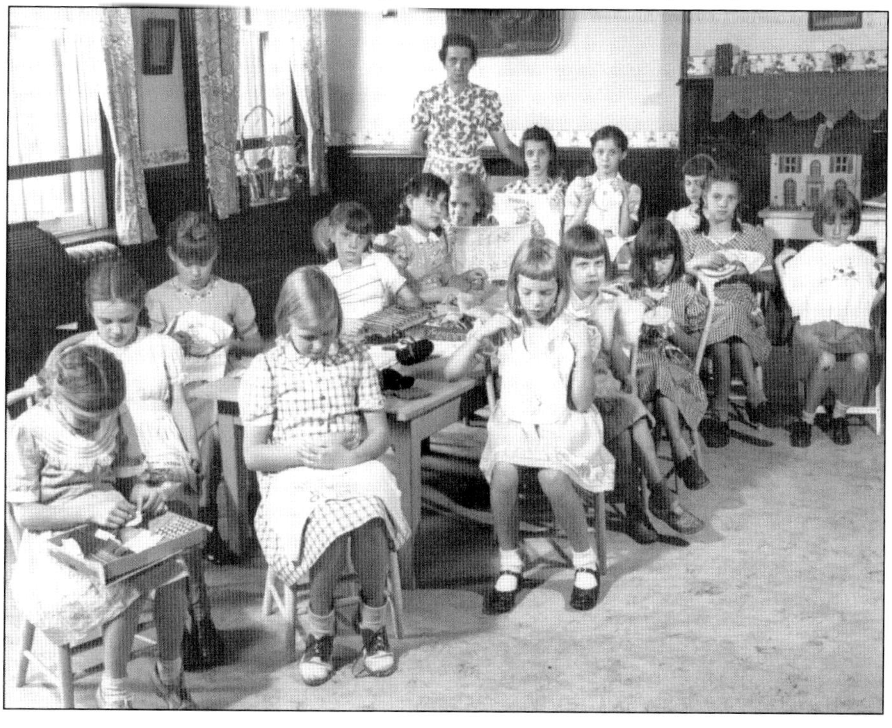

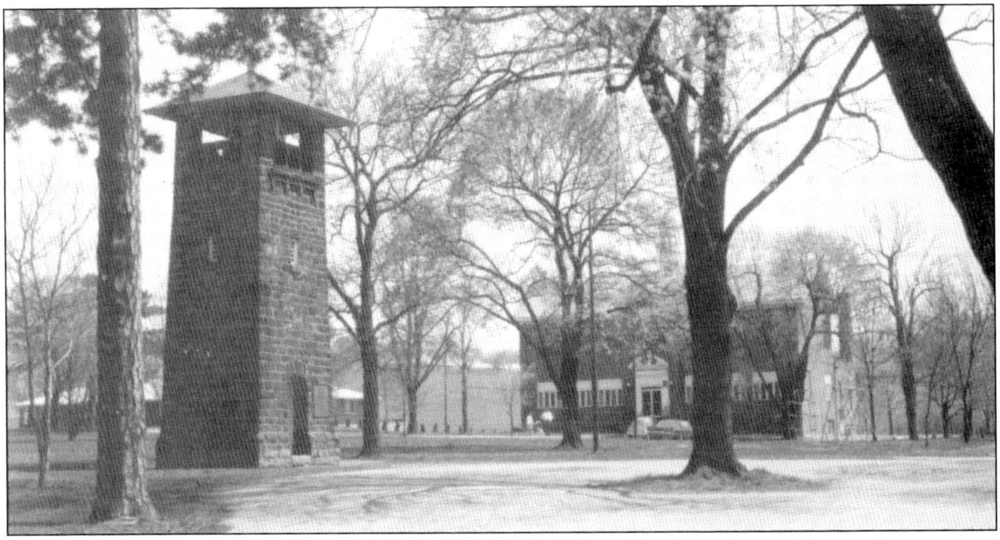

The 1909 bell tower still houses the original 1854 bell from the founding of the orphanage and a brass plaque paying tribute to Rev. William Passavant. The 1925 school in the background was attended by many orphans, and later by residents in town during the 1950s, when classroom space at the Zelienople Elementary School was at a premium. Today, it is used for facility offices. (Larry Parisi.)

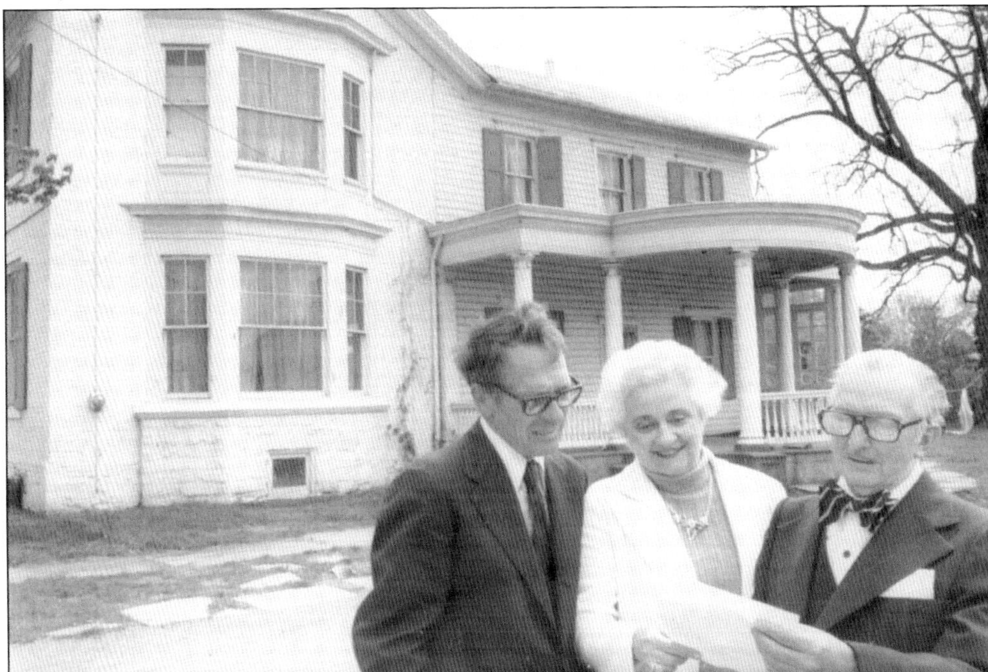

The 1808 home of Philipp and Zelie Passavant was almost lost forever, as no one seemed to want the somewhat tattered home along Main Street. In 1975, local historian Lester Mohr stepped in, bought the home, and donated it to the newly formed Zelienople Historical Society. The photograph shows society president Gertrude Ziegler, center, accepting the deed to the home from Lester Mohr, on the right. (ZHS.)

About the Zelienople Historical Society

Over the years, there have been several local contributing historians, including Nell Campbell, Nell Goehring, Carl Hartman, Yvonne Johnson, Lester Mohr, Blair Zeigler, and Gertrude Ziegler. They shared stories, research, photographs, and the common interest they had in the town's early days. Individually, they wrote articles, books, and booklets about various historical aspects of Zelienople, but there was no historical society.

The Zelienople Historical Society was founded in 1975 by Gertrude Ziegler and a small group of historically minded people to better record and share the local history. They were able to acquire the 1808 home of Philipp and Zelie Passavant as their museum, library, and office. In 1991, the society acquired the 1805 Christian Buhl House as a second museum site. The history of the Basse, Passavant, and Buhl families is quite unique for a little town in the wilds of western Pennsylvania. The society hosts informative tours for students and adults and participates in various community activities that help residents understand their local history. Please consider donating your time and talents to help this small group of volunteers keep the Buhl and Passavant homes in good condition so they will properly represent the history of our town and the founding families for years to come.

The society has records, photographs, newspaper articles, genealogy, and historical books, and only a donation is required for their use. The office is open daily in the mornings, and tours can be arranged by calling 724-452-9457. The society can be contacted at 243 South Main Street, Zelienople, Pennsylvania, 16063 or at www.zelienoplehistoricalsociety.com. Anyone with additional historical photographs to be scanned, please contact Tom Nesbitt at tomnesbitt@zoominternet.net.